Brian Hart
with Mario Rinvolucri, Herbert Puchta & Jeff S

English in Mind
Second edition

Teacher's Resource
Book Starter

CAMBRIDGE
UNIVERSITY PRESS

Unit	Grammar	Vocabulary	Pronunciation
1 He's a footballer	The verb *be* (singular): statements and questions Question words: *who, what, how old, where?*	Countries and nationalities Vocabulary bank: countries and nationalities	*from*
2 We're a new band	The verb *be* (plural): negatives and questions *I (don't) like ... / Do you like ...?* Object pronouns	Positive and negative adjectives Everyday English Vocabulary bank: positive and negative adjectives	/ɪ/ and /iː/
CHECK YOUR PROGRESS			
3 She lives in Washington	Present simple: positive and negative; questions and short answers Possessive *'s* Possessive adjectives	Family Vocabulary bank: family	/s/, /z/ and /ɪz/
4 Where's the café?	*there's / there are* Positive imperatives Prepositions of place	Places in towns Numbers 100 + Everyday English Vocabulary bank: places in towns	/ð/ and /θ/
CHECK YOUR PROGRESS			
5 They've got brown eyes	*has / have got* *Why ... ? Because ...*	Parts of the body Vocabulary bank: parts of the body	/v/ *they've*
6 This is delicious!	*I'd like / Would you like ... ?* Countable and uncountable nouns *this/that/these/those*	Food Everyday English Vocabulary bank: food	/w/ *would*
CHECK YOUR PROGRESS			
7 I sometimes watch TV	Present simple with adverbs of frequency	Days of the week TV programmes Telling the time	Compound nouns
8 Don't do that!	Negative imperatives	Adjectives to describe feelings Everyday English Vocabulary bank: adjectives to describe feelings	Linking sounds
CHECK YOUR PROGRESS			
9 Yes, I can	*can/can't* (ability) *like / don't like + -ing*	Sports Vocabulary bank: sports	*can/can't*
10 A bad storm's coming	Present continuous	House and furniture Everyday English Vocabulary bank: house and furniture	/h/ *have*
CHECK YOUR PROGRESS			
11 Special days	*can/can't* (asking for permission) Prepositions: *at, in, on* *one/ones*	Months of the year and seasons Clothes Vocabulary bank: clothes	/æ/ and /e/
12 He was only 22	Past simple: *was/wasn't; were/weren't*	Time expressions Ordinal numbers and dates Everyday English Vocabulary bank: materials	*was/wasn't* and *were/weren't*
CHECK YOUR PROGRESS			
13 What happened?	Past simple: regular and irregular verbs (questions and negatives)	Verb and noun pairs Vocabulary bank: verb and noun pairs: *make/do/take/have*	*-ed* endings
14 Things change	Comparison of adjectives *than*	Adjectives and opposites Everyday English Vocabulary bank: adjectives and opposites	/ðən/ *than*
CHECK YOUR PROGRESS			

Pronunciation • Vocabulary bank • Get it Right! • Projects • Irregular verbs and phonetics

Speaking & Functions	Listening	Reading	Writing
Saying where you are from Talking about your hero	My hero/heroine	Dialogue: In a queue Culture in Mind: heroes and heroines	Writing about yourself
Talking about likes and dislikes Talking about singers and bands Last but not least: asking a celebrity questions	People talking about likes and dislikes Song: *Are We Alone?*	Dialogue: members of a band Photostory: Just a little joke	Email about your favourite band
Talking about your family Talking about the present	Dialogue about free-time activities	Article: America's First Lady Culture in Mind: British families	Paragraph about your family
Talking about places in a town Giving directions Last but not least: conversation between tourists and a local person	Asking for and giving directions	Web page: Things to see and do in London Photostory: A charity run	Text about your town or city
Describing people Giving personal information	Descriptions of people	Article: Sally or Paula? Culture in Mind: Different cultures – different pets	Description of a friend or family member
Ordering food in a restaurant Last but not least: talking about food you like and dislike	Dialogue in a restaurant	Article: Unusual food around the world Photostory: Enjoy your lunch!	Email to an English family about food likes and dislikes
Talking about routines Talking about TV programmes	Dialogues about TV likes, dislikes and habits	Article: Different places – different lives Culture in Mind: What British teenagers watch	Paragraph for a school magazine about the TV programmes you like
Talking about how you feel Last but not least: Simon says	A picture story Song: *Don't stop*	Email about feelings Photostory: Kate looks great!	Email about your friends and your likes and dislikes
Talking about abilities Talking about likes and dislikes	Amazing abilities Conversation about sport	Article: We never win, but we always win	Email about sport
Describing what is happening now Talking about your house or flat Everyday English Last but not least: talking about a holiday	A telephone conversation about what is happening now	Article: Round the world – alone Photostory: A kickabout	A holiday postcard
Talking about times and dates Describing what someone is wearing Talking about clothes and shopping	Description of models in a fashion show	Article: Scotland – a land of traditions Culture in Mind: The Edinburgh Festival	Email about a festival
Talking about the past Last but not least: talking about when you were young	Conversation about the Beatles	Article: The Day the Music Died Photostory: An accident in the park	Email about a past holiday
Asking and answering questions in a questionnaire	Radio quiz show about historic events	Article: She said 'No' Culture in Mind: The daughter of a lion	Paragraph for a school magazine about a famous person from the past
Comparing people and things in the classroom Describing things using adjectives Comparing things Last but not least: giving a presentation about your country, comparing past and present	Conversation comparing the 1960s with the present	Article: From London bank to Thailand hotel Photostory: So sorry	Competition text comparing life in the past and present

Introduction

'*If you can teach teenagers, you can teach anyone.*' Michael Grinder

Teaching teenagers is an interesting and challenging task. A group of adolescents can be highly motivated, cooperative and fun to teach on one day, and the next day the whole group or individual students might turn out to be truly 'difficult' – the teacher might, for example, be faced with discipline problems, disruptive or provocative behaviour, a lack of motivation, or unwillingness on the students' part to do homework assigned to them.

The roots of these problems frequently lie in the fact that adolescents are going through a period of significant changes in their lives. The key challenge in the transition period between being a child and becoming an adult is the adolescent's struggle for identity – a process that requires the development of a distinct sense of who they are. A consequence of this process is that adolescents can feel threatened, and at the same time experience overwhelming emotions. They frequently try to compensate for the perceived threats with extremely rude behaviour, and try to 'hide' their emotions behind a wall of extreme outward conformity. The more individual students manage to look, talk, act and behave like the other members of their peer group, the less threatened and insecure they feel.

Insights into the causes underlying the problems might help us to understand better the complex situation our students are in. However, such insights do not automatically lead to more success in teaching. We need to react to the challenges in a professional way[1]. This includes the need to:

- select content and organise the students' learning according to their psychological needs;
- create a positive learning atmosphere;
- cater for differences in students' learning styles and intelligence(s), and facilitate the development of our students' study skills.

English in Mind second edition has been written taking all these points into account. They have significantly influenced the choice of texts, artwork and design, the structure of the units, the typology of exercises, and the means by which students' study skills are facilitated and extended.

The importance of the content for success

There are a number of reasons why the choice of the right content has a crucial influence over success or failure in the teaching of adolescents. Teachers frequently observe that teenagers are reluctant to 'talk about themselves'. This has to do with the adolescent's need for psychological security. Consequently, the 'further away' from their own world the content of the teaching is, the more motivating and stimulating it will be for the students. The preference for psychologically

remote content goes hand in hand with a fascination with extremes and realistic details. Furthermore, students love identifying with heroes and heroines, because these idols are perceived to embody the qualities needed in order to survive in a threatening world: qualities such as courage, genius, creativity and love. In the foreign language class, students can become fascinated with stories about heroes and heroines to which they can ascribe such qualities. *English in Mind* treats students as young adults, offering them a range of interesting topics and a balance between educational value and teenage interest and fun.

As Kieran Egan[1] stresses, learning in the adolescent classroom can be successfully organised by starting with something far from the students' experience, but also connected to it by some quality with which they can associate. This process of starting far from the students makes it easier for the students to become interested in the topic, and also enables the teacher finally to relate the content to the students' own world.

A positive learning atmosphere

The creation of a positive learning atmosphere largely depends on the rapport between teacher and students, and the one which students have among themselves. It requires the teacher to be a genuine, empathetic listener, and to have a number of other psychological skills. *English in Mind* supports the teacher's task of creating positive learning experiences through: clear tasks; a large number of carefully designed exercises; regular opportunities for the students to check their own work; and a learning process designed to guarantee that the students will learn to express themselves both in speaking and in writing.

Learning styles and multiple intelligences

There is significant evidence that students will be better motivated, and learn more successfully, if differences in learning styles and intelligences are taken into account in the teaching-learning process.[2] The development of a number of activities in *English in Mind* has been influenced by such insights, and students find frequent study tips that show them how they can better utilise their own resources.[3]

The methodology used in *English in Mind*

Skills: *English in Mind* uses a communicative, multi-skills approach to develop the students' foreign language abilities in an interesting and motivational way. A wide range of interesting text types is used to present authentic use of language, including magazine and newspaper clippings, interviews, narratives, songs and engaging photostories.

1   An excellent analysis of teenage development and consequences for our teaching in general can be found in Kieran Egan: *Romantic Understanding*, Routledge and Kegan Paul, New York and London, 1990. This book has had a significant influence on the thinking behind *English in Mind*, and the development of the concept of the course.

2   See for example Eric Jensen: *Brain-Based Learning and Teaching*, Turning Point Publishing, Del Mar, CA, USA, 1995, on learning styles. An overview of the theory of multiple intelligences can be found in Howard Gardner: *Multiple Intelligences: The Theory in Practice*, Basic Books, New York, 1993.

3   See Marion Williams and Robert L. Burden: *Psychology for Language Teachers*, Cambridge University Press, 1997 (pp. 143–162), on how the learner deals with the process of learning.

Grammar: *English in Mind* is based on a strong grammatical syllabus and takes into account students' mixed abilities by dealing with grammar in a carefully graded way, and offering additional teaching support.

Vocabulary: *English in Mind* offers a systematic vocabulary syllabus, including important lexical chunks for conversation and extension of the vocabulary in a bank at the back of the book.

Culture: *English in Mind* gives students insights into a number of important cross-cultural and intercultural themes. Significant cultural features of English-speaking countries are presented, and students are involved in actively reflecting on the similarities and differences between other cultures and their own.

Consolidation: Seven **Check your progress** revision pages per level will give teachers a clear picture of their students' progress and make students aware of what they have learned. Four **projects** give students the opportunity to use new language in a less controlled context and allows for learner independence.

Teacher support: *English in Mind* is clearly structured and easy to teach. The Teacher's Resource Book offers step-by-step lesson notes, background information on content, culture and language, additional teaching ideas, tapescripts, photocopiable materials for further practice and extra lessons, taking into consideration the needs of mixed-ability groups by providing extra material for fast finishers or students who need more support, as well as an entry test.

Student support: *English in Mind* offers systematic support to students through: Study help sections and Skills tips; classroom language; guidance in units to help with the development of classroom discourse and the students' writing; lists of irregular verbs and phonetics (at the back of the Student's Book); and a Grammar reference (at the back of the Workbook).

English in Mind: components

Each level of the *English in Mind* series contains the following components:

- Student's Book with accompanying DVD-ROM
- Audio CDs
- Workbook
- Teacher's Resource Book
- Testmaker Audio CD / CD-ROM
- DVD
- Classware DVD-ROM
- Website resources

The Student's Book

Student's Book Starter has a **Welcome section** at the beginning. This is to allow teachers to check, reasonably quickly, some of the key areas of language which students may have covered in their previous learning. An alternative use of the Welcome section might be as diagnostic exercises, allowing teachers to gauge the strengths and weaknesses of their particular group of students before embarking on the material.

The **units** have the basic following structure, although with occasional minor variations depending on the flow of an individual unit:

- an opening **reading** text
- a **grammar** page, often including pronunciation
- two pages of **vocabulary** and **skills** work
- either a **photostory** or a **Culture in mind** text, followed by **writing skills** work and extra speaking

The **reading texts** aim to engage and motivate the students with interesting and relevant content, and to provide contextualised examples of target grammar and lexis. The texts have 'lead-in' tasks and are followed by comprehension tasks of various kinds. All the opening texts are also recorded on the Audio CDs, which allows teachers to follow the initial reading with a 'read and listen' phase, giving the students the invaluable opportunity of connecting the written word with the spoken version, which is especially useful for auditory learners. Alternatively, with stronger classes, teachers may decide to do one of the exercises as a listening task, with books closed.

Grammar follows the initial reading. The emphasis is on active involvement in the learning process. Examples from the texts are isolated and used as a basis for tasks, which focus on both concept and form of the target grammar area. Students are encouraged to find other examples and work out rules for themselves. Occasionally there are also **Look!** boxes which highlight an important connected issue concerning the grammar area, for example, in Unit 1, work on adjectives has a Look! box showing how *a* and *an* are used with adjectives. This is followed by a number of graded exercises, both receptive and productive, which allow students to begin to employ the target language in different contexts and to produce realistic language. Next, there is usually a speaking activity, aiming at further personalisation of the language.

Each unit has at least one **Vocabulary** section, with specific word fields. Again, examples from the initial text are focused on, and a lexical set is developed, with exercises for students to put the vocabulary into use. Vocabulary is frequently recycled in later texts in the unit (e.g. photostories or Culture in mind texts), and also in later units

Pronunciation is included in every unit. There are exercises on common phoneme problems such as /ɪ/ in *big* vs. /iː/ in *three*, as well as aspects of stress (within words, and across sentences) and elision. Vital areas are often dealt with in relation to a grammar area, for example, the pronunciation of *than* when comparatives are taught.

Language skills are present in every unit. There is always at least one **listening skills** activity, with listening texts of various genres and at least one (but usually several) **speaking skills** activity for fluency development. **Reading skills** are taught through the opening texts and also later texts in some units, as well as the Culture in mind sections. There is always a **writing skills** task, towards the end of each unit.

The final two pages of each unit have either a **photostory** (even-numbered units) or a **Culture in mind** text (odd-numbered units). The **photostories** are conversations between teenagers in everyday situations, allowing students to read and listen for interest and also to experience the use of common everyday language expressions. These Everyday English expressions are worked on in exercises following the dialogue. The photostories are expanded with videostories on the DVD/DVD-ROM, where students can follow the progress of the characters through a term at school. The **Culture in mind** texts are reading texts which provide further reading practice, and an opportunity for students to develop their knowledge and understanding of the world at large and in particular the English-speaking world. They include a wide variety of stimulating topics: heroes and heroines, British families, pets in different cultures, TV viewing habits, school sports, the Edinburgh festival and Queen Elizabeth I.

Towards the end of each unit there is a **writing skills** task. These are an opportunity for students to further their control of language and to experiment in the production of tasks in a variety of genres (e.g. letters, emails, reports, etc.). There are model texts for the students to aid their own writing, and exercises providing guidance in terms of content and organisation. Through the completion of the writing tasks, students, if they wish, can also build up a bank of materials, or 'portfolio', during their period of learning: this can be very useful to them as the source of a sense of clear progress and as a means of self-assessment. A 'portfolio' of work can also be shown to other people (exam bodies, parents, even future employers) as evidence of achievement in language learning. Many of the writing tasks also provide useful and relevant practice for examinations such as Cambridge ESOL or Trinity Integrated Skills Examinations.

At the end of every even unit there is an extra speaking section, titled 'Last but not least' where students are given the opportunity for freer practice of the grammar and vocabulary that they have learnt in the unit.

There is a **Check your progress** section after every two units. Here the teacher will find exercises in the Grammar and Vocabulary that were presented in the previous two units. The purpose of these (as opposed to the more formal tests offered on the Testmaker CD-ROM) is for teachers and students alike to check quickly the learning and progress made during the two units just covered; they can be done in class or at home. Every exercise has a marking scheme, and students can use the marks they gain to do some simple self-assessment of their progress (a light 'task' is offered for this).

Beyond the units themselves, *English in Mind* offers at the end of the Student's Book a further set of materials for teachers and students. These consist of:

- **Vocabulary bank:** extension of vocabulary from the units in the main body of the Student's Book for students to build on their vocabulary. This section is attractively illustrated and the words are taught through either definitions or pictures. This section is particularly useful for those students who want to learn more.

- **Get it right!** This section is based on the Cambridge Learner Corpus and concentrates on typical errors that students often make at this level. These errors are dealt with through a variety of exercises and activities which correspond with the grammar studied in the units in the Student's Book. They allow students to focus on the errors they make and give them the opportunity to correct them.

- **Projects:** activities which students can do in pairs or groups (or even individually if desired), for students to put the language they have learned so far into practical and enjoyable use. They are especially useful for mixed-ability classes, as they allow students to work at their own pace. The projects produced could also be part of the 'portfolio' of material mentioned earlier.
  Project 1, **A tourist leaflet**, can be done after students have finished the first four units of the Student's Book. Project 2, **A class survey**, fits in after students have finished Unit 8 of the Student's Book.
  Project 3, **A poster presentation about a band or singer**, should be done once students have finished Unit 11 of the Student's Book, and finally, Project 4, **A presentation on changes in your country**, is an enjoyable way for students to round off the whole course.

- An **irregular verb** list for students to refer to when they need.

- A listing of **phonetic symbols**, again for student reference.

The DVD-ROM

The Student's Book includes a DVD-ROM which contains the listening material for the Workbook (listening texts and pronunciation exercises) in MP3 format and a range of carefully graded grammar and vocabulary exercises to provide further practice of the language presented in each unit. It also contains the 'Free Time' videostories corresponding to the seven photostories in the Student's Book. These complement the photostories by dealing with the same themes and reflecting the same values, but they contain separate stories and scenes to them. They may take place before, at the same time as or after the photostories. There are four exercises for each videostory on the DVD-ROM, including a 'videoke' one in which students record their voices onto a short section of the videostory and can then play it back, either solo or as a pair with a friend. This provides a fun, sociable element, but also good practice of spoken English. The DVD-ROM also includes games for students to practise in an enjoyable and motivating way.

The Workbook

The Workbook is a resource for both teachers and students, providing further practice in the language and skills covered in the Student's Book. It is organised unit-by-unit, following the Student's Book. Each Workbook unit has six pages, and the following contents:

Remember and check: this initial exercise encourages students to remember the content of the initial reading text in the Student's Book unit.

Exercises: an extensive range of supporting exercises in the grammatical, lexical and phonological areas of the Student's Book unit, following the progression of the unit, so that teachers can use the exercises either during or at the end of the Student's Book unit.

Everyday English and **Culture in mind:** extra exercises on these sections in alternating units, as in the Student's Book.

Study help: these sections follow a syllabus of study skills areas, to develop the students' capacities as independent and successful learners. After a brief description of the skill, there are exercises for the students to begin to practise it.

Skills in mind: these pages contain a separate skills development syllabus, which normally focuses on two main skill areas in each unit. There is also a skill tip relating to the main skill area, which the students can immediately put into action when doing the skills task(s).

Unit check: this is a one-page check of knowledge of the key language of the unit, integrating both grammar and vocabulary in the three exercise types. The exercise types are: a) a cloze text to be completed using items given in a box; b) a sentence-level multiple choice exercise; c) sentences to be completed with given vocabulary items.

At the end of the Workbook, there is a **Grammar reference** section. Here there are explanations of the main grammar topics of each unit, with examples. It can be used for reference by students at home, or the teacher might wish to refer to it in class if the students appreciate grammatical explanations.

The audio for the Workbook is available on the Audio CDs as well as on the Student's Book DVD-ROM in MP3 format.

The Teacher's Resource Book

The Teacher's Resource Book contains:

- clear, simple, practical teaching **notes** on each unit and ideas for how to implement the exercises as effectively as possible.
- complete **tapescripts** for all listening and pronunciation activities.
- complete **answers** to all exercises (grammar, vocabulary, comprehension questions, etc.).
- **optional further activities**, for stronger or weaker classes, to facilitate the use of the material in mixed-ability classes.
- **background notes** relating to the information content of reading texts (where appropriate). You can use these to set homework research tasks on the texts.
- **language notes** relating to grammatical areas, to assist less-experienced teachers who might have concerns about the target language and how it operates (these can also be used to refer to the Workbook Grammar reference section).
- a complete **answer key** and **tapescripts** for the **Workbook**.
- A '**Memo from Mario**' page at the end of each unit of teaching notes and ideas for further exploitation of the material in the Student's Book written by the well-known methodologist Mario Rinvolucri.
- an **entry test** which has been designed with two purposes. It can be used purely as a diagnostic entry test, or teachers can use it for remedial work before beginning the Welcome section or after completing it.
- **photocopiable communication activities**: one page for each unit reflecting the core grammar and/or vocabulary of the unit. The communication activities recycle the key grammar and/or vocabulary in each unit. They are designed to activate the new language in a communicative context. They cover a range of fun and motivating activity types: board games; quizzes; information gap activities; descriptions; 'Find someone who … ', etc.

- **photocopiable grammar practice exercises:** extra exercises for each unit, reflecting the key grammar areas of the unit. They are intended for fast finishers or students who need extra practice.
- **teaching notes** for the photocopiable communication activities which contain clear step-by-step instructions for all the activities. In addition, there are answers for the Communication Activities, where relevant, and answers for all of the Grammar Practice Exercises.

Other resources

Testmaker Audio CD / CD-ROM: This allows you to create and edit your own texts, choosing from unit tests, which can be combined in unit pairs to match the course syllabus, or end-of-year tests. The tests offer 'standard' and 'more challenging' levels of testing, and can be created in A and B versions to avoid the sharing of answers. The listening test recordings are provided in audio CD format.

DVD: This contains both the 'Free Time' videostories and the complete 'EiMTV' material from the original edition.

Classware DVD-ROM: This contains the Student's Book in digital format to project on a whiteboard or via a computer with projector. You can enlarge parts of the page for a clearer focus. The 'Free Time' videostories and class listenings are also included, together with scripts.

Web resources: In addition to information about the series, the *English in Mind* website contains downloadable pages of further activities and exercises for students as well as interactive activities for students and wordlists with multiple translations. It can be found at this part of the Cambridge University Press website:

www.cambridge.org/elt/englishinmind

Introductory note from Mario Rinvolucri

As you read through the Teacher's Resource Book you will, at the end of each unit, find small contributions of mine that offer you alternative ways of practising a structure, of dealing with a text or of revising words.

- I want to stress that the ideas presented are simply alternatives to the ways of working proposed to you by the authors. I strongly recommend that you try the authors' way first.
- When you teach the book through for the second or third time you may be ready then to try something a bit different. The authors and I believe that options are important but options are not useful if they confuse you.
- Maybe you could think of my contributions as a sort of sauce with a slightly different flavour to be tried for variety's sake.

Mario Rinvolucri, Pilgrims, UK, guest methodologist.

Welcome section

This section is designed to serve as a review, giving students the opportunity to revise and practise language they already know. It is also a tool for teachers to find out how much students know already and which areas students may need to do more work on before continuing with the course.

A GREETINGS

1 Saying *hello* and *goodbye*

Warm-up

Books closed. In order to introduce yourself to a group of new students at beginner level, say: *Hello, my name is ...* and encourage individual students to respond. Many students will know the word *Hello* in English. Go round the class introducing yourself to the students and encourage them to say *Hello, my name is ...* to each other.

a ▶ CD1 T2 Books open. Read through the dialogues with students and ask them to guess which words go in the gaps. Listen to some of their ideas but do not comment at this stage. Play the recording for students to listen and check their answers.

TAPESCRIPT

See dialogues on page 4 of the Student's Book.

> **Answers**
> 1 this 2 How; thanks 3 morning; Goodbye
> 4 See you

✱ OPTIONAL ACTIVITY

Play the recording again, pausing after every second sentence and asking students to respond. With stronger classes, get students to respond without looking at their books. For further practice, ask students to work in pairs to recreate the dialogues. One student can look at the book while the other tries to remember the responses.

2 The day

a Ask students to look at the pictures and match them to the words.

> **Answers**
> 2 night 3 morning 4 afternoon

b ▶ CD1 T3 Students match the expressions to the speech bubbles. Play the recording for students to check their answers. To practise pronunciation, ask students to repeat the expressions after the recording.

TAPESCRIPT

A Good afternoon
B Goodbye
C Goodnight
D Good morning
E Good evening

> **Answers**
> B 5 C 4 D 1 E 3

B THE WORLD, THE CLASSROOM

1 International words

Warm-up

Books closed. Ask students if they can think of any words in English which are also international words. Elicit suggestions and put them on the board.

a Students open their books at page 6 and read through the words in the box. Check understanding and see if any students' predictions from the Warm-up are in the list. Go through the first item as an example, if necessary. Students complete the exercise. Do not check answers at this stage.

b ▶ CD1 T4 Play the recording for students to listen and check their answers to Exercise 1a. If your students are complete beginners, you may need to translate the numbers on the recording. Play the recording a second time, pausing after each word for students to repeat. If students are having problems with some words, drill these as a class.

TAPESCRIPT/ANSWERS

1 city 2 football 3 airport 4 computer
5 sandwich 6 bus 7 music 8 taxi 9 cinema
10 restaurant 11 museum 12 hamburger
13 DVD 14 TV 15 hotel 16 phone
17 pizza 18 café

✱ OPTIONAL ACTIVITY

Weaker classes: Call out one of the numbers from the pictures on page 6 and a student's name. The student must name the object using the correct pronunciation.

Stronger classes: Give students a few minutes to memorise the pictures on page 6. Books closed. Call out the number of an object from page 6 and a student's name. The student must name the object using the correct pronunciation.

Vocabulary notebook

In their vocabulary notebooks, students can start a section called *International words*. They should note down any new words from this section and add any new words as they come across them.

② Classroom objects

a **Stronger classes:** Students look at the pictures on page 7. In pairs, they ask each other the example question and try to answer as many questions as possible with the correct English word. If they are having problems, they can ask you the question. Remind students not to write anything down at this stage.

Weaker classes: Give students a few minutes to look at the pictures. Ask a student to demonstrate the question and then give them the answer. Remind students not to write anything down at this stage.

b ▶ **CD1 T5** Students now read through the words in the box and write the correct words under the pictures in Exercise 2a. Give them a few minutes to complete the activity. Play the recording for students to listen and check answers. If your students are complete beginners, you may need to translate the numbers on the recording.

Play the recording a second time, pausing after each word for students to repeat.

TAPESCRIPT/ANSWERS

1 pen   2 book   3 board   4 CD   5 pencil
6 chair   7 door   8 window   9 notebook
10 desk

Vocabulary notebook

In their vocabulary notebooks, students can start a section called *Classroom objects*. They should note down any new words from this section and add any new words as they come across them.

✳ OPTIONAL ACTIVITY

Collect eight to ten small classroom objects (e.g. pen, pencil, notebook, CD) and put them on a tray. Give students a few minutes to look at the tray and memorise the items. Ask one student to come out and remove an object, while the others close their eyes. The students must then try and guess which object has been removed from the tray. The first person to get it right can come out and remove the next object.

③ Plural nouns

Stronger classes: Students look at the pictures and identify each one. Remind them of the words they have just learnt in Exercise 2. Explain that there is more than one of each item in each picture so they must write the plural form of each noun. Go through the example as a class, asking a student to explain how the plural is formed (by adding an -s). Give students a few minutes to write their answers. Check answers as a class.

Weaker classes: Books closed. Ask students how many of the words they can remember from Exercise 2a and write them on the board. Explain to students that these are all singular words and ask them how they would form the plural of them. Elicit or explain that they would add an -s and ask a student to come out and add an -s to the words on the board to demonstrate how this works. Students now open their books at page 9 and write the plural forms of the nouns in the pictures in Exercise 3.

Check answers as a class, making sure students are using the correct pronunciation.

> **Answers**
> 2 seven pencils   3 five chairs   4 four CDs
> 5 six books   6 three notebooks

Language note

Explain to students that the plurals they have seen so far are regular (add an -s). There are other spelling rules for regular plurals which students may find it useful to know at this stage:

If a noun ends in *s, z, x, ch, sh*: add -es (*bus/buses*).

If a noun ends in *y*, change the *y* to *i* and add -es (*baby/babies*).

Exceptions to the rule are: *potato/potatoes, tomato/tomatoes*.

b Books closed. Write the words *man, woman, person, child* on the board and ask students to write the plurals. Students may try to write *mans, womans*, etc. Explain that these plurals are irregular. Books open. Students match the singular and plural nouns. Check answers and make sure students are pronouncing the words correctly.

> **Answers**
> 1 b   2 d   3 a   4 c

✳ OPTIONAL ACTIVITY

Call out some singular nouns from this lesson or some others of your own and ask students to provide the correct plural form, asking them to spell them out if necessary.

Grammar notebook

Students should note down the plural rules and some examples of their own in their grammar notebooks.

 ## Syllables and word stress

a ▶ **CD1 T6** Students read through the words in each column. Play the recording, pausing after each word for students to repeat. Ask students to explain the number of syllables in each column (A = 1 syllable, B = 2 syllables, C = 3 syllables). Remind them that they should repeat the words with the same stress as on the recording.

TAPESCRIPT

bus phone desk taxi teacher hotel computer cinema hamburger

b ▶ **CD1 T7** Explain that students will hear some other words. They must listen and decide how many syllables are in each and then write them under the appropriate column. Do the first item with them as an example, if necessary. Students listen and write the words in the appropriate column. Play the recording again for students to listen and check answers. Play the recording a third time, pausing after each word for students to repeat.

TAPESCRIPT

sandwich door museum pen restaurant window

> **Answers**
> A: door, pen
> B: sandwich, window
> C: museum, restaurant

C THINGS, LETTERS, COLOURS

 ## Adjectives

a Students read through the phrases in the box. Check any problems. Ask a stronger student to explain what an adjective is (it describes a noun). Ask students to point out the adjectives in the box. Go through the example as a class, making sure students understand what *cheap* means. Students complete the exercise. Do not check answers at this stage.

b ▶ **CD1 T8** Play the recording for students to listen and check their answers. Pause after each phrase for students to repeat.

TAPESCRIPT/ANSWERS

1 a cheap computer
2 an old man
3 a big TV
4 a new book
5 a small hotel
6 an interesting DVD
7 a bad café
8 a good hamburger

c Ask students what they notice about the position of the adjectives in the phrases (the adjectives are all before the noun). Go through the example as a class, then give students a few minutes to complete the exercise. Monitor and check students are putting the adjective in the correct position. Check answers.

> **Answers**
> 2 a good CD
> 3 an expensive restaurant
> 4 an interesting museum
> 5 a good football team
> 6 an interesting computer game

> ### Language note
> It may be useful to point out to students at this stage that adjectives in English do not change with the noun. The adjective stays the same whether the noun is singular or plural. We say: *A good book / three good books* NOT ~~three goods books~~.

d Go through the example as a class and then, in pairs, students can provide an example for each item in Exercise 1c. Ask pairs to read out their examples to the rest of the class.

e Students read through the list of adjectives. Go through the example as a class. Students complete the exercise. Check answers.

> **Answers**
> 2 d 3 a 4 b 5 e

✳ OPTIONAL ACTIVITY

Ask students to look round the class and find an object for each of the adjectives in Exercise 1e, e.g. a big television, an old chair, etc.

Vocabulary notebook

Remind students to note down the adjectives from this section in their notebooks.

② a/an

Warm-up

Books closed. Write three gapped words on the board, e.g.

_ c _ _ _ _   c _ _ _ _ _ _ _

Ask students to guess what the words are (a cheap computer), then ask them to point to the noun, the adjective and the article. Repeat the exercise with

_ _ o _ _ m _ _ (an old man)

a Books open. Look at the examples with students and ask them to complete the rule. If necessary, use L1 to help weaker students.

> **Answer**
> a, e, i, o, u

b Students complete the exercise. Check answers in open class, paying attention to pronunciation. Make sure students are not stressing the article.

> **Answers**
> 2 an 3 an 4 a 5 a 6 an

③ The alphabet

a ▶ CD1 T9   Play the recording for students to listen. Play the recording a second time, pausing after each letter for students to repeat.

TAPESCRIPT

See page 9 of the Student's Book.

b Write the sounds of the alphabet on the board. Go through each sound as a class, making sure students can hear each sound clearly.

Stronger classes: They can classify the remaining letters. Do not check answers at this stage.

Weaker classes: It may be helpful to go through each sound individually with them, replaying the recording from Exercise 6a for them to listen again. Do not check answers at this stage.

c ▶ CD1 T10   Play the recording for students to listen and check their answers.

TAPESCRIPT/ANSWERS

/e/	f, l, m, n, s, x, z
/eɪ/	a, h, j, k
/iː/	b, c, d, e, g, p, t, v
/aɪ/	i, y
/əʊ/	o
/uː/	q, u, w
/ɑː/	r

d Go through the example as a class. Point out to students that we can also say 'double …' in English when there are two letters the same in a word, e.g. R-I-H-A-double N-A. In pairs, students think of names and spell them out to their partner, who must work out if the spelling is correct.

✳ OPTIONAL ACTIVITY

Make up various bingo cards using the letters of the alphabet. Copy and give these out to students. Call out the letters of the alphabet in a random order (keeping a note of the letters you have called out). The first student to cross off all the letters on their card and to call out *Bingo!* is the winner. Alternatively, this can be done as a small group or pair activity.

④ Colours

a Ask students if they know the names of any colours in English. Ask them if a colour is an adjective or noun (adjective) and whether it goes before or after a noun (before). Students write the colours under the football shirts. Let them compare answers with a partner but do not check at this stage.

b ▶ CD1 T11   Play the recording for students to listen and check their answers to Exercise 4a. Repeat the recording, pausing after each colour for students to repeat.

TAPESCRIPT/ANSWERS

1 white 2 black 3 brown 4 pink 5 grey
6 red 7 green 8 purple 9 silver 10 yellow
11 blue 12 orange

c Point to various objects in the classroom and ask students to say the colour. Encourage students to use articles and nouns as well.

Vocabulary notebook

Encourage students to start a section called *Colours* and to note down the colours from this section.

✳ OPTIONAL ACTIVITY

Whole class or small groups. Students think of colours which are used with famous brands, organisations or TV characters, e.g. the Red Cross, the Pink Panther. If this is done in small groups, set a time limit and the group with the most words after the time limit is the winner.

D ASKING AND ANSWERING

1 Problems

Warm-up

Books closed. Draw a large question mark on the board. Speak very quickly to the students on a topic of your choice. Encourage them to say they don't understand and try to elicit some of the expressions from the dialogues.

a ▶ **CD1 T12** Books open. Read through the dialogues with students and ask them to guess the correct words. Play the recording while students listen and check their predictions. Check answers. Play the recording again, pausing for students to repeat. In pairs, students can act out the dialogues. Listen to some of the best examples in open class.

> **Answers**
> 2 Sorry 3 don't 4 you 5 Excuse me 6 No

b Ask students to cover the dialogues in Exercise 1a and to make phrases using one word from each column. Check answers.

> **Answers**
> 2e Excuse me.   3a I don't know.
> 4c What does this mean? 5d I can help you.

✳ OPTIONAL ACTIVITY

As this is useful classroom language, ask students to work in pairs and prepare a poster using some of the expressions. Display the best ones around the class.

2 Numbers 0-20

a ▶ **CD1 T13** Books closed. Elicit as many numbers from 0 to 20 as students know and write them on the board (or ask students to come out and write them up if time permits). Students open their books at page 11 and quickly read through the numbers. Play the recording, pausing after each number for students to repeat.

TAPESCRIPT

See page 11 of the Student's Book.

> **Language note**
> Make sure students are pronouncing the -teen numbers correctly; they should put the stress on the second syllable (e.g. fourteen). If you feel this is a problem, call out a few -teen numbers for them to practise in isolation.

b Prepare a list of numbers between one and twenty to read to the class, pausing after the first item to go through as an example, if necessary. Read the rest of the list for students to listen and tick the numbers they hear. Check answers, reading your list of numbers again as necessary.

c ▶ **CD1 T14** Explain to students that they will hear four phone numbers. It may be useful to explain to them (or elicit) that in English we say phone numbers in two ways, e.g. 712345 = *seven one two/three four five* or *seven one/two three/four five*. Also explain to students that where there are two numbers the same we say 'double ...'. Play the recording, pausing after the first phone number, if necessary. Play the rest of the recording for students to listen and write down the numbers they hear.

TAPESCRIPT/ANSWERS

1 My phone number is 272 3454. That's 272 3454.

2 My phone number is 681 7595. Once more: 681 7595.

3 Hi John? It's Tom. Phone me, can you? It's 923 6931. OK? 923 6931.

4 Hi. This is 717 4930. Please leave a message after the tone.

d Divide the class into pairs. Ask a stronger pair to demonstrate the example question and answer. Give students a few minutes to ask and answer.

✳ OPTIONAL ACTIVITY

You can give students some simple sums using the numbers 0 to 20.

3 Numbers 20-100

a ▶ **CD1 T15** Books closed. Elicit as many numbers between 20 and 100 as students know and write them on the board. Students open their books at page 11 and quickly read through the numbers. Play the recording, pausing after each number for students to repeat.

TAPESCRIPT

See page 11 of the Student's Book.

b ▶ **CD1 T16** Students read through the numbers. Ask them how to pronounce them. Play the recording for students to listen and check their pronunciation. Pause the recording after each number for students to repeat.

TAPESCRIPT

1 twenty-six 2 twenty-nine 3 thirty-five
4 forty-seven 5 fifty-eight 6 sixty-four

Vocabulary notebook

Remind students to make a note of all the numbers from this section in their notebooks.

Give students the following extra exercise for practice in distinguishing between -*teen* numbers and -*ty* numbers. Write the following on the board:

1   13 or 30?
2   90 or 19?
3   18 or 80?
4   50 or 15?
5   17 or 70?

Choose which number you are going to call out, making a note of it each time and then ask students to read out their answers.

Alternatively, you can give them some more sums using all the numbers from 0 to 100.

Messages

a ▶ **CD1 T17** Ask students who the first message is to (Lucy) and who is it from (Mrs Hurley). Students quickly read through the message. Play the recording while students read the text again.

TAPESCRIPT

Hello, this is Mrs Hurley with a message for Lucy. The homework is on page 78. If there are any problems, my number is 01437 651464. Bye now.

b ▶ **CD1 T18** Students read the gapped message. Ask them what information is missing (person's name, page number and phone number). Students listen to the recording and complete the missing information.

Weaker classes: They may find it helpful to listen to the whole message first, then it can be played and paused after each gap. Check answers.

TAPESCRIPT

Girl: Hello?

Woman: Hello, it's Mrs Booker. Is Rob there please?

Girl: No sorry. Can I take a message?

Woman: Oh, yes please. My name is Mrs Booker, that's B-double O-K-E-R, I'm Rob's English teacher. Please tell him the homework is on page 85.

Girl: Page 85. OK.

Woman: And my phone number is 01763 208956.

Girl: 01763. Er …

Woman: 208956. Thanks very much.

Girl: OK. Bye Mrs Booker.

Woman: Goodbye.

> **Answers**
> 1 Booker   2 85   3 01763 208956

1 He's a footballer

Unit overview

TOPIC: Countries and nationalities

TEXTS
Reading and listening: a dialogue about famous people
Listening: a text about heroes and heroines
Writing: a text about yourself

SPEAKING AND FUNCTIONS
Talking about nationalities and where people are from

LANGUAGE
Grammar: the verb *be* (singular): statements and questions; question words: *who, what, how old, where?*
Vocabulary: countries and nationalities
Pronunciation: *from*

1 Read and listen

If you set the background information as a homework research task, ask students to tell the rest of the class what they found out.

BACKGROUND INFORMATION

Fernando Torres (born 20 March 1984) is a footballer who plays for Liverpool and Spain. He scored the winning goal in Spain's 1–0 win over Germany in the Euro 2008 final.

Kakà (born Ricardo Izecson dos Santos Leite, 22 April 1982) is a Brazilian footballer who plays for Real Madrid and Brazil. He was FIFA World Player of the Year in 2007.

Rafael Nadal (born 3 June 1986) is a Spanish tennis player. He has won six Grand Slam titles and is recognised as the world's best player on clay.

Angelina Jolie (born 4 June 1975) is an American actress, star of films such as *Mr & Mrs Smith* and *Lara Croft: Tomb Raider*. She lives with Brad Pitt with whom she has six children.

Matt Damon (born 8 October 1970) is an American actor, star of films such as *The Bourne Ultimatum, The Talented Mr Ripley* and *The Departed*.

Brad Pitt (born 18 December 1963) is an American actor, famous for such films as *Fight Club, Ocean's Eleven* and *Troy*.

Kelly Clarkson (born 24 April 1982) is an American pop singer. She won the first season of the television series *American Idol* in 2002. Her biggest hit is *My Life Would Suck Without You,* which reached No. 1 in the US.

Lily Allen (born 2 May 1985) is an English singer. Her first album *Alright, Still* sold over 2.6 million copies and included the No. 1 hit *Smile.*

Warm-up

Give students a few minutes to look at the picture. Ask them: *What is happening?* (Two girls are waiting to go into a concert) and *Who are they thinking about?*

a ▶ **CD1 T19** Students read the question. Play the recording while students listen and read. Check answers. Play the recording again, pausing as necessary to clarify any problems

TAPESCRIPT

See the dialogue on page 12 of the Student's Book.

> **Answer**
> Emma

b ▶ **CD1 T20** Give students a few minutes to look at the pictures and names of the stars in the box. Tell them that they must match the names to the pictures. Play the recording, pausing to give students time to write the names in the spaces. Students can compare answers in pairs before checking as a class.

TAPESCRIPT

Emma: Who's your favourite celebrity, Olivia?

Olivia: Well, Rafael Nadal is my favourite sportsman.

Emma: Who's your favourite singer? Is it Taylor Swift?

Olivia: No, it isn't. It's photo number 2, Lily Allen. She's my favourite. What about you ... oh ... is it Beyoncé?

Emma: No way! My favourite singer is Kelly Clarkson, photo number 1. She's great.

Olivia: Yeah, she's OK.

Emma: What about actors?

Olivia: Guess who is my favourite actor.

Emma: Er ... Will Smith? Or Matt Damon, number 4?

Olivia: No.

Emma: OK – a clue. He's blonde and good looking.

Olivia: Oh, yeah! Brad Pitt, number 3.

Emma: Yes, and who's your favourite?

Olivia: Matt Damon, of course! He's the best!

Answers
1 Kelly Clarkson   2 Lily Allen   3 Brad Pitt
4 Matt Damon

2 Grammar
✱ The verb *be* (singular)

a **Stronger classes:** Students look at the sentences. Ask them which sentences are positive, negative and questions. Ask them what they notice about the verb in each one (positive: *I'm, it is*), negative (uses *n't*), question (subject and verb inverted). This can be done in L1 if necessary.

Weaker classes: Books closed. Write some example sentences of your own on the board, e.g. *I'm (your name). Am I a teacher? You're a student. I'm not a singer.* Ask students what they notice about the verb in each sentence and elicit the positive, negative and question forms. Students now open their books at page 13 and look at the examples from Exercise 1. Ask them which person each verb is for (*I'm* = first person, *Is it/it is* = third person, *He isn't* = third person) and then ask them to identify the different forms.

b Students read through the table quickly and fill in the missing verbs. Give them a few minutes to do this, reminding them to refer back to the examples from Exercise 2a to help them. Check answers.

Answers
Positive: You're, She's, It's
Negative: She isn't, It isn't
Question: Are, Is, Is, Is
Short answer: are, aren't, is, is, isn't, is, isn't

Language note
Remind students that we use the word *not* to make a positive verb negative. If you feel it would be useful for students, explain that the short form is usually used when speaking and the full form when writing more formally.

c This exercise can be set for homework. Students read through sentences 1 to 4. Go through the first item as an example, if necessary. Students complete the exercise. Check answers.

Answers
2 's 3 're 4 's

d This exercise can be set for homework. Students read through sentences 1 to 4. Go through the

example as a class, if necessary. Students complete the exercise. Remind students they are using the negative form this time. Check answers.

Answers
2 She isn't a film star.
3 You're not the winner.
4 I'm not a tennis player.

LOOK!

Students read the examples in the box. Ask them what they notice about the positive and the question form in English (to make the question form we invert the subject and the verb).

e This exercise can be set for homework. Students read through questions 1 to 4. Go through the example with students. Students complete the exercise. Remind them to look carefully at the subject of each sentence before they choose the verb. Check answers.

Answers
2 Are 3 Is 4 Is

f Divide the class into pairs. Ask a stronger pair to demonstrate the example question and answer. Give students a few minutes to ask and answer and then ask a few pairs to feedback to the class.

Language note
Explain to students that in English we use the verb *be* when asking about someone's age. We say: *I am 15* NOT ~~I have 15 years~~.

Grammar notebook
Remind students to note down the verb forms from this unit in their notebooks.

3 Vocabulary
✱ Countries

Warm-up

Books closed. Ask students how many countries they know the names of in English. Elicit the names and put them on the board. Check the pronunciation of each country they have given.

Alternatively, you could use a large wall map and ask students to come and identify the countries they know the names of in English.

a ▶ **CD1 T21**   Give students a few minutes to read through the names of the countries. Play the recording, pausing after each country for students to repeat. Point out the stress marks above each country. If students have produced countries in the Warm-up which are not in this exercise, ask them to identify the number of syllables in each country.

TAPESCRIPT

Spain Belgium Britain Poland Brazil Switzerland

b ▶ **CD1 T22** Give students a few minutes to read through the countries in the box.

Stronger classes: They can pronounce the countries themselves and decide on the number of syllables and fit them into the table. They can listen and check their answers.

Weaker classes: Play the recording once for students to listen only. Play the recording a second time, pausing to give students time to fill in the table.

TAPESCRIPT/ANSWERS

China Russia Turkey Japan Italy Canada Germany

c Divide the class into pairs. Give students a few minutes to look at the map. Ask a stronger pair to demonstrate the example question and answer. Students complete the exercise. Students can compare answers with another pair, but do not check answers at this stage.

d ▶ **CD1 T23** Play the recording for students to listen and check their answers to Exercise 3c.

TAPESCRIPT/ANSWERS

1 Canada 2 Brazil 3 Britain 4 Spain
5 Belgium 6 Germany 7 Poland
8 Switzerland 9 Italy 10 Turkey 11 Russia
12 China 13 Japan

> **Language note**
> Remind students that we always use a capital letter when we write a country in English.

e Give students a few minutes to look at the photos. Go through the example as a class.

> **Answers**
> 1 Japan 2 Italy 3 Britain 4 Brazil 5 Turkey
> 6 Poland

✳ OPTIONAL ACTIVITY

Whole class or small groups. You will need a large wall map. Point to a country and ask a student to name it in English and then spell the name out. The student who answers correctly can come out and choose another country. You can award points for each correct country and spelling.

Vocabulary notebook

Encourage students to start a section called *Countries* in their vocabulary notebooks and to note down the countries from this section and any others they come across later in the course.

4 Grammar

✳ *Where are you from?*

Warm-up

Give students a few minutes to read the dialogue. Can students predict any of the missing words? Accept all suggestions at this stage but do not give the answers.

a ▶ **CD1 T24** Play the recording for students to complete the dialogue and check their predictions from the Warm-up.

Weaker classes: Play the recording once and then play it a second time, pausing after each gap to give them time to fill in the answers. Check answers.

TAPESCRIPT/ANSWERS

Andrea: Hi! I'm Andrea. I'm from Switzerland.
Tomasz: Hi, Andrea. I'm Tomasz.
Andrea: Where are you from, Tomasz?
Tomasz: Poland.

b Students read through items 1 to 3. Students complete the exercise. Check answers.

> **Answers**
> 1 'm 2 are 3 from

Grammar notebook

Remind students to note down the new structures from this section in their notebooks.

5 Pronunciation

See notes on page 107.

6 Vocabulary

✳ Nationalities

Warm-up

Write the countries from Exercise 3b on the board. Ask students if they know or can work out the nationality adjectives for any of them. Students can come and write the nationalities they know beside the relevant country if there is time.

a Give students a few minutes to read through the countries in the box. Go through the examples as a class, making sure students can see which endings go in which column. Students complete the exercise. They can then add in any other countries from the Warm-up to the table. Do not check answers at this stage.

Language note

Explain to students that they may need to make some spelling changes from the country to the nationality. If necessary, practise the change in stress from country to nationality as a class.

b ▶ CD1 T26 Play the recording for students to check their answers. Alternatively, write the column headings on the board and ask students to come and write the nationalities under the correct heading. Check spelling. Play the recording a second time, pausing after each adjective for students to repeat. Make sure students are using the correct stress when pronouncing the nationality adjectives.

TAPESCRIPT/ANSWERS

Italian Belgian Brazilian Russian
Polish British Turkish Spanish
Chinese Japanese Portuguese

c Give students a few minutes to look at the flags and read through the nationalities. Go through the first item as an example, if necessary. Students complete the exercise. Do not check answers at this stage.

d Divide the class into pairs. Ask a stronger pair to demonstrate the example. Give students a few minutes to discuss their answers to Exercise 6c.

e ▶ CD1 T27 Play the recording for students to check answers.

TAPESCRIPT/ANSWERS

1 Belgian 2 Chinese 3 Polish 4 Russian
5 Turkish 6 Italian 7 British 8 Brazilian

LOOK! 🔍

Students read through the examples in the box. Elicit the rule for nationality adjectives which start with a vowel and a consonant. Students may remember this rule from Welcome section C, Exercise 2.

Vocabulary bank Refer students to the vocabulary bank. Read through the words and phrases in open class and check understanding.

Get it right! Refer students to the Get it right! section. These exercises can be used as homework or for fast-finishers.

Vocabulary notebook

Encourage students to start a section called *Nationalities* and to note down the nationalities from this section.

✳ OPTIONAL ACTIVITY

In small groups, students take turns to choose a famous person and the other students must guess who the person is. The person who has chosen

must give information to the rest of the group. For example:

S1: *I am from [country]. I am not American. I am a film star.*

The student who guesses correctly takes the next turn and so on.

7 Grammar
✳ Wh- question words

a Students read through the question words. Elicit how they say them in their own language. Ask them if they know which words apply to the following things: people (*who*), places (*where*), things (*what*) and manner (*how*), and elicit the answers.

b Students read through items 1 to 6. Go through the example as a class, asking students what they notice about these questions (the verb goes immediately after the question word). Students complete the exercise. Check answers.

Answers
2 Where 3 What 4 Where 5 How 6 Who

✳ OPTIONAL ACTIVITY

A fun way to practice *who*, *what* and *where* is to cover a magazine picture with nine post-its (numbered 1–9). Ask *Who/Where/What is it?* depending on the picture. Divide the class into two teams. Students call out a number which is then removed from the picture. Students guess the object, person or place using *It is ...* . Continue until someone guesses correctly.

Grammar notebook

Encourage students to start a section called *Wh-question words* and to note down these question words and others that they come across.

8 Speak

If you set the background information as a homework research task, ask students to tell the rest of the class what they found out.

BACKGROUND INFORMATION

Lionel Messi (born 24 June 1987) is an Argentine footballer who plays for Barcelona and Argentina. In 2004 he became the youngest player ever to play professionally in Spain. In 2008–2009 he scored 38 goals.

Lorena Ochoa (born 15 November 1981) is a Mexican golfer, ranked the number one female golfer in the world. She won the Women's British Open in 2007 and the Kraft Nabisco Championship in 2008.

Dinara Safina (born 27 April 1986) is a Russian tennis player, formerly ranked World No. 1. She has been runner-up in three Grand Slam competitions. Her brother Marat Safin has been ranked World No. 1 men's player.

Kanye West (born 8 June 1977) is an American rapper. He has released four albums including *Graduation* (2007). His biggest hits are *Gold Digger* and *Stronger*, both of which made No. 1 in the US.

Sertab Erener (born 4 December 1964) is a Turkish pop star. She released her first album in 1992 and has since made 11 more. In 2003 she won the Eurovision song contest with *Every Way That I Can*.

Rodrigo Santoro (born 22 August 1975) is a Brazilian actor. He began acting in soap operas, before making films in the United States such as *Charlie's Angels: Full Throttle*, *300* and *Che*. He also starred in the TV show *Lost*.

Queen Latifah (born Dana Owens, 18 March 1970) is an American actor and rapper. She released her first album *All Hail The Queen* in 1989. She starred in the US TV comedy *Living Single* before moving on to films. She won the Oscar for Best Actress in a Supporting Role for her role in *Chicago* (2002).

Warm-up

Ask students if they know any of the famous people in the pictures and where they come from. Divide the class into pairs. Give students a few minutes to read through the information and check any problems. Go through the example sentence as a class, drawing students' attention to the use of the third person singular *be* form. Students complete the exercise. Monitor and check students are using the third person singular forms correctly, noting down any repeated errors to go through as a class after the exercise. Do not check answers at this stage.

> **Answers**
> 1 Sertab Erener is a singer. She's from Istanbul. She's Turkish.
> 2 Queen Latifah is a film star. She's from Newark. She's American.
> 3 Kanye West is a rap singer. He's from Chicago. He's American.
> 4 Lionel Messi is a football player. He's from Rosario. He's Argentinean.
> 5 Rodrigo Santoro is an actor. He's from Rio de Janeiro. He's Brazilian.
> 6 Lorena Ochoa is a golfer. She's from Guadalajara. She's Mexican.

9 Listen

a ▶ **CD1 T28** Play the recording for students to listen and check their answers to Exercise 8.

TAPESCRIPT/ANSWERS

1 Sertab Erener is my heroine. She's a singer from Istanbul in Turkey.
2 My heroine is an actress. She's from Newark, New Jersey in the USA. Her name is Queen Latifah.
3 My hero is a rap singer. He's from Chicago, in the USA. He's Kanye West.
4 My hero is a football player from Rosario in Argentina. His name is Lionel Messi.
5 My hero is Brazilian. He's from Petropolis near Rio de Janeiro and he's an actor. Can you guess his name? Yes, it's Rodrigo Santoro.
6 My heroine is a golfer. Her name is Lorena Ochoa. She's Mexican. She's from Guadalajara.

b Students read through sentences 1 to 7. Go through the example as a class, reminding students to correct the information if it is false. Remind them to use their answers from Exercise 9a to help them. Students complete the exercise. Check answers.

> **Answers**
> 2 No, he isn't. He's from Rosario.
> 3 No, she isn't. She's from Istanbul.
> 4 No, she isn't. She's Mexican.
> 5 No, he isn't. He's an actor.
> 6 No, she isn't. She's from Newark.
> 7 No, he isn't. He's from Chicago.

c In pairs, students discuss who their hero or heroine is. They must say where the person is from and what they do. Ask pairs to feedback to the rest of the class about their partner.

10 Write

Warm-up

a Give students a few minutes to read the example text and answer the questions.

> **Answers**
> Joanna is from Manchester. She's 14. Her heroine is Alicia Keys.

b This part of the writing can be set for homework. Encourage students to make notes on the areas the text covers: name, age, nationality, where from, address, phone number, hero/heroine and where hero/heroine is from. Students can draft their notes before checking them and writing the full text.

Memo from Mario

He's a footballer

1 Extra practice of *Is it a ...?*

▶ Tell the students you are going to draw an everyday object line by line and at each stage of the process you want them to ask you: *Is it a ...?*

▶ Suppose the picture you have in mind is a bicycle. Start by drawing two back wheel spokes, then look at the class to invite hypotheses. Then draw the front mudguard, and so on.

▶ Be ready to help students with the English words for the objects that they imagine (there is no better time to teach vocabulary than when the student is reaching out for the word).

▶ Play the game twice (two different objects) with the whole class.

▶ Teach the students these new patterns:

Is it maybe a ...?

Could it be a ...?

I guess it's a ...?

▶ Put the students in groups of four. They play the game four times. Each time a different student takes the role of picture-maker. Encourage them to try out the new patterns.

> **RATIONALE**
> This activity will appeal to students who have strong spatial awareness, some of whom may not even like learning English.
>
> The exercise allows real human interaction using the very limited language resources the students have so far.

2 Extra practice of the verb *be*

▶ Preparation: you need one sticky label for each person in the class. Put the name of one hero/heroine or profession on each label. Use the famous names given in the text and/or the names of people who are really familiar to your students. Depending on the size of your class, you may end up with more than one label with the same name/profession.

▶ In the lesson, pick a student to put a label on each of their classmates' backs. The students must **not** see what's written on the label on their own backs.

▶ Ask the students to get up and move around the room. Their task is to ask other people questions using *Am I ...?* to find out who they are, e.g.

Am I an actor?

▶ The students mingle until they discover who is on their label.

▶ Then ask the students to swap identities (labels) and to hide their new labels. They continue mingling and ask each other questions using *Are you ...?* to find out who they are, e.g.

Are you Kanye West?

Are you a footballer?

▶ When the students have had a chance to interact with about half their classmates, tell them to go up to somebody whose identity they think they know and say: *But aren't you X?*

▶ In the last phase of the exercise they go up to a classmate, point to another and ask:

Is s/he X?

> **RATIONALE**
> Apart from practising the unit's grammar, the students are up and moving, making fluid, though brief, contact with all their classmates. The students are practising English as they approach and leave other people in the group. The exercise is a useful way of getting students to meet their classmates and start building a group.

2 We're a new band

Unit overview

TOPIC: Likes and dislikes; music

TEXTS

Reading and listening: an interview with a pop star; photostory: Just a little joke
Listening: people talking about things they like and things they don't like
Writing: an email about your favourite band

SPEAKING AND FUNCTIONS

Expressing likes and dislikes

LANGUAGE

Grammar: the verb *be*: plural, negatives and questions; *I (don't) like... / Do you like ...?*; object pronouns
Vocabulary: positive and negative adjectives
Pronunciation: /ɪ/ and /iː/

1 Read and listen

If you set the background information as a homework research task, ask students to tell the rest of the class what they found out.

BACKGROUND INFORMATION

Birmingham (population c. 1 million) is the second-biggest city in England. During the nineteenth century, Birmingham was home to much industry. Manufacturing has declined now, but Birmingham is still a major commercial centre. The town is known as 'Brum' and people from Birmingham are called 'Brummies'.

Coventry (population c.309,800) is the ninth-biggest city in England. It is farthest from the coast of any city in Britain.

Warm-up

Ask students which bands or pop singers they enjoy listening to. Ask them if they can tell the rest of the class the country the singer/group comes from and their nationality.

a Discuss the question as a class or in small groups. Ask groups to feedback. Are there any interesting results? Is there a song or band/singer which most students prefer?

b ▶ CD1 T29 Students read through the two questions. Play the recording while students read and listen. Check answers. Play the recording a second time, pausing after each answer if necessary.

Weaker classes: Ask students to predict the kind of information they are likely to need to listen for in each answer.

TAPESCRIPT
See reading text on page 18 of the Student's Book.

> **Answers**
> 1 The Targets
> 2 There are four people in the band.

c ▶ CD1 T29 Students read through statements 1 to 5. Check any problems. Go through the first item as an example if necessary.

Stronger classes: Students can answer the questions without reading or listening again. They can read and listen to check their answers only. They can then correct the false sentences.

Weaker classes: Play the recording again before students answer the questions. Check answers.

> **Answers**
> 1 T (Chuck plays lead guitar, Matt plays bass.)
> 2 F (One person (Chuck) is not from Birmingham.)
> 3 T
> 4 F (Chuck and Matt are 19, Kate and Connor are 18.)
> 5 F (It's a new song.)

2 Grammar

★ The verb *be*: plural, negatives and questions

If you set the background information as a homework research task, ask students to tell the rest of the class what they found out.

BACKGROUND INFORMATION

The Killers are a rock band from Las Vegas, formed in 2002. Their first album *Hot Fuss* (2004) was a big success and they have since released two more: *Sam's Town* (2006) and *Day & Age* (2008).

Daniel Craig (born 2 March 1968) is an English actor. He has starred in films such as *Elizabeth* and *Layer Cake*, but is most famous for being the sixth actor to play James Bond. He has made two films as Bond: *Casino Royale* and *Quantum of Solace*.

Camden Market is a market in North London selling clothing, crafts and jewellery. It is the fourth most popular visitor attraction in London, with 100,000 visitors each weekend.

Christian Bale (born 30 January 1974) is an English actor. His first role was in *Empire of the Sun* at the age of 13, and he has gone on to star in major films such as *American Psycho* and *Shaft*. He played Batman in *Batman Begins* and *The Dark Knight*.

Hugh Jackman (born 12 October 1968) is an Australian actor. He is best known for his role as *Wolverine* in the X-Men series; other films include *Van Helsing*, *The Prestige* and *Australia*.

Chessington World of Adventures is a theme park and zoo near London. The zoo originally opened in 1931, and a theme park was added in 1987.

Kia Motors is an automobile manufacturer based in Seoul, South Korea. Its most popular vehicles are the *Forte*, the *Optima* and the *Sportage*.

a Stronger classes: Students read through the three examples. Ask them to identify the positive, negative and question forms. Then ask them to provide an example of their own for each form. Ask them what they notice about the difference between the three forms.

Weaker classes: Books closed. Write the following examples (or some of your own) on the board: *We're in an English class. We aren't (nationality). Are you from (country)?* Ask students to identify the positive, negative and question forms. Students open their books at page 19 and read through the examples. Ask them what they notice about the difference between the three forms.

Language note

Remind students that we use *not* in the negative form of the verb *be* and that in English we invert the subject and the verb in questions. For example, we say: *Are you ...?* NOT ~~You are ...?~~

b Students read through the gapped table. Go through the first item with them as an example. Remind them that they are completing the plural form. Students complete the exercise. Check answers.

> **Answers**
> Positive: 're, 're
> Negative: aren't, aren't
> Question: Are, Are
> Short answers: are/aren't, are/aren't, are/aren't

✷ OPTIONAL ACTIVITY

To check understanding of plural forms, call out a person and a form, and ask students to give you the correct form.

c Students read through items 1 to 3. Go through the example, making sure students remember they are practising plural forms. Students complete the exercise. Check answers.

> **Answers**
> 1 aren't; 're
> 2 Are; aren't
> 3 Are; aren't; 're

d This exercise can be set for homework. Students read through items 1 to 4. Go through the first item as an example, making sure students are aware that they are practising singular and plural forms. If necessary, elicit the singular forms quickly before they start. Students complete the exercise. Check answers.

> **Answers**
> 1 he's
> 2 it isn't
> 3 Are; they're
> 4 Are; they aren't

e This exercise can be set for homework. Students read through questions 1 to 6 and look at the pictures. Go through the example as a class, drawing students' attention to the use of the third person singular question form. Remind them that they may also need to use the plural question form. Students complete the exercise. Check answers.

> **Answers**
> 2 Is 3 Is 4 Are 5 Is 6 Is

f In pairs, students try to answer the questions. Listen to some of their ideas, but do not give answers at this stage. For homework, students research the answers on the internet. Check answers in the following class.

> **Answers**
> 1 Students' own answer.
> 2 He's British.
> 3 Yes, it is.
> 4 Yes, they are.
> 5 No, it isn't. It's South Korean.
> 6 Yes, it is.

✷ OPTIONAL ACTIVITY

Students can write some more questions of their own, similar to those in Exercise 2f, for their partner to answer.

❸ Vocabulary

✷ Positive and negative adjectives

a Write the headings *very good* and *very bad* on the board. Students read the words in the box. Ask volunteers to come and classify the words in the box under the relevant headings. Then ask students to give an example of their own for each adjective.

Weaker classes: Write the headings on the board but then put each adjective into a sentence of your own and ask students to classify each adjective.

> **Answers**
> Very good: fantastic, excellent, great
> Very bad: awful, terrible

Language note
Remind students that in English adjectives go before the noun and that they do not change if the noun is singular or plural.

b Divide the class into pairs. Students read through the words in the box. Check any problems. Go through the example as a class if necessary. Give students a few minutes to decide on their examples. Monitor and check students are using the example phrase correctly, and that they are using the adjectives correctly. Ask pairs to feedback to the class. Are there any interesting answers? If so, ask students to give more information.

✳ OPTIONAL ACTIVITY

Weaker classes: Books closed. Call out an adjective from the box in Exercise 3a. Ask a student to give you its opposite. That student can then call out another adjective from the box and ask another student to give the opposite.

Stronger classes: You can do this with other adjectives if students know more.

Vocabulary bank Refer students to the vocabulary bank. Read through the words and phrases in open class and check understanding.

④ Grammar and speaking

✳ *I (don't) like ... / Do you like ...?*

If you set the background information as a homework research task, ask students to tell the rest of the class what they found out.

BACKGROUND INFORMATION
The Black Eyed Peas are an American hip hop band formed in Los Angeles in 1995. Since their first album *Elephunk* in 2003, they have sold 29 million albums. Their hits include *Where Is The Love?*, *Boom Boom Pow* and *I Gotta Feeling*.

Pink (born Alicia Moore, 8 September 1979) is an American singer and songwriter. She has released five albums, selling over 32 million records worldwide. Her big hits include *Lady Marmalade* and *Get The Party Started*.

Miley Cyrus (born Destiny Hope Cyrus, 23 November 1992) is an American singer and actress. She found fame as Hannah Montana before releasing her first solo album *Meet Miley Cyrus* in 2007. The album included her first top 10 single *See You Again*. She released her second album *Breakout* in July 2008. Both albums reached No. 1 in the US. Miley earned $25 million in 2008.

Pussycat Dolls are an American pop group formed in L.A. in 1995. Their big hits include *Don't Cha*, *Buttons* and *Stickwitu*. It is rumoured that only one of the five group members sings on their records.

Coldplay are an English rock band formed in 1998. Their first big hit was *Yellow* from the album *Parachutes*. They have now released four albums and sold more than 50 million records. The lead singer Chris Martin is married to Gwyneth Paltrow, with whom he has two children, Apple and Moses.

Justin Timberlake (born 31 January 1981) is an American pop musician and actor. He started his career as a child actor on *The New Mickey Mouse Club* television show. He went on to be lead singer of the band 'N Sync, before releasing his first solo album *Justified* in 2002. He also owns a record label, a fashion label and two restaurants.

a **Stronger classes:** Students read the two sentences and look at the faces. Give them a few minutes to classify each sentence under the appropriate face. Ask students to identify which is the positive and which is the negative form. Students can give you an example of their own using each expression.

Weaker classes: Books closed. Give students an example of your own using *I like* and *I don't like*. Ask students to identify which is the positive and which is the negative form. Students open their books at page 22. Follow the procedure for stronger classes.

b Students read through the sentences. Give them a few minutes to write their answers. Students then read through the examples in the table. Ask them what they notice about the questions and short answer forms (they both use the auxiliary *do/don't*).

Language note
Students may produce statements like *I like swim*. Remind them that in English we either use the *-ing* form or the *to* infinitive after *like/don't like*. We never use the bare infinitive after *like/don't like*.

c Divide the class into pairs. Students take turns to tell their partner their answers to Exercise 4b. Monitor and check students are using the verb *like* correctly, making a note of any repeated errors to go through as a class after the exercise.

d Students can work with the same partner as they did in Exercise 4c or they can work with a different partner. Students read through the box and look at the illustrations. Check any problems. Ask a stronger pair to demonstrate the example dialogue, drawing students' attention to the use of the question and short answer forms and the positive and negative adjectives from Exercise 3. Give students a few minutes to ask and answer questions about the items in the box. Monitor and check students are asking and answering using the correct forms and make a note of any repeated errors to go through as a class after the exercise. Ask pairs to feedback to the rest of the class.

Get it right! Refer students to the Get it right! section. These exercises can be used as homework or for fast-finishers.

5 Grammar

✱ Object pronouns

If you set the background information as a homework research task, ask students to tell the rest of the class what they found out.

BACKGROUND INFORMATION

Kanye West: see Background Information Unit 1, Exercise 8.

Jonas Brothers are an American boy band from New Jersey, made popular on the Disney Channel television network. The band consists of three brothers: Kevin, Joe and Nick Jonas. They have released four albums including *It's About Time* (2006) and *Lines, Vines and Trying Times* (2009).

Eminem (born Marshall Mathers III, 17 October 1972) is an American rapper and actor. His first album *The Slim Shady LP* (1999) won a Grammy award and the follow-up *The Marshall Mathers LP* was the fastest-selling rap LP in history. He has sold more than 80 million albums and also played the lead role in the film *8 Mile*.

Green Day are an American rock band formed in California in 1987. Their most popular albums are *Dookie* (1994) and *American Idiot* (2004).

Lily Allen: see Background Information Unit 1, Exercise 1.

Jennifer Aniston (born 11 February 1969) is an American actress. She became famous for her role as Rachel in the US TV comedy *Friends*. She has also starred in many films, including *Bruce Almighty*.

Lindsay Lohan (born 2 July 1986) is an American actress. She started her career as a child model before moving on to acting in films such as *The Parent Trap, Freaky Friday* and *Mean Girls*.

---

a ▶ **CD1 T30** Play the recording while students read through the dialogue. Then ask students who *him* and *them* refer to in the dialogue (Kanye West and the Jonas Brothers). Explain that these words are object pronouns and are used to refer to someone or something which has already been mentioned.

TAPESCRIPT

See dialogue on page 21 of the Student's Book.

b **Stronger classes:** Students read through the words in the box. Explain that these are all the object pronouns. Go through the example, if necessary. Students complete the table. Check answers.

Weaker classes: Write the headings *Subject* and *Object* on the board and ask a student to come and fill in the example items from Exercise 5a. Follow the procedure for stronger classes above.

Answers
me, you, her, him, it, us, them

To check understanding at this point, call out a subject pronoun and a student's name. The student must give the correct object pronoun.

c This exercise can be set for homework. Students read through items 1 to 4. Do the first item as an example, if necessary. Students complete the exercise. Remind students to look carefully at the subject of each sentence before they decide which object pronoun to choose. Check answers.

Answers
1 him 2 them 3 her 4 me

---

6 Pronunciation

See notes on page 107.

7 Listen and speak

If you set the background information as a homework research task, ask students to tell the rest of the class what they found out.

BACKGROUND INFORMATION

Jensen Button (born 19 January 1980) is an English Formula One driver. He first drove in Formula One in the 2000 season. He won his first race in 2006 after 113 races. In 2009, he won six of the first seven races and went on to become World Champion.

Madonna (born Madonna Louise Ciccone, 16 August 1958) is an American singer and actor. Her biggest hits include *Holiday* and *Ray of Light*. She has sold more than 200 million albums. She has also starred in several films, including *Evita* (1996).

Halle Berry (born 14 August 1966) is an American actress and fashion model. Her biggest film roles have been in the X-Men series and *Monster's Ball*, for which she won an Oscar.

Jennifer Aniston: see Background Information Unit 2, Exercise 5.

Pink: see Background Information Unit 2, Exercise 3.

a ▶ **CD1 T34** Give students a few minutes to look at the pictures. Check any pronunciation problems, if necessary. Explain that students will hear four people talking about famous people or things they like and don't like. Play the recording for students to listen.

Stronger classes: Explain that students must now complete the table with information from the recording. They can complete the table and then listen and check only.

Weaker classes: Play the recording again for students to listen only. Then play the first part of the recording again, pausing after Speaker 1 to give students time to complete this part of the table. Continue in this way until students have completed the table. Check answers, playing and pausing the recording again as necessary.

TAPESCRIPT

Speaker 1: I like rock music. And I like a lot of the female singers. I like Madonna and I like Pink. She's great.

Speaker 2: Yeah, I like sport. Well, I don't like all the teams, of course. I don't like Manchester United – the Reds. But I like the Blues – Chelsea!

Speaker 3: I don't like football but I like car racing. I like Formula One – it's my favourite sport. I like Jensen Button – he's amazing.

Speaker 4: My favourite actresses are Jennifer Aniston and Halle Berry. I really like them. Do you?

Answers
Speaker 1 *Like*: Pink
Speaker 2 *Like*: Chelsea (the Blues) *Don't like*: Manchester United (the Reds)
Speaker 3 *Like*: car racing, Formula One, Jensen Button *Don't like*: football
Speaker 4 *Like*: Halle Berry, Jennifer Aniston

b Divide the class into pairs. Ask a stronger pair to read out the example dialogue. Draw students' attention to the use of question and short answer forms and also the use of positive and negative adjectives. Monitor and check students are asking and answering correctly, making a note of any repeated errors to go through as a class after the exercise.

c ▶ **CD1 T35** Tell students they are going to listen to a song called *Are we alone?* Read through the lyrics and ask students to complete the gaps with the correct form of the verb *be*. Tell them it is not necessary to understand every word. Let them compare answers with a partner before checking in open class.

Answers
2 's 3 's 4 are 5 is 6 's 7 're 8 're
9 're 10 's

Photostory: Just a little joke

8 Read and listen

Warm-up
Introduce the characters to students. They are two boys, Darren and Mark, and two girls, Izzie and Kate, from the same school. Tell students the characters will appear regularly throughout the book.

Look at the title with students and check understanding. Look at the first picture together. Ask students where the people are (at the entrance to the youth centre) and what they might be talking about (a concert).

a ▶ **CD1 T36** Read the instructions and question with students and ask them to look at the photos. Play the recording for students to read and listen to find the answers.

TAPESCRIPT
See the text on page 22 of the Student's Book.

Answer
Nobody is on the phone.

b Students read through items 1 to 5. Check any problems. Go through the first item with students as an example. Allow students to go back through the dialogue if they can't remember what happened. Students complete the exercise. Check answers and then ask students to correct the false statements.

Answers
1 T
2 F (The concert is on Saturday.)
3 F (They both want to go.)
4 T
5 F (Nobody is on the phone.)

✳ OPTIONAL ACTIVITY

In groups, students can act out the dialogue from the photostory.

9 Everyday English

a Read through the expressions from the dialogue with students. Do the first item as an example. Ask students if they can remember who said this (Kate). Students complete the exercise, only looking back at the dialogue if they need to. Check answers.

b Ask students to look at the expressions in the dialogue and in L1, discuss what they think they mean. Is a direct translation possible in their language? If not, discuss how they might express a similar meaning.

c ▶ **CD1 T37** Read through the sentences with students and clarify any problems with understanding. In pairs, students decide on the correct order for the dialogue. Check answers and ask students to practise the correct dialogue.

TAPESCRIPT/ANSWERS

Alex: The new *Matrix* film is on at the cinema this weekend.

Sally: I know. And *Matrix* films are great! Let's go together!

Alex: OK – cool! Let's go on Friday.

Sally: Oh, Alex – I'm sorry, not Friday. It's my mum's birthday.

Alex: No problem. Is Saturday OK?

Sally: Of course! Saturday's great. See you there!

d Ask students to read through the dialogues and check they understand them. Check any vocabulary problems. Go through the first item as an example. Students complete the exercise and compare answers in pairs before a whole class check.

Vocabulary notebook

Students should start a section called *Everyday English* in their vocabulary notebooks and note down these expressions.

10 Improvisation

Divide the class into pairs. Tell students they are going to create a dialogue between Darren and Izzie. Read through the instructions with students. Give students two minutes to plan their dialogue. Circulate and help with vocabulary as necessary. Encourage students to use expressions from Exercise 9. Students practice their dialogue in pairs. Listen to some of the best dialogues in open class.

11 Free Time ⦿ DVD Episode 1

a Look at the photo with students and ask them to describe what is happening and answer the questions. Divide the class into pairs and ask students to create a short dialogue for the people in the photo. Circulate and help with vocabulary as necessary. Listen to some of the dialogues in open class as feedback.

b Read through the sentences with students and check understanding. Ask students to match the sentences to the photographs. Students check their answers with a partner before feedback in open class. Play Episode 1 of the DVD for students to find out what happens.

12 Write

Warm-up

Ask students if they send emails. If so, how often do they send them? What do they write about and who do they send them to and receive them from?

a Ask students the name of Anna's favourite CD (*Lost*). Students read the email. Check answers.

b Students can prepare this exercise in class and write the email for homework. Students read through the instructions. Elicit, or remind them, how an email is structured:

Informal openings: *Hi!, Hello!*

Content: Does not have to be split into paragraphs as in a letter.

Signing off: Does not need a full sentence and can just have a name or an informal signing off expression.

Weaker classes: Give them time to plan a draft of their email using the headings from the Student's Book. They can then swap plans and check them before writing up a final version.

Vocabulary notebook

Students can start a section called *Writing emails*. They should note down the key points about writing emails.

13 Last but not least: more speaking

a In preparation for this activity, bring some photos of famous people to class. Divide the class into pairs. Students write questions that they would like to ask the star, and also think of things they would like to tell the star if they met them. Draw attention to the prompts to help students prepare questions. Monitor and deal with any problems.

b Ask a student to come to the front of the class and pretend that they are the star in their photo. The rest of the class ask the questions they have prepared in Exercise 13a. Pay attention to question intonation where necessary. Repeat the activity with other students.

★ OPTIONAL ACTIVITY

As an extension to this activity, ask students to imagine they are the star in their photo and that they are all at a glamorous party. Ask students to mingle (without their photos), to introduce themselves to other students and to ask some of the questions from Exercise 13a.

Check your progress

1 Grammar

a 2 My friends are great singers
3 London is a fantastic city.
4 Polish restaurants are really good.

b 2 don't 3 Are 4 isn't 5 Do 6 Is 7 aren't
8 don't

c 2 How 3 Who 4 What 5 Where

2 Vocabulary

a 2 Belgium 3 Britain 4 Italy 5 Poland 6 Turkey
7 Japan 8 Canada

b 2 Belgian 3 British 4 Italian 5 Polish 6 Turkish
7 Japanese 8 Canadian

c 2 fantastic 3 awful 4 terrible

How did you do?

Check that students are marking their scores. Collect these in, check them as necessary, and discuss any further work needed with specific students.

Memo from Mario

We're a new band

Extra practice of *I like ...*, *I don't like ...*, *D'you like ...?*

▶ Once you have done the exercises on this grammar in the Student's Book, demonstrate this activity to the class.

▶ At the top left side of the board write I LIKE and at the top right side write I REALLY DON'T LIKE. Divide the board in two with a vertical line down the middle:

I LIKE	I REALLY DON'T LIKE

▶ Under I LIKE draw two quick, minimal things, people or situations you like. Label each drawing with a word or phrase, e.g. *my cat*, *swimming*, etc.

▶ Draw similar labeled pictures on the right hand side under I REALLY DON'T LIKE.

▶ Tell the students to take a piece of paper and divide it into two columns: the left hand side for good things, and the right hand side for bad things.

▶ Ask them to draw five pictures under the heading I LIKE and five pictures under the heading I REALLY DON'T LIKE. Give them 30 seconds for each picture.

▶ Ask the students to write a word or phrase under each picture that describes the person, thing or situation in the picture. To do this they ask their classmates, they use their bi-lingual dictionaries, and they ask you, especially for help with pronunciation.

▶ Ask the students to get up, move around, pair off and read their likes and dislikes to at least six other people. This gives lots of repetitive practice in a communicative framework.

▶ Then ask the students to work with different people, using this pattern:

I like X.

D'you like it/him/her/them?

▶ Make it clear to the students that this exercise only makes sense with general objects. Since people may not know each other well, you can't reasonably say *I like my sister. D'you like her?* However, you can say *I like skate-boarding. D'you like it?*

▶ Demonstrate the activity with a couple of students.

▶ The students return to their seats and freely ask you about *your* likes and dislikes.

> **RATIONALE**
> This activity is a firmly guided pattern drill but its content is student-generated. It is reasonable to hope that this realism will help the students absorb the patterns into their subconscious minds. This sort of assimilation is what we are after as language teachers.

3 She lives in Washington

Unit overview

TOPIC: Family

TEXTS

Reading and listening: a magazine article about a famous person
Listening: someone talking about their family
Reading: a text about two British families
Writing: a paragraph about your family

SPEAKING AND FUNCTIONS

Talking about your family
Asking about habits

LANGUAGE

Grammar: present simple: positive and negative; questions and short answers; possessive *'s*; possessive adjectives
Vocabulary: family
Pronunciation: /s/, /z/ and /ɪz/

1 Read and listen

If you set the background information as a homework research task, ask students to tell the rest of the class what they found out.

BACKGROUND INFORMATION

Michelle Obama (born 17 January 1964) is the first African American First Lady of the United States. She graduated from Princeton University and Harvard Law School and was working as a lawyer when she met her husband Barack Obama. They married in 1992 and have two daughters, Malia and Sasha.

Barack Obama (born 4 August 1961) is the 44th President of the United States, the first African American to hold the office. He was previously the junior US Senator from Illinois. He was awarded the 2009 Nobel Peace Prize.

Chicago (population 2.8 million) is the third-largest city in the USA. It is a major industrial and communications hub and its airport is the second biggest in the world. It is often called the Windy City.

Washington D.C. is the capital of the USA. It is named after George Washington, the first President of the United States.

The White House is the official residence and workplace of the President of the USA. It was built in 1800, and has six storeys and the famous East and West wings. The West Wing houses the Oval Office, the president's official office.

Portuguese water dogs are long-haired working dogs originally bred in Portugal to herd fish into fishermen's nets and to retrieve objects from the water. US Senator Ted Kennedy owned three Portuguese water dogs.

Warm-up

Books closed. Ask students to think of famous Americans and to say why they are famous, e.g. *Johnny Depp. He's an actor.* Write the word *President* on the board and elicit the name of the US President (Barack Obama). Ask students what they know about him.

a Books open. Students read the question. Elicit suggestions but do not give the answer at this point. Students read the magazine article to check their answer.

> **Answer**
> Michelle Obama, Barack Obama's wife.

b ▶ **CD1 T38** Students read through statements 1 to 6. Go through the first item as an example, if necessary. Play the recording while students listen and read the article again. Students then complete the exercise. Check answers.

Stronger classes: They can do this from memory and then correct the false statements.

Weaker classes: They can listen and read the text again before completing the exercise. Play the recording again, pausing after each answer to allow students time to check their answers.

TAPESCRIPT

See text on page 26 of the Student's Book.

> **Answers**
> 1 F (She comes from the USA.)
> 2 T
> 3 F (Her mother's name is Marian.)
> 4 F (She lives in Washington D.C.)
> 5 T
> 6 T

c In small groups, students discuss the President of the USA. If they did the Warm-up, remind them of the things they said then and see if they can expand their opinions. Ask groups to feedback to the class.

★ OPTIONAL ACTIVITY

In pairs, students can think of famous people and what they are famous for. They then give their partner either the name of the person or the reason for their fame and their partner has to guess the other piece of information.

2 Grammar

✱ Present simple: positive and negative

a **Stronger classes:** Students read through sentences 1 to 4 and underline the verbs. Ask students to identify the positive and negative verb forms in the sentences and to explain the difference between the two forms (the negative form uses the auxiliary *don't/doesn't*). Ask them too what they notice about the verb form in item 3 (it is third person singular and has an *-s* on the end).

Weaker classes: Books closed. Write two present simple positive and two negative sentences of your own on the board (e.g. *I like English. / They don't like English. / He speaks English. / She doesn't speak English.*). Ask for volunteers to come and underline the verb in each sentence. Then ask them what they notice about the verbs in each sentence and elicit the difference between positive and negative and singular and plural forms. Students then open their books at page 27, read through the example sentences and underline the verbs.

> **Answers**
> 2 doesn't live 3 helps 4 don't use

b Students read through the gapped table. Give them a few minutes to complete it. Remind them to think carefully about the verb endings they will need. Check answers.

> **Answers**
> Positive: read
> Negative: don't, doesn't

c Students read through the table and complete the missing spellings. Check answers.

> **Answers**
> +s: stops, lives, plays
> +es: finishes, goes

┌───┐
Language note
Remind students that in the present simple, the third person singular is the only form which changes. We add one of the endings from the box in Exercise 2c to form it.
└───┘

d This exercise can be set for homework. Students read through sentences 1 to 6. Check any problems. Go through the example as a class. Students complete the exercise. Remind them to look carefully at the subject of the sentence before they choose the verb form they need. Check answers.

> **Answers**
> 2 don't like
> 3 studies
> 4 doesn't speak
> 5 doesn't listen
> 6 don't study

✱ Present simple: questions and short answers

e Students read through the four questions. Ask them what they notice about the present simple question form in English and elicit that the auxiliary *do* or *does* is used.

f Students read through the gapped table. Give them a few minutes to complete it. Check answers.

> **Answers**
> Question: Do
> Short answer positive: does, do
> Short answer negative: don't

g This exercise can be set for homework. Students read through items 1 to 5. Check any problems. Go through the example as a class, if necessary. Students complete the exercise. Check answers.

> **Answers**
> 2 Does 3 Do 4 Does 5 Do

Get it right! Refer students to the Get it right! section. These exercises can be used as homework or for fast-finishers.

Grammar notebook

Remind students to start a section called *Present simple* in their notebooks and to note down some example sentences and the rules from the section.

3 Pronunciation

See notes on page 107.

4 Speak

a Divide the class into pairs. Ask a stronger pair to demonstrate the example dialogue. Remind students of the different short answer forms or elicit them. Students complete the exercise. Monitor and check students are asking and answering correctly, making a note of any repeated errors to go through as a class after the exercise.

b Students read through items 1 to 5. Check any problems. Students complete the exercise. Check answers.

c Divide the class into pairs, or students can work in the same pairs as they did in Exercise 4a. Go through the example as a class, pointing out the use of the third person singular verb forms. Students ask their partner their questions and then note their answers. Monitor and check students are taking turns to ask and answer and gather the information. Then ask pairs to report back to the rest of the class on what they found out about their partner. If students are still having problems with the third person singular forms, then revise this area after the exercise.

5 Vocabulary

✱ Family

Warm-up

This can be done in L1 if necessary. Ask students how many people are in their family and if they have brothers and sisters. If so, how many? Do they have grandparents?

a Books closed. Elicit any words students know for members of the family in English and write them on the board. Students then open their books at page 28 and look at the words in the box in Exercise 5a. If students have not produced those words already, ask a stronger student to explain what they are. Students then read through the gapped text. Go through the first item as an example. Students complete the exercise. Remind them they can refer back to the reading text on page 26 if necessary. Check answers.

Answers
2 mother 3 grandmother 4 daughters
5 sister

Vocabulary bank Refer students to the vocabulary bank. Read through the words and phrases in open class and check understanding.

b ▶ CD1 T40 Students read through the words in the box. Check any problems. Go through the example as a class. Students complete the exercise.

Play the recording for students to check their answers.

TAPESCRIPT

My family's not very big, but it's not small either! My grandfather's called James (we call him Grandad), and my grandmother's called Elizabeth, but we call her Gran. Then there's my mother, Claire, and my father, Jonathan. Of course, we call them Mum and Dad! My dad has a brother, he's called Uncle Mike, and he's married to Sarah, so she's our aunt and they've got a son, who's our cousin, Joseph. Um, I've got a brother, William, and a big sister, Olivia, so I'm in the middle! They're nice, but sometimes William is a pain.

Answers
Grandmother – Elizabeth
Mother – Claire
Father – Jonathan
Uncle – Mike
Aunt – Sarah
Brother – William
Sister – Olivia
Cousin – Joseph

Vocabulary notebook

Remind students to start a section called *Family* and to note down the new words from this section.

✱ OPTIONAL ACTIVITY

Pairs or small groups. Students must describe a family member without using the relationship word. For example:
S1: I am my mother's brother.
S2: Uncle.
The student who guesses correctly takes the next turn. Monitor and check students are taking turns to ask and answer.

Weaker classes: Students can write down their definitions before they start the activity.

6 Grammar

✱ Possessive 's

a **Stronger classes:** Students read the examples. Ask them to explain why the possessive 's is used in both cases (it is the name belonging to Sally's father / they are the parents belonging to Sally's father). Ask students to give a few examples of their own using the possessive 's and some of their classmates' personal belongings.

Weaker classes: Books closed. Write the words: *Sally's family* on the board. Elicit or explain why the possessive 's is used in this example (because it is referring to the family belonging to Sally). Students now open their books at page 28 and look at the examples on the page. Follow the procedure for stronger classes from this point.

b Students look at the pictures. Check any problems. Students complete the exercise. They can then compare answers in pairs before a whole-class check.

Answers
2 Emily's house
3 Mr Black's car
4 My father's computer
5 My sister's bike
6 My brother's school

Language notes
1 Students may find it useful to note down the following rules for the possessive *'s*. It is used with:
- person + thing: *John's book*
- person + person: *my Mum's brother*

It is not used with:
- thing + thing: We say: *The start of the TV programme* NOT ~~*The TV programme's start*~~.

2 Students may produce statements like *the sister of Sally* so it may be useful for them to think about how they express the possessive in their language to make them more aware of the differences in English.

✳ OPTIONAL ACTIVITY

Go round the class picking up various items belonging to students. Hold them up and ask *Whose is it?* Ask a student to reply using the possessive *'s*. For example:
T: Whose is it? (holding up bag)
S1: It's Maria's.

You can either give the next object to the student, who asks the question and chooses who is to reply, or you can continue asking the question yourself.

✳ Possessive adjectives

c **Stronger classes:** Students read through the examples. Ask them to underline the possessive adjective in each example and ask students to explain why each one is used (because it refers back to the subject and depending on whether the subject is male or female, singular or plural, *his, her* or *their* is used).

Weaker classes: Books closed. Write the following examples (or one of your own) on the board: *I like your bike. He likes her pen.* Ask a student to come out and underline the possessive adjective in each example, and then elicit or explain why each one is used. Students open their books at page 29 and read through the example sentences. Follow the procedure for stronger classes.

d Students read through the gapped table. Go through the examples as a class, pointing out the subject pronouns and the possessive adjectives. Students complete the table.

Weaker classes: It may be useful to write the subject pronouns on the board and the possessive adjectives in a jumbled order. Ask students to come out and write the relevant possessive adjective beside the subject pronoun.

Check answers.

Answers
Singular: my, your, his, its
Plural: your, their

e This exercise can be set for homework. Students read through items 1 to 6. Go through the example as a class, asking students to explain why the answer is *My*. Students complete the exercise. Check answers, asking students to justify their choice of possessive adjective.

Answers
1 your 2 His 3 Their 4 her 5 our 6 your

Grammar notebook

Remind students to start a section for *Possessive 's and Possessive adjectives* and to note down the examples from this section or some of their own.

✳ OPTIONAL ACTIVITY

You can do a similar activity here as for Possessive *'s*. Collect up some small belongings from students. This time students must point to the person it belongs to and answer using the possessive adjective. For example:
T: Whose is it?
S1: It's her bag.

7 Speak

a Divide the class into pairs. Ask a stronger pair to demonstrate the example dialogue. Remind students to refer back to Sally's family tree in Exercise 5 to help them with their questions. Students ask and answer questions. Monitor and check students are taking turns to ask and answer, and that they are using the correct possessive adjectives and the possessive *'s*. Make a note of any repeated errors to go through as a class after the exercise.

b Students draw their family tree, using Sally's one as a model. Remind them not to write in the names of the members of their family, only *father, mother*, etc.

c Divide the class into pairs or students can work in the same pairs they did in Exercise 7a. Ask a stronger pair to read out the example using their own family trees. Remind students that they must ask the question and then fill in the information in the correct place in their partner's family tree. Students complete the exercise. Ask pairs to feedback to the class about their partner's family.

⁕ OPTIONAL ACTIVITY

Students can decorate their family trees for homework or add photos of the members of the family. These can then be displayed on the classroom wall. Students could vote for the best family tree.

8 Listen

a Students read through items 1 to 6 and look at the pictures. Check any problems. Go through the first item as an example, if necessary. Students complete the exercise. Check answers.

Answers
2 E 3 F 4 C 5 D 6 A

b ▶ CD1 T41 Explain that students will hear Paul and Ben talking about Paul's family using the expressions in Exercise 8a. Students must put the expressions in the order he mentions them. Play the recording for students to listen. Play the recording again, pausing as necessary for students to note down the correct order. Check answers, playing and pausing the recording again as necessary.

TAPESCRIPT

Paul: I have a great time with my cousins! We all get on really well.

Ben: Really? Do you like the same things?

Paul: Yes, we do. Well, actually Jason, Jamie and I all like going bowling, but Kelly doesn't like that so much. She likes going to the cinema or going to museums.

Ben: Does she go bowling with you at all?

Paul: No, she doesn't.

Ben: What do you all do together, then?

Paul: We go shopping together at weekends, and we go to the internet café together.

Ben: What about your sister, Jess? Does she go with you?

Paul: Yeah, sometimes. She works in a shop at the weekends, so she doesn't have a lot of time.

Answers
E, C, A, B, F

Culture in mind

9 Read and listen

If you set the background information as a homework research task, ask students to tell the rest of the class what they found out.

BACKGROUND INFORMATION

Birmingham: see Background Information Unit 2, Exercise 1.

Bangladesh (population c.162 million) is a country in South Asia. It is bordered by India on all sides apart from a small border with Burma. It is among the most densely populated countries in the world and has a high poverty rate.

Liverpool is a city in northwestern England (population 444,500). Liverpool was a very wealthy port in the nineteenth century, but suffered heavy bombing during the Second World War. It is the home of The Beatles and has named its airport *John Lennon International*.

Chester (population 77,040) is a city in England, close to the border with Wales. Chester was founded nearly 2000 years ago by the Romans, and has the most complete city walls in Great Britain.

Manchester (population 437,000) is a city in the North West of England. It is a centre of the arts, the media, higher education and big business. The city is world-famous for its football, being home to Manchester City and Manchester United FC.

Warm-up

Ask students how many people are in their family and how many people live at home with them (e.g. grandparents and parents or only parents?).
Ask students to discuss the types of houses/flats they live in. This can be discussed in L1, if necessary.

a ▶ CD1 T42 Pre-teach any necessary vocabulary before students read and listen to the texts, e.g. *grocery shop, flat, looks after, factory, secretary.*

Stronger classes: Students read the texts quickly. Check any problems. Give students a few minutes to match the texts to the pictures.

Weaker classes: The texts can be read aloud as a class and the matching can be done in pairs.

Check answers.

Answers
The Siddiqui family is from Birmingham and the Jackson family is from Chester.

b Stronger classes: Students can read the text again if necessary and complete the information in the table.

Weaker classes: Divide the class into pairs. Go through the table headings and look at the example. Students complete the exercise. Check answers.

c In small groups, students discuss the question. Ask groups to feedback to the rest of the class.

10 Write

If you set the background information as a homework research task, ask students to tell the rest of the class what they found out.

BACKGROUND INFORMATION
Bristol (population 416,400) is a city in South West England. It is England's sixth most populous city. Bristol is a cultural centre and is home to many musicians, such as Massive Attack, and street artists, including Banksy.
Reading (population 143,096) is a town in England 65 km west of London. It is an important commercial centre with strong links to IT and insurance. It has a large student population with two universities.

Warm-up

Ask students if they have a personal webpage or know anyone who has. Ask them to predict the kind of information they might find on a personal webpage.

a Stronger classes: Students look at the pictures and read the text, then write the names under the appropriate picture.

Weaker classes: The text can be read aloud as a class. Elicit the first name as an example. Students complete the exercise. Check answers.

b Stronger classes: Students plan and write a webpage based on the model in the Student's Book. Remind them to look carefully at the

structure of the text and to identify the topic of each paragraph before they begin.

Weaker classes: Go through each paragraph with the students, eliciting the main topic for each. Put the topic headings on the board. Students then plan and draft their information. Students can write their final versions for homework.

Memo from Mario

She lives in Washington

Extra practice of the present simple (positive and negative)

▶ Preparation: photocopy the question grid (opposite), one for each student.

▶ Put words that may be new to the students up on the board, e.g.
  sleep
  dream
  in colour
  in black and white
  early
  late
  go to bed
  get up

▶ Elicit the meanings of the words using the students' prior knowledge, mime, pictures and translation.

▶ Give out the question grid and demonstrate the exercise. Pick a student and ask them all the relevant questions from the grid. Put these ways of answering up on the board:

Yes, I do.	*No, I don't.*
Yeah, I do.	*Not really.*
Sure, yes.	*Nah!*

▶ When the student answers affirmatively, note their name down next to the question.

▶ The students mingle and ask relevant questions from the grid. They note other students' names next to the questions answered affirmatively.

▶ After the mingling phase, call out a student's name and ask people to tell you about this student's night time habits, e.g.
  Vladimir sleeps 8 hours.
  He dreams in colour.
  He doesn't go to bed early.
  He gets up late.

▶ Check that the final *-s* of the four verbs is being pronounced correctly. Go through five or six students in this way.

▶ Then call out two names and see if these two students have given any common answers to generate: *They both get up late.*

▶ Round the exercise off with students coming to the board and writing their own most interesting answers.

Questions	Name
Do you sleep six hours?	....
Do you sleep seven hours?	....
Do you sleep eight hours?	....
Do you sleep nine hours?	....
D'you dream?	....
D'you dream in colour?	....
D'you dream in black and white?	....
Do you go to bed early?	....
Do you go to bed late?	....
D'you get up early?	....
D'you get up late?	....

RATIONALE

Here you have a simplified version of *Find someone who ...* , which I first learnt from Gertrude Moskowitz's book *Caring and Sharing in the Foreign Language Classroom* (Newbury House, 1978).

To my mind the virtue of the activity is that it brings the present simple off the page and into the group, with students talking about themselves, in however limited a way.

A frequent way of affirming in UK English, and across the age groups, is *Yeah*.

If you listen to the negating habits of UK English speakers between the ages of 12 and 25, *Nah* is a form you will frequently hear. Many of our students will meet such usage when emailing, blogging and social networking.

4 Where's the café?

Unit overview

TOPIC: People and places

TEXTS

Reading and listening: a webpage about things to do in London; photostory: A charity run
Listening and reading: people giving and asking for directions
Writing: a short text about your town or city

SPEAKING AND FUNCTIONS
Giving directions

LANGUAGE
Grammar: *There's / there are*; positive imperatives
Vocabulary: places in towns; numbers 100 +
Pronunciation: /d/ and /t/

1 Read and listen

If you set the background information as a homework research task, ask students to tell the rest of the class what they found out.

> **BACKGROUND INFORMATION**
> **The Tower of London** is a fortress in central London, on the north bank of the River Thames. It is the oldest building used by the British government. There has been a tower on the site since 1078. In medieval times, the tower was used as a prison (particularly for royal prisoners). Since 1303, it has been the home of the Crown Jewels of the UK.
>
> **Trafalgar Square** is a square in central London. At its centre is Nelson's Column, which is guarded by four lion statues at its base. Other statues and sculptures are on display in the square and it is also a site of political demonstrations. Trafalgar Square ranks as the fourth most popular tourist attraction on earth, with more than 15 million annual visitors.
>
> **Buckingham Palace** is the official London residence of the British monarch. Originally built in 1703, it has belonged to the Royal Family since 1761. The Buckingham Palace Garden is the largest private garden in London. The state rooms, used for official and state entertaining, are open to the public each year for most of August and September.

Pablo Picasso (25 October 1881 – 8 April 1973) was a Spanish painter and sculptor. He is one of the most recognised figures in twentieth-century art. He is best known for co-founding the Cubist movement. Among his most famous works is *Guernica* (1937), his portrayal of the German bombing of Guernica during the Spanish Civil War.

Salvador Dalí (11 May 1904 – 23 January 1989) was a Catalan surrealist painter. His work includes film, sculpture and photography, and contains symbolic, fantastical images. He was as famous for his eccentric behaviour and flamboyant appearance as for his work.

The Globe Theatre was a theatre in London associated with William Shakespeare. It was built in 1599 by Shakespeare's theatre company, the Lord Chamberlain's Men, and was destroyed by fire on 29 June 1613. A second Globe Theatre was built on the same site by June 1614 and closed in 1642. A modern reconstruction, named 'Shakespeare's Globe', opened in 1997. It is approximately 230 metres from the site of the original theatre.

Madame Tussauds is a museum in London. It was set up by wax sculptor Marie Tussaud in 1835 and contains hundreds of wax models of famous people which look quite real. The models cost around £30,000 each and take six months to make. They use real human hair.

Hard Rock Café is a restaurant chain founded in 1971 in London. In 1979, the cafe began covering its walls with rock'n'roll memorabilia, a tradition which expanded to others in the chain. Currently, there are 140 Hard Rock locations in over 36 countries.

Covent Garden is a district in central London. The area is dominated by shops, street performers and entertainment facilities, and it contains an entrance to the Royal Opera House, which is also widely-known simply as 'Covent Garden'.

Warm-up

▶ **CD1 T43** Ask students if they have ever been to London. If so, ask them to tell the class what they saw and where they went. If not, ask them to name some of the major attractions in London.

Pre-teach any necessary vocabulary, e.g. *tour, open-top buses, wax models, jugglers, clowns.*

Stronger classes: Students can read the texts quickly and match the paragraphs to the pictures.

Weaker classes: Give students a few minutes to read the texts or read them aloud as a class. Do the first item as an example. Students complete the exercise.

Play the recording for students to listen and check their answers.

TAPESCRIPT
See reading text on page 32 of the Student's Book.

> **Answers**
> 2 B 3 E 4 A 5 C

Vocabulary

✶ Numbers 100 +

▶ CD1 T44 Books closed. Elicit as many numbers as students know in English above 100 and write the numbers and words on the board. Students now open their books at page 33 and look at the numbers. Play the recording, pausing after each number for students to repeat.

TAPESCRIPT
See page 33 of the Student's Book.

> **Language note**
> Remind students that we can say *a hundred* or *one hundred* in English. We always add *and* after *a hundred* if the number is bigger, e.g. *a hundred and one*.

 OPTIONAL ACTIVITY

Stronger classes: In pairs, students can give each other some sums using numbers above 100. Monitor and check students are taking turns to ask and answer, and that they are giving the right answers.

Weaker classes: Divide the class into pairs. You can give pairs sums and the first pair to get the most sums correct in a time limit is the winner.

Vocabulary notebook
Remind students to make a note of these new numbers in their *Numbers* section.

 # Pronunciation

See notes on page 107.

 # Grammar

✶ *There's / there are*

a **Stronger classes:** Students read through the examples. Ask them to identify the positive forms and the question forms. Ask them what they notice about the verbs in each sentence and elicit that *are* is used with plural nouns and *is* with singular nouns.

Ask students if they can work out how to form the negative and elicit the rule from them. Students then complete the table and the rule.

Weaker classes: Books closed. Write some examples of your own on the board, e.g. *There are thirty students in this class. There's a bird in the garden. Is there a book on your desk? Are there any students outside?* Ask students to identify the different forms and elicit or explain when each is used. Students open their books at page 33 and look at the examples. Go through the table as a class, asking students for the correct words to complete it. Students can then complete the rule.

Check answers.

> **Answers**
> Singular nouns: is
> Plural nouns: are, Are, are, aren't
> Rule: is, are, questions

b Students read through sentences 1 to 7. Go through the examples as a class. Students complete the exercise. Remind them to check the form they need carefully before they fill in the verb. Check answers.

> **Answers**
> 3 There isn't 4 There are 5 There's
> 6 There aren't 7 There aren't any

  Refer students to the Get it right! section. These exercises can be used as homework or for fast-finishers.

Vocabulary

✶ Places in towns

Warm-up

Books closed. Elicit any names of places in towns that students know in English. Are there any similarities with their own language?

a **▶ CD1 T46** Students open their books at page 34 and look at the pictures and the list of words in the box. Go through the example as a class. Students complete the exercise. Play the recording for students to listen and check their answers. Play the recording a second time if necessary, pausing for students to repeat.

TAPESCRIPT/ANSWERS
1 library 2 railway station 3 newsagent
4 supermarket 5 chemist 6 bank
7 bookshop 8 park 9 post office

b Divide the class into pairs. Ask a stronger pair to demonstrate the example dialogue. Draw students' attention to question and answer forms with *there is/ are*. Students ask and answer questions about their town. Monitor and check students are taking turns and that they are using the correct question and answer forms. Make a note of any repeated errors to go through as a class after the exercise.

c Divide the class into pairs. Students read through the items in the box. Check any problems. Do the first item as an example, encouraging students to refer back to the places in Exercise 5a. Students complete the exercise. Check answers.

Answers
2 You send a parcel in a post office.
3 You catch a train at a railway station.
4 You buy stamps at a post office.
5 You change money in a bank.
6 You buy milk in a supermarket.
7 You play football in a park.
8 You buy a magazine in a newsagent.

Language notes
You can explain to students that sometimes in English we refer to *the chemist's* or *the newsagent's* and explain that the word has an apostrophe (') *s* at the end. This refers to the chemist's shop or the newsagent's shop.

Students may find it useful to look at the words for places in towns and see if any are similar in their own language.

 Refer students to the vocabulary bank. Read through the words and phrases in open class and check understanding.

Vocabulary notebook
Encourage students to start a section called *Places in towns* and to note down the new words from this section. Students could also write translations or illustrate each word.

6 Grammar
✱ Positive imperatives

a **Stronger classes:** Students read through the examples. Before they look at the rule box, see if they can work out the rule.

Weaker classes: Books closed. Give students a few simple instructions in English, e.g. *Stand up! Sit down! Touch your nose!* Ask students what they noticed about the verb you used in each instruction and elicit that it is the base form without *to*. Students now open their books at page 34 and read through the examples and the rule.

Language note
Students may find it useful to compare how positive imperatives work in their own language. Remind them that we always use the infinitive

without *to* for all persons in English, and that the positive imperative does not change.

b Students read through items 1 to 6 and a to f. Check any problems. Go through the example as a class, if necessary. Students complete the exercise. Check answers.

Answers
2 b 3 e 4 a 5 c 6 d

c Explain to students that you are going to give them some simple instructions using positive imperatives. When you say [*your name*] *says Stand up!* students must perform the action. If you give an instruction without saying your name first, students should not follow it. If a student follows the instruction when you have not given your own name before it, they must sit out of the rest of the game.

Grammar notebook
Remind students to note down the rules for positive imperatives and some examples from this section in their notebooks.

7 Listen and read
✱ Directions
LOOK! 🔍
Go through the prepositions in the Look! box with students before they start Exercise 7a.

a ▶ **CD1 T47** Students look at the map and quickly read through the dialogue. Check any problems. Play the recording for students to listen and read. Give them a few minutes to write the places on the map before checking answers.

Weaker classes: If necessary, play the recording a second time, pausing after each place is mentioned to give them time to write the names on the map. Check answers.

Play and pause the recording again as necessary to clarify any problems.

TAPESCRIPT
See dialogues on page 35 of the Student's Book.

Answers
The tourists are looking for the post office and the railway station.

Vocabulary notebook
Students should start a section called *Prepositions of place* and note down the new words from this section. Encourage them to write translations or to illustrate each preposition.

⁎ OPTIONAL ACTIVITY

Divide the class into pairs. Students take turns to choose a place on the map without telling their partner. They then describe the place to their partner using directions and prepositions of place, and their partner must guess where they are. Monitor and check students are taking turns to ask and answer, and that they are using the correct directions and prepositions.

Photostory: A charity run

8 Read and Listen

Warm-up

Ask students to look at the photo story and tell you who the characters are (Kate, Izzie, Mark and Darren). What can they remember about the story from Unit 2? (They wanted to go to a concert. Mark, Kate and Izzie played a joke on Darren). Explain the title of the story and ask students to predict what is going to happen, in L1 if necessary.

a ▶ **CD1 T48** Read through the instructions and the questions with students. Play the recording for students to read and listen. You may like to pre-teach difficult vocabulary: *half-marathon, charity, late, over*. Check answers.

> **Answer**
> **They are late because they get lost.**

b Ask students to read through the beginnings and endings and check understanding. Do the first item with students, then ask them to complete the exercise. Allow them to look back at the story if necessary. Allow them to discuss their answers with a partner before open class feedback.

TAPESCRIPT

See the text on page 36 of the Student's Book.

> **Answers**
> 2 e 3 f 4 a 5 b 6 d

9 Everyday English

a Students must decide who said these expressions from the photo story. Do the first one as an example, if necessary.

Stronger classes: Ask students to complete the exercise without looking back at the photo story.

Weaker classes: Allow students to refer back to the photo story.

> **Answers**
> 1 Kate 2 Mark 3 Darren 4 Jo

b Discuss the expressions in Exercise 9a as a class and ask students to try and work out how they would say these things in their own language. Are there any similarities with English?

c ▶ **CD1 T49** Read through the sentences with students and clarify any problems with understanding. In pairs, students decide on the correct order for the dialogue. Check answers and ask students to practise the correct dialogue.

TAPESCRIPT/ANSWERS

Julie: Where are we, Dan?

Dan: I have no idea. Let's look at the map again.

Julie: OK. The map's in my backpack. Here it is.

Dan: Well, actually Julie, that's the wrong map.

Julie: Really? Oh yes – I'm sorry. Wait a minute. OK, here's the right map.

Dan: Good. Now …

d Students read the dialogues. Check any problems. Go through the first dialogue as an example, if necessary. Students complete the exercise. Check answers.

> **Answers**
> 2 actually 3 I have no idea 4 Wait a minute

Vocabulary notebook

Students should note down the Everyday English expressions in that section of their vocabulary notebooks. Encourage them to use translations or other expressions from this unit to help them remember each one.

10 Improvisation

Divide the class into groups of four. Tell students they are going to create a role play. Read through the instructions with students. Give students two minutes to plan their role play. Circulate and help with vocabulary as necessary. Encourage students to use expressions from Exercise 9. Students practise their role plays. Listen to some of the best role plays in open class.

11 Free Time ⊙ DVD Episode 2

a Look at the photo with students and ask them to describe what is happening and answer the questions. Divide the class into pairs and ask students to create a short dialogue for the people in the photo. Circulate and help with vocabulary as necessary. Listen to some of the dialogues in open class as feedback.

b Divide the class into pairs. Read through the
question with students and elicit some ideas. In
pairs, students discuss the questions. Listen to
some of their ideas in open class as feedback.

c Play Episode 2 of the DVD for students to check
their predictions.

12 Write

The writing task can be set for homework or the
preparation can be done in class and Exercise 12b
can be set for homework.

If you set the background information as a
homework research task, ask students to tell the
rest of the class what they found out.

BACKGROUND INFORMATION

Cambridge (population 126,000) is a city in the
east of England on the river Cam. It is an ancient
market town with a lot of high-tech and computer
businesses. It is also home to Cambridge University,
founded in the twelfth century.

Midsummer Common is an area of common land
in Cambridge. The Cambridge Midsummer Fair held
on the common is one of the oldest fairs in the UK
and at one point was among England's largest. The
common borders the River Cam, houseboats are
typically moored on the common's bank, and many
university boathouses are located on the opposite
bank. Despite being in the centre of the city, the
common is still used by a herd of cows.

The Fitzwilliam Museum is the art museum of
Cambridge University. It was founded in 1816
and it houses magnificent collections of art and
antiquities of international importance.

a Students read the text silently and match the
paragraphs with the headings. Check answers.

b **Stronger classes:** Give students time to plan and
draft notes about their own town or city. Remind
them to use Rob's text as a model.

Weaker classes: They can discuss their drafts in
pairs and then write a rough version of their text.
They can swap texts with a partner to check before
writing the final version.

✳ OPTIONAL ACTIVITY

Students can add a photo or an illustration of their
town or city to their writing and the class could
vote for the best one.

13 Last but not least: more speaking

Divide the class into groups of four. Tell students
they are going to prepare a short play. Read
through the instructions with the class and check
understanding. Ask students to write down the
script as they prepare it. Circulate and help with
vocabulary. Students practise their plays. Encourage
them to use their notes as little as possible. As
feedback, ask students to act out their plays for
the rest of the class. Hold a class vote to decide
on the best play.

Check your progress

1 Grammar

a 2 our 3 my; your 4 Her 5 their

b 2 speaks 3 watch 4 finishes 5 goes 6 listen

c 2 There is 3 There are 4 Is there 5 Are there
6 Are there

2 Vocabulary

a **Places in towns:** chemist, railway station, bookshop,
post office, newsagent, library

Family: parents, aunt, father, daughter, cousin, uncle,
mother

Numbers: twenty-one, fourteen, thirteen, seventy,
eight, two, thirty

b 2 a thousand 3 eighty four 4 thirteen
5 nineteen 6 a hundred

How did you do?

Check that students are marking their scores.
Collect these in, check them as necessary, and
discuss any further work needed with specific
students.

Memo from Mario

Where's the café?

1 Fun practice (for some) of numbers between 0 and 1000

► Once you have worked on the numbers in the ways suggested by the authors, try this short activity.

► Don't explain, demonstrate:
Student: *zero*
You: *one thousand*
Student: *fifty*
You: *nine hundred and fifty*
Student: *one hundred*
You: *nine hundred*
Student: *one hundred and fifty*
You: *eight hundred and fifty*

► Then explain that one person goes up by 50 each time, starting from zero, while the other comes down by 50, each time, starting from 1000. The exercise ends when both people simultaneously reach 500.

► Pair the students and ask them to do what you have demonstrated.

► Get the students to work with two new partners, and do the exercise twice more, hopefully becoming more fluent each time.

> **RATIONALE**
>
> I cordially dislike this activity and have met plenty of language teachers who feel the same! However, to select exercises according to one's own prejudices alone is a bit simplistic.
>
> I have found that this type of number work helps logically-mathematically switched-on students to come into their own in the language class. Helping students who are strong in areas where I am weak is one of my greatest joys as a teacher.

2 Extra practice of *there is, there's, there are, there're*

► Divide the board in two down the middle.

► Tell the students that on one half of the board they are going to create a group picture. The rule is that volunteer A comes and draws **one** item, e.g. a bird or a chair. Volunteer B then comes up and draws **two** of the same item, e.g. two houses or two TVs. In this way the students create a picture full of single items and pairs of items.

► The drawing phase is done in silence (culture permitting!) and you the teacher make no content suggestions.

► Get the students to come to the board and write in the words they know under the items.

► Help them to name what they do not yet have words for.

► Then ask students to come to the other side of the board and write as many descriptive sentences as they can, e.g.
There's a tree.
There're two houses.
There's a chair and two children.

► Round off the activity by asking students to copy the pictures into their books with the words written in.

► Even if you have an IWB, still ask the students to make their own copies manually as the process helps fix the new words.

5 They've got brown eyes

Unit overview

TOPIC: Describing people

TEXTS

Reading and listening: an article about people and chimpanzees
Listening: descriptions of people; personal information
Reading: a magazine article about pets in different cultures
Writing: descriptions of your friends or family

SPEAKING AND FUNCTIONS

Asking and answering questions with *have got*
Describing people
Giving personal information

LANGUAGE

Grammar: *has/have got; Why ...? because ...*
Vocabulary: parts of the body
Pronunciation: /v/ *they've*

1 Read and listen

If you set the background information as a homework research task, ask students to tell the rest of the class what they found out.

> **BACKGROUND INFORMATION**
> DNA (deoxyribonucleic acid) is a nucleic acid that contains the genetic instructions used in the development and functioning of all living organisms. DNA is often compared to a code or a recipe, since it contains the instructions needed to construct other components of cells, such as proteins and molecules.

a Pre-teach any necessary vocabulary, e.g. *intelligent, fingers, thumb, chocolate, chimpanzee, forests, DNA*.

Students read the questions and look at the pictures. Ask them to predict their answers. Students then read the text and check their answers. Were their predictions correct?

> **Answers**
> Chimpanzee: Sally
> Girl: Paula

b ▶ **CD1 T50** Students read through statements 1 to 4. Check any problems.

Stronger classes: They can do this from memory and then listen to check their answers. They can then correct the false statements.

Weaker classes: Play the recording for students to read and listen. Students complete the exercise. Play the recording again, pausing after each answer for students to check. Students can then correct the false statements.

TAPESCRIPT
See reading text on page 42 of the Student's Book.

> **Answers**
> 1 F (They haven't got big families.)
> 2 F (She's got two sisters.)
> 3 F (She loves her sisters.)
> 4 F (It's 98% the same.)

2 Grammar

✱ *Why ...? Because ...*

a **Stronger classes:** Students read the example questions and answer. Point out the use of *why* in the question and *because* in the answer. Elicit or explain that *because* answers the question *why* and is followed by a reason. Students then read the second question and re-read the text on page 40 to find the answer. Check answers.

Weaker classes: Books closed. Write the following question and answer on the board (or an example of your own): *Why are we here? Because we want to learn English.* Draw students' attention to the use of the question word *why* and the answer with *because*. Students open their books at page 41. Follow the procedure for stronger classes.

Check answers as a class.

> **Answer**
> Because she loves chocolate.

✱ *has / have got*

b Go through the examples as a class. Ask students to identify the positive and negative singular forms and the positive plural form. Ask them what they notice about each verb and elicit that the positive singular form is *has got*, the positive plural form is *have got*, and negative singular is *hasn't got*.

Ask students to work out at this point what they think the plural negative form is (*haven't got*). Students read through the table and complete the gaps. Check answers.

Answers
Negative: haven't got
Question: Has
Short answer: have/haven't, has/hasn't

Language notes
Explain to students that in short answers with *has/ have got*, the *got* is dropped and only the *have/has* is used.

[c] Read through the sentences with students and check understanding. Go through the example. Students compare answers with a partner before feedback in open class.

Answers
2 has got   3 've got   4 Has; got   5 've got
6 haven't got   7 Have; got   8 haven't got

[d] This exercise can be set for homework. Students read through sentences 1 to 6. Go through the first item as an example, if necessary. Students complete the exercise. Ask students to compare with a partner and then students can feedback to their partner.

Answers
Students' own answers.

Get it right! Refer students to the Get it right! section. These exercises can be used as homework or for fast-finishers.

3 Pronunciation

See notes on page 108.

4 Speak

Divide the class into pairs. Ask a stronger pair to demonstrate the example dialogue. Students ask and answer about their families. Remind them to use the information they completed in Exercise 2b. Monitor and check students are taking turns asking and answering, and that they are using the questions and answer forms correctly. Ask pairs to feedback to the class with the information they found out about their partner. If anyone has found out any interesting information, ask them to give the class more details.

5 Vocabulary
✱ Parts of the body

Warm-up
Elicit as many parts of the body as students know in English. Refer students back to the reading text on page 40 to find some of the parts of the body vocabulary there (*eyes, nose, fingers, thumb*).

▶ **CD1 T53**   Students read through the words in the box. In pairs, students label the diagram. Play the recording for students to listen and check their answers, pausing after each word for students to repeat.

TAPESCRIPT/ANSWERS
1 eye   2 ear   3 face   4 thumb   5 hand   6 hair
7 nose   8 mouth   9 arm   10 finger   11 leg
12 foot

Vocabulary notebook
Students should start a section called *Parts of the body*. Encourage them to note down the words from this section and to translate them into their own language or to illustrate them.

✱ OPTIONAL ACTIVITY

Whole class. This activity revises positive imperatives and parts of the body. Give students instructions, e.g. *Touch your head. Put your hands on your knees.* You can speed things up once students have got the hang of the game. If a student carries out the wrong instruction, they must sit out of the game. You can ask students to come and call out the instructions.

Vocabulary bank   Refer students to the vocabulary bank. Read through the words and phrases in open class and check understanding.

6 Listen and speak
✱ Describing people 1

[a] ▶ **CD1 T54**   Students read through the words in the box. Go through the examples, if necessary. Writing in their notebooks, students complete the lists with the words from the box. Play the recording for students to listen and check their answers. Play the recording a second time, pausing after each word for students to repeat.

TAPESCRIPT/ANSWERS
Hair colour: blonde, brown, red, grey, fair, black.
Hair style: straight, short, curly, wavy, medium-length, long.
Eye colour: brown, blue, grey, green.

b Divide the class into pairs. Students look at the pictures. Ask a stronger pair to demonstrate the example dialogue. Draw students' attention to the use of *has got* in each sentence. Students ask and answer in pairs. Monitor and check students are taking turns to ask and answer, and that they are using the third person singular form *has got* correctly. Note down any repeated errors to go through as a class at the end of the exercise. Ask pairs to feedback to the rest of the class.

Vocabulary notebook

Encourage students to start a section called *Describing people* and to make a note of all the words from this section. They can write translations or illustrate them.

✳ OPTIONAL ACTIVITY

Divide the class into pairs. Give students a few minutes to look at their partner. Students then stand back to back and describe their partner to the rest of the class. They must describe their hair colour, eye colour, etc. The rest of the class must decide if they are correct.

⑦ Listen and speak

✳ Describing people 2

a ▶ CD1 T55   Before students listen, ask them to describe each picture using the words from Exercise 5d. Explain that they will only need to tick three of the four pictures. Play the recording for students to listen and tick the pictures described. Check answers.

TAPESCRIPT

1

Boy 1: John? Do you know the new girl in class 4A?

Boy 2: The girl in 4A? No, I don't know her. Why?

Boy 1: She's really pretty. She's got dark hair.

Boy 2: Uh huh. What — long dark hair?

Boy 1: No, no, it's short. And, erm, blue eyes I think. She's got really big eyes. She's got a great smile, too.

Boy 2: Oh, right. So — what's her name?

2

Girl 1: So, what's your new friend like?

Girl 2: Oh, he's wonderful! He's really tall, and he's got fair hair, not very short, sort of medium length.

Girl 1: Long blonde hair!

Girl 2: No! Medium length and fair, not blonde — quite wavy. And he's got lovely big brown eyes. He's really good-looking!

Girl 1: Oh! So, when can I meet him?

3

Boy 1: My cousin's here from America.

Boy 2: Right! What's she like?

Boy 1: Oh, she's lovely. She's tall with blond hair.

Boy 2: Is it long?

Boy 1: No, it isn't. It's short and spiky.

Boy 2: What colour are her eyes?

Boy 1: They're, um, green and she's got freckles. She's very pretty.

Boy 2: Really? When can I come round and meet her?

Answers
Pictures 1, 2 and 4
---

b Go through the example as a class, drawing students' attention to the use of *has got* and the adjectives used to describe people. Give students a few minutes to find a person to describe and to ask and answer questions. Monitor and check students are using the verbs and adjectives correctly, making a note of any repeated errors to go through as a class after the exercise.

✳ Giving personal information

Warm-up

Books closed. Ask students if they have filled in any forms recently. If so, what were they for and what type of information did they have to fill in? If not, then ask them what sort of information they think they would need to give to apply for a Saturday job.

c ▶ CD1 T56   Students read through the form. Check any problems. Play the recording for students to listen only. Play the recording a second time for students to complete the form. Students can compare answers in pairs before a whole-class check. Play the recording again, pausing after each answer if necessary.

TAPESCRIPT

Man: So, you want to work in the dogs' home at weekends?

Nina: Yes, I do, please.

Man: Great! How old are you?

Nina: I'm seventeen.

Man: Right ... and ... what's your name?

Nina: My first name's Nina.

Man: Anna?

Nina: No, Nina — N-I-N-A.

Man: OK, thanks. And your surname?

Nina: It's Torrington.

Man: How do you spell that?

Nina: T-O-double R-I-N-G-T-O-N.

Man: Right — Nina Torrington. And what's your address, Nina?

Nina: 129, Lincoln Street. Oxford.

Man: Sorry, can you repeat the street name, please?

Nina: Lincoln Street – L-I-N-C-O-L-N.

Man: L-I-N-C-O-L-N ... OK – that's fine. And have you got a phone, Nina? At home, I mean.

Nina: Yes, it's four eight nine two double seven. And I've got a mobile.

Man: Good. Tell me that too, please.

Nina: It's oh seven nine four three double two nine eight six nine.

Man: OK, now, let me see what jobs we've got ...

Answers
Surname: Torrington
Age: 17
Address: 129 Lincoln Street
Phone: 489277
Mobile: 07943 229869

d This exercise can be set for homework. Students read through items 1 to 6. Check any problems. Go through the example, if necessary. Students complete the exercise. Check answers.

Answers
2 What's your first name
3 How do you spell that, please
4 What's your address
5 Can you repeat that, please
6 What's your telephone number, please

e Divide the class into pairs. Students ask and answer questions from Exercise 7d.

Monitor and check students are taking turns to ask and answer, and that they are using the correct question and answer forms.

✱ OPTIONAL ACTIVITY

Stronger classes: They could change their identities and ask and answer using different information.

Weaker classes: Ask pairs from Exercise 7e to imagine they are completing a form for a Saturday job. Students can act out their dialogues.

Culture in mind

If you set the background information as a homework research task, ask students to tell the rest of the class what they found out.

BACKGROUND INFORMATION

China (population 1,345,751,000) is officially known as The People's Republic of China and is situated in East Asia. It is the world's third-largest country and the world's most highly populated country. The capital is Beijing and other major cities include Shanghai and Tianjin.

Japan (population 127,590,000) is situated off the coast of Asia and consists of four main islands: Hokkaido, Honshu, Shikoku, Kyushu. Two-thirds of Japan's surface is covered with mountains, including a number of volcanoes. The most famous mountain in Japan is Mount Fuji.

Inuit is a term for a group of indigenous peoples in the Canadian Arctic region. Inuit people are traditionally hunters and fishers and their traditional diet is very high in fat (75%).

Canada (population 34 million) is a country in the north of North America. The country's border with the United States is the longest border in the world. Canada is a country of forest and mountains with long cold winters. The capital is Ottawa and other large cities are Toronto, Montreal and Vancouver.

Madagascar (population 19,625,000) is an island nation in the Indian Ocean off the southeastern coast of Africa. It is the fourth-largest island in the world and is home to 5% of the world's plant and animal species. Two-thirds of the population live below the international poverty line.

Australia is the world's oldest, smallest and flattest continent and the only continent occupied by a single nation. Its capital city is Canberra. It has five states on the mainland (Queensland, New South Wales, Victoria, South Australia and Western Australia) and also Tasmania, an island just off its south coast. The Aborigines (Australian native people) are thought to have come to Australia from Southeast Asia at least 49,000 years ago.

Indonesia (population 230 million) is a country in Southeast Asia and Oceania. Indonesia comprises 17,508 islands. It is the world's fourth most populous country, with the world's largest population of Muslims. Despite being densely populated, Indonesia has vast areas of wilderness that support the world's second highest level of biodiversity.

8 Read and listen

Warm-up

Ask students if they have any pets. If so, what kinds of animals do they have? Do they know anyone who has a strange or unusual pet? If so, ask students to give you more information. This can be done in L1.

a ▶ **CD1 T57** Students look at the photos. Go through the names of each pet before students start the exercise.

Stronger classes: They can read the article silently and answer the question. Go through the first item as an example, if necessary.

Weaker classes: Read the article aloud as a class. Go through the first item as an example, then students complete the exercise in pairs.

Answers
China, Japan, Canada, Australia, Indonesia

b Students read through questions 1 to 6. Check any problems.

Stronger classes: They can answer these questions without reading the text and then check their answers.

Weaker classes: Go through the first item as an example. In pairs, students read the text again and complete the exercise.

Check answers as a class.

Answers
1 budgies
2 dogs, cats, birds, fish
3 China and Japan
4 northern Canada
5 no
6 a pouch

c In pairs or small groups students discuss the question. Ask for feedback. Are there any interesting answers? If so, encourage students to give more information to the rest of the class.

⭐ OPTIONAL ACTIVITY

Individual or pairs. Students choose their ideal pet and write about what it is, how they would look after it, what they would call it, what it eats, etc. They can then read out their descriptions to the rest of the class without saying what the animal is. The other students can guess what the animal is.

⑨ Write

If you set the background information as a homework research task, ask students to tell the rest of the class what they found out.

BACKGROUND INFORMATION
Red Hot Chili Peppers is an American rock band formed in Los Angeles, California, in 1983. For most of the band's existence, the members have been vocalist Anthony Kiedis, guitarist John Frusciante, bassist Michael 'Flea' Balzary, and drummer Chad Smith. The band's varied musical style has fused traditional funk with punk rock. They have sold over 55 million albums worldwide. Their most famous albums are *Blood Sugar Sex Magik* (1991) and *Californication* (1999).

a Students read through the two descriptions and match them with the pictures. Check any problems.

Answers
1 B   2 A

b This can be set for homework. Encourage students to read Anna's text again, noting down all the things she mentions about the people she is describing (name, age, eye colour, hair colour and style, things he/she likes, one extra piece of information).

Stronger classes: They can use Anna's models to write their own descriptions.

Weaker classes: Encourage them to write a draft version and to swap with a partner to check. They can then write their final versions.

⭐ OPTIONAL ACTIVITY

Students can add photos or illustrations to their descriptions and these can be displayed around the class.

Memo from Mario

They've got brown eyes

1 An activity using *I've got* and *X has got*

► Organise your class into seated circles of eight to twelve people. If the furniture is fixed, have the students form standing circles in among the desks.

► Ask each student to think of something they own that defines them. Explain (in L1 if necessary) that shoes, in a society where most people wear shoes, do not define them. The object chosen needs to be special in some sort of way. Make sure that everybody has chosen an object and that they can name it in English.

► Demonstrate the exercise with one of the circles, with all the others gathered round:

Student A says: *I'm Luca and I've got a stuffed bird.*

Luca then chooses Student B who repeats what A has said and then declares what they have got:

He's Luca and he's got a stuffed bird. I'm Sonia and I've got a very old book.

Sonia then chooses the next person who repeats what the first two students have got and then says what they have got.

► After the demonstration, ask all the circles to do the exercise simultaneously. The last person in each circle has to remember between 9 and 11 sentences.

> **RATIONALE**
> Providing the students choose genuinely defining objects, this activity helps them, in a small way, to meet each other differently.

2 Animal vocabulary revision

► Dictate the animals from Culture in mind on pages 44–45 (dog, fish, cat, budgie, kangaroo, sugar glider, fox, bear cub, baby seal, fighting cricket, Madagascar hissing cockroach). Taking down dictation is, in itself, quite useful revision.

► Put these headings on the board:

The animal I know best
The most silent animal
The most dangerous animal

► Check that the students understand *best*, *silent* and *dangerous*.

► Tell the students to turn their papers landscape way round and to copy the headings across the top of the page.

► Then ask them to rank the animals from the most familiar animal to least familiar, most silent to noisiest, and most dangerous to least dangerous.

► Ask the students to work in groups of four and compare their three column rankings.

> **RATIONALE**
> Ranking exercises are excellent for helping students to commit vocabulary sets to long term memory, since ranking forces detailed thought about meaning.

This is delicious!

Unit overview

TOPIC: Food

TEXTS

Reading and listening: an article about unusual food from around the world; photostory: Enjoy your lunch!

Listening and speaking: ordering food in a restaurant

Writing: an email about yourself

SPEAKING AND FUNCTIONS

Ordering food in a restaurant

LANGUAGE

Grammar: countable and uncountable nouns; *this/that/these/those*; *I'd like … / Would you like …?*

Vocabulary: food

Pronunciation: /w/ *would*

1 Read and listen

If you set the background information as a homework research task, ask students to tell the rest of the class what they found out.

BACKGROUND INFORMATION

Slovenia (population c.2 million) is a mountainous country in Central Europe. Slovenia borders Italy to the west, Croatia to the south and east, Hungary to the northeast, and Austria to the north. The capital and largest city of Slovenia is Ljubljana. Slovenia is a member of the European Union and the eurozone.

Indonesia: see Background Information Unit 5, Exercise 8.

China: see Background Information Unit 5, Exercise 8.

Japan: see Background Information Unit 5, Exercise 8.

Warm-up

Ask students what their favourite food is. Do they have a favourite food from another country? If so, what is it?

a Students look at the pictures and the countries (a–d). Go through each item as a class, making sure students know how to pronounce each word. Go through the first item as an example, if necessary. In pairs, students work out which countries the other items come from. Do not check answers at this stage.

b ▶ **CD1 T58** Pre-teach any difficult vocabulary, e.g. *raw*, *stews*, *beef*, *meat*, *dragonfly*. Play the recording for students to read and listen and check their answers to Exercise 1a. Play the recording again, pausing as necessary after each answer.

TAPESCRIPT

See reading text on page 46 of the Student's Book.

> **Answers**
> **1** a **2** d **3** b **4** c

✱ OPTIONAL ACTIVITY

Students can research other countries for homework and find out if there are any other interesting foods people like to eat. They can report their findings in the next lesson.

2 Vocabulary

✱ Food

Warm-up

Books closed. Ask students if they know the English names for any food items. Elicit suggestions.

a ▶ **CD1 T59** Students open their books at page 47, look at the pictures and read through the words in the box. They can check their predictions from the Warm-up. Check they understand the different categories. Play the recording, pausing after each item. Go through the first item from the box as an example, if necessary. Students classify the other items. Check answers.

TAPESCRIPT/ANSWERS

1 chicken
2 eggs
3 bread
4 cheese
5 onions
6 tomatoes
7 bananas
8 apples
9 strawberries

b Divide the class into pairs. Ask a stronger pair to demonstrate the example dialogue. Students ask and answer about what they like and don't like. Monitor and check students are taking turns to ask and answer. Ask pairs to feedback to the rest of the class about their partner.

Vocabulary bank Refer students to the vocabulary bank. Read through the words and phrases in open class and check understanding.

Vocabulary notebook

Students should start a section called *Food* and note down the words from this section. They can either write translations for the items or illustrate each one.

OPTIONAL ACTIVITY

Small groups or whole class. One student begins by saying a food item. The next student must repeat the first item and add a new item. The game continues in this way until someone can't remember an item in the correct order. For example:

S1: In my bag I have apples.
S2: In my bag I have apples and bananas.
S3: In my bag I have apples and bananas and [new item], etc.

3 Grammar

✱ Countable and uncountable nouns

a **Stronger classes:** Students read through the words in the box and look at the table. Ask them what they notice about the words in the *Countable* column and elicit that they all have *a/an* in front of them. Ask them which word appears before the uncountable nouns (*some*). Ask a student to explain the difference between countable and uncountable nouns if they can. Students now complete the table with the words from the box.

Weaker classes: Books closed. Write the headings *Countable* and *Uncountable* on the board and the nouns *apple* and *cheese*. Ask students if we can count apples and elicit the response, then do the same with cheese. Ask a student to come out and write each noun under the appropriate heading. At this point, elicit which words precede countable nouns (*a/an*) and which words precede uncountable nouns (*some*). Ask students to provide another example for each column. Students then open their books at page 50 and look through the list of words in the box. Ask volunteers to come out and write the nouns under the relevant heading on the board.

Check answers.

Answers
Countable: tomato, egg, strawberry, orange, onion
Uncountable: bread, chicken, sugar, beef, rice

OPTIONAL ACTIVITY

To check understanding at this point, call out a few food nouns of your own and ask students to tell you if they are countable or uncountable.

b Students can read and complete the rule based on the information they supplied in Exercise 3a.

Answers
an; some

Get it right! Refer students to the Get it right! section. These exercises can be used as homework or for fast-finishers.

Grammar notebook

Encourage students to note down the rules and some examples of countable/uncountable nouns from this section.

OPTIONAL ACTIVITY

Give students the following items (or others of your own choice) to classify as Countable (*C*) or Uncountable (*U*):

Potatoes (*C*), apples (*C*), cheese (*U*), pasta (*U*), water (*U*), orange (*C*)

✱ *this/that/these/those*

Stronger classes: Students look at the pictures and the sentences. Ask them which words are singular and which are plural and elicit that *this/that* are singular and *these/those* are plural. Then ask a student to explain the difference between them. *This/these* are used when we refer to something closer to the speaker while *that/those* are used when something is further away from the speaker.

Weaker classes: Books closed. Using items in the classroom, give students some examples using *this/that/these/those*. Ask students if they can tell you which are the singular words and which are the plural words. Then elicit or explain when we use *this/these* and *that/those*. Students now open their books at page 50 and look at the pictures and examples.

c Students look at pictures 1 to 4. Go through the first item as an example, if necessary. Students complete the sentences. Check answers.

Answers
1 These 2 that 3 Those 4 this

Grammar notebook

Encourage students to note down the rules and some examples from this section. They can write translations for each item if it will help.

✱ *I'd like ... / Would you like ...?*

d ▶ **CD1 T60**   Students read through the dialogue quickly. Check any problems. Play the recording for students to read and listen to find the answers. Check answers, playing and pausing the recording again as necessary.

TAPESCRIPT

See dialogue on page 49 of the Student's Book.

> **Answers**
> cheese, tomatoes, lettuce, cucumber, potatoes, strawberries and cherries.

e   Students read through items 1 to 3. Go through the first item as an example, drawing students' attention to the expressions in the dialogue in Exercise 3d. Students complete the answers. Students can check answers in pairs before a whole-class check.

> **Answers**
> 1 like; please
> 2 Would you like
> 3 Would you like?; thanks

✱ OPTIONAL ACTIVITY

Stronger classes: Students can change the items they want to buy and then act out the dialogue in Exercise 4d in pairs.

Weaker classes: Students can act out the dialogue from Exercise 4d in pairs.

4 Pronunciation

See notes on page 108.

5 Listen and speak

Warm-up

Ask students if they have ever eaten in a restaurant. If so, when did they eat there? What did they choose from the menu and who were they with?

a ▶ **CD1 T62**   Students read through the menu. Check any problems. Ask students to predict what they think the man and woman on the recording will choose. Play the recording for students to listen, tick the items the people order, and check their predictions. Check answers, playing and pausing the recording again as necessary.

TAPESCRIPT

Waiter: Good evening. Would you like to order now?

Man: Yes, please. Wendy, what would you like to start with?

Woman: Hmm. I'd like the mixed salad, please.

Waiter: OK.

Man: I'd like the goat's cheese with mushrooms, please.

Waiter: Right. And, for your main course?

Woman: What do you recommend?

Waiter: Well, the chef's special today is the baked salmon with rice or potatoes.

Woman: That sounds perfect. I'd like that with rice, please.

Waiter: Certainly.

Man: And I'd like the chicken in lemon sauce.

Waiter: With rice or potatoes?

Man: Rice, please.

Waiter: No problem. Would you like anything else? Desserts? Drinks?

Woman: No thanks. Just water, please.

Waiter: OK, thank you. I'll bring your water and starters right away.

b   Students read through the phrases in the box. Check any problems.

Stronger classes: Ask them if they can remember any phrases the waiter or the customer used in the dialogue in Exercise 5a. Remind them to use these when acting out their dialogues.

Weaker classes: Before students begin, play the recording from Exercise 5a again to remind students of the language and structures used.

In groups of three, students take turns to order and take the order in a restaurant. Monitor and check students are taking turns and are asking and answering correctly.

✱ OPTIONAL ACTIVITY

Stronger classes: Students can plan and write their own ideal menus and decorate them. Students can then vote for the best menu.

Weaker classes: Ask groups to act out their dialogues for the rest of the class.

Photostory: Enjoy your lunch!

6 Read and Listen

Warm-up

Ask students to look at the title of the photostory and the photos, and to predict what they think this episode will be about (food). You could also ask

a ▶ **CD1 T63** Read through the instructions with students and see if students can guess the answer to the question. Play the recording for students to read and listen. Check answers. Play the recording again, pausing as necessary for students to clarify any problems.

TAPESCRIPT

See the text on page 50 of the Student's Book.

b Read through the sentences with students. Ask students to read the story in Exercise 6a again and decide on the correct order of the sentences. Do the first one as an example if necessary. Students order the sentences, discussing their answers with a partner before feedback. Check answers.

Answers
Correct order: 2 b 3 e 4 f 5 a 6 d

7 Everyday English

a Read the expressions aloud with the class. Tell them to find them in the photostory and to try to match them with their meaning. Allow students to check answers with a partner before open class feedback.

Answers
1 Izzie 2 Kate 3 Mark 4 Mark

b Ask students to look at the expressions in the dialogue and in L1, discuss what they think they mean. Is a direct translation possible in their language? If not, discuss how they might express a similar meaning.

c ▶ **CD1 T64** Read through the sentences with students and clarify any problems with understanding. In pairs, students decide on the correct order for the dialogue. Check answers and ask students to practise the correct dialogue.

TAPESCRIPT/ANSWERS

Samantha: What's that – in your sandwich?

Andy: It's cheese. It's called Gorgonzola. Would you like some?

Samantha: No thanks. I don't like cheese very much. And that cheese is blue!

Andy: Yes, it's blue, but don't worry. It's really delicious!

Samantha: Oh, right. But I think I'll just eat my chips. Do you want one?

Andy: Yes, please! I love chips!

d Students read through the dialogues. Check any problems. Go through the first item as an example, if necessary, showing students how only one option is possible. Students complete the exercise. They can compare answers in pairs before a whole class check.

Answers
1 No thanks 2 Oh right 3 Yes, please
4 Don't worry

8 Improvisation

Divide the class into groups of four. Tell students they are going to create a role play. Read through the instructions with students. Give students two minutes to plan their role play. Circulate and help with vocabulary as necessary. Encourage students to use expressions from Exercise 7, but do not let them write down the text. Students practise their role plays. Listen to some of the best role plays in open class.

9 Free Time ⊙ DVD Episode 3

a Look at the photo with students and ask them to describe what is happening and answer the questions. Divide the class into pairs and ask students to create a short dialogue for the people in the photo. Circulate and help with vocabulary as necessary. Listen to some of the dialogues in open class as feedback.

Answers
They are Kate, Izzie, Darren, Mark and Jo.
Students' own answers.

b Read through the sentences with students and check understanding. Students tick the statements which are true for them. Divide the class into pairs and ask students to compare their answers. Listen to some of their ideas in open class.

c Play Episode 3 of the DVD for students to find out what happens.

10 Write

a Explain to students that the email is from an English family. Ask them where the family lives and what they want to know. Ask them if they know what *P.S.* means (post script, when you add something to the end of a letter or email that you forgot to include in the main body). Students read the email and find the answers.

Answers
They live in London. They want to know about the food you like and what you want to do in London.

b This exercise can be set for homework. Encourage students to answer all the questions from the email on page 52. Students should make notes first and then draft a version of their email. Remind them of some of the conventions of more formal emails:

- Opening: *Dear*
- New paragraphs for different topics
- Signing off phrases: *Best wishes, Yours sincerely,*
- *P.S.*: This can be added if you forget something in the main body of the email.

Students complete their emails. They can swap with a partner to check and then write a final version.

Vocabulary notebook

Remind students to note down any new expressions and any points to remember for more formal email writing.

11 Last but not least: more speaking

Read through the instructions with students and check understanding. Divide the class into groups of four and ask each member of the group to write four things to eat. Students choose one of the lists and make four sentences, two of which are true and two not true. Circulate and help with vocabulary as required. You may like to give students an example of your own to get them started. Students decide which sentences are true or false. As feedback, listen to some examples in open class.

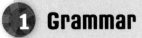

Check your progress

1 Grammar

a 2 haven't got 3 have got 4 've got 5 haven't got

b 1 some 2 some 3 an 4 a

c 2 a 3 e 4 b 5 c

d 2 those 3 these 4 this

2 Vocabulary

Parts of the body: arm, finger, mouth
Animals: kangaroo, cockroach, seal
Food: butter, chicken, sugar

How did you do?

Check that students are marking their scores. Collect these in, check them as necessary and discuss any further work needed with specific students.

Memo from Mario

This is delicious!

An activity to revise *Unusual food around the world*

▶ Write a simple sentence from the reading text on page 46 on the board, e.g.

^ *Jiro* ^ *likes* ^ *food* ^

▶ Ask a student to come and add one word replacing any of the carets. The resultant sentence must be grammatically correct and meaningful, e.g.

Young Jiro ^ *likes* ^ *food* ^

▶ Ask the person who added *young* to read the whole sentence. The point of the reading is to allow the student time to correct the sentence if it is wrong. If they do not realise there is a mistake all you have to do is to silently delete the wrongly placed word.

▶ Then another student comes out and adds a word, and so on.

▶ End the expansion work before the utterance becomes too unwieldy.

▶ Here are some minimal sentences from the reading text on page 46 that may be suitable for the exercise:

^ *they* ^ *eat* ^ *raw* ^ *eggs* ^

^ *they* ^ *have   stews* ^

^ *put* ^ *it* ^ *on* ^ *plate* ^

^ *they* ^ *wouldn't* ^ *like* ^ *what* ^ *I* ^ *eat* ^

▶ After the sentence expansion phase ask the students to re-read the text on page 46.

RATIONALE

Sentence expansion of this sort has two aims: (i) to help students revise the previous reading passage and its vocabulary and (ii) to allow discovery grammar and syntax work.

It is vital that you do not correct the volunteering student until they have had time to stand back and read the new sentence aloud and check it against their own growing inner language criteria.

This simple technique, from the Silent Way work of Caleb Gattegno, allows the student to do useful trial and error work, developing their sense of autonomy.

7 I sometimes watch TV

Unit overview

TOPIC: TV programmes and viewing habits

TEXTS

Reading and listening: an article about different ways of life
Listening: an interview about TV and TV programmes
Reading and listening: a text about what British teenagers watch on TV
Writing: a paragraph about TV

SPEAKING AND FUNCTIONS

Talking about regular activities and daily routine
Talking about TV programmes

LANGUAGE

Grammar: present simple with adverbs of frequency
Vocabulary: days of the week; TV programmes; telling the time
Pronunciation: compound nouns

1 Read and listen

If you set the background information as a homework research task, ask students to tell the rest of the class what they found out.

> **BACKGROUND INFORMATION**
>
> **The Outer Hebrides** is an island chain off the west coast of Scotland. Scottish Gaelic remains widely spoken on the islands, even though in some areas it has now been largely replaced by English.
>
> **Scotland** is a country that is part of the United Kingdom. Occupying the northern third of the island of Great Britain, it shares a border with England to the south. After the creation of the devolved Scottish Parliament in 1999, the first ever Scottish Government was elected in 2007.
>
> **West Java** (population c. 41.5 million) is the most populous province of Indonesia, located on Java Island. Its capital city is Bandung.

Warm-up

Ask students if they like watching TV, and what types of programmes they watch.

a Pre-teach any vocabulary students may need to know, e.g. *fisherman, housework, temporary, storms, rain*. Students read the five statements. Check any problems. They then look at the pictures and decide which activities they think each person does. This can be done in pairs.

Stronger classes: Students then read the text individually and check their ideas.

Weaker classes: Read the text aloud as a class to check ideas.

> **Answers**
> Calvin: 1,2,5
> Mawar: 3,4

b ▶ **CD1 T65**   Students read through questions 1 to 4. Check any problems.

Stronger classes: They can answer the questions and then listen to check their answers.

Weaker classes: Play the recording for students to read and listen. Give students a few minutes to complete the exercise. Check answers, playing and pausing the recording again as necessary.

TAPESCRIPT

See the reading text on page 54 of the Student's Book.

> **Answers**
> 1 Calvin is from Vatersay, an island in the Outer Hebrides, Scotland. Mawar is from Kertajaya, West Java.
> 2 She never watches TV because they haven't got a TV.
> 3 He never goes to school because Vatersay hasn't got a school.
> 4 His father is a fisherman, his mother is a housewife.

2 Vocabulary

✳ Days of the week

Warm-up

Books closed. Ask students if they know any of the days of the week in English. If so, write them on the board.

▶ **CD1 T66**   Students open their books at page 55 and read through the days of the week in the box. Play the recording, pausing after each day for students to repeat. If students are having problems with any particular day, drill as a class.

Monday Tuesday Wednesday Thursday Friday
Saturday Sunday

Language note
Listen carefully for students' pronunciation of
Wednesday and make sure they are pronouncing
it /ˈwenzdeɪ/ and not /wednezdeɪ/. If there are
problems, drill this word a few times in isolation.

Vocabulary notebook
Tell students to start a section called *Days of the
week* and to note down the words in English with
a translation.

3 Grammar
✱ Adverbs of frequency

a Give students a few minutes to read through the
words in the box. Elicit or give an example of your
own for the first adverb of frequency, then ask
students to provide an example of their own for
the others. Students then read through items 1 to 7.
Check any problems. Go through the example as a
class, if necessary. Students complete the exercise.
Remind them to refer back to the reading text on
page 54 if they need to. Check answers.

> **Answers**
> 2 always 3 often 4 sometimes
> 5 never 6 often

b **Stronger classes:** Students read through the rule
and complete it. Ask them to provide an example
of their own or from Exercise 3a for each part of
the rule to check they understand.

Weaker classes: They may find it useful to refer
back to their completed answers in Exercise 3a to
help them complete the rule.

> **Answers**
> after; before

c Students read through the information in the table
and then look at the examples. Ask a few students
to give examples of their own using the expressions
in the table.

Language note
Students may find it useful to compare the position
of these expressions with the same expressions
in their own language. It may also be useful for
students to translate the adverbs of frequency
and these expressions.

d ▶ **CD2 T2** Students look at the pictures and
sentences 1 to 4. Check any problems. Go through
the example as a class, drawing students' attention
to the use of the adverbs of frequency expressions.
Students complete the exercise. Make sure they
understand that the sentence they write must
mean the same as the first one and must include
a frequency expression. Play the recording while
students listen and check their answers.

TAPESCRIPT/ANSWERS
1 My mum checks her email twice a day.
2 Tom eats fruit every day.
3 Susan goes shopping three times a week.
4 Harry plays football once a week.

Get it right! Refer students to the Get it right!
section. These exercises can be used as homework
or for fast-finishers.

Grammar notebook
Encourage students to start a section called
Adverbs of frequency and to note down the
expressions and rules from this section. They may
find it useful to write translations of some of the
expressions.

4 Speak

Divide the class into pairs. Students read through
the items in the box. Check any problems. Ask a
stronger pair to demonstrate the example dialogue,
drawing students' attention to the use of the
adverbs of frequency. Give students a few minutes
to ask and answer questions about the items in the
box. Monitor and check students are taking turns to
ask and answer, and that they are using adverbs of
frequency correctly. Make a note of any repeated
errors to go through as a class after the exercise.
Ask a few pairs to feedback to the class about
their partner.

5 Vocabulary
✱ TV programmes

Warm-up
Books closed. Ask students how often they
watch TV each week. Encourage them to use an
expression of frequency from this unit.

a Students read through the questions. Discuss these
as a class, and in L1 if appropriate. If there are any
interesting answers, discuss these as a class.

b ▶ **CD2 T3** Give students a few minutes to look
at the pictures and read the programme types. Play
the recording, pausing after each word for students
to repeat.

Divide the class into pairs. Students now decide
on an example for each picture and discuss their

favourite type of programme. Ask pairs to feedback to the rest of the class.

TAPESCRIPT

1 soap operas
2 documentaries
3 sports programmes
4 the news
5 chat shows
6 comedies
7 cartoons
8 game shows

6 Pronunciation

See notes on page 108.

7 Listen and speak

a ▶ **CD2 T5** Students look through the information in the chart. Explain that the answers are expressions of frequency. Play the recording, pausing after the examples to make sure students understand what they have to do. Remind them that each interviewee may not mention every type of programme in the table. Continue with the recording while students listen and complete the chart.

Weaker classes: If necessary, play the recording for Interview 1 and give students time to write their answers then play it a second time for Interview 2, giving students time to complete the table for that part.

Check answers, playing and pausing the recording again as necessary.

TAPESCRIPT

Dialogue 1

Speaker 1: Do you often watch TV, Dan?

Speaker 2: Well, no, not really.

Speaker 1: How often do you watch it? Every day? Three times a week?

Speaker 2: Hmm, every day I think. Yes, I watch TV every evening.

Speaker 1: And what sort of programmes do you watch?

Speaker 2: Well, I watch a lot of films, and I love documentaries. I watch films two or three times a week.

Speaker 1: Great! Do you watch the news at all?

Speaker 2: No, not very often. I don't like the news very much. But I like chat shows – I often watch them.

Speaker 1: What do you think of soap operas, then, Dan?

Speaker 2: I don't like them much. I never watch them. But I love drama series. I usually watch them.

You know, series like *House* and *Grey's Anatomy*.

Speaker 1: Do you know what I think? I think you watch a lot of TV!

Dialogue 2

Speaker 1: I really like watching TV. Do you?

Speaker 2: Er ... yes, I do.

Speaker 1: Well, how often do you watch TV, then? Do you watch something every day?

Speaker 2: No, I don't watch TV every day. I only watch a few programmes during the week. But I always watch TV at the weekend.

Speaker 1: Really? So, what programmes do you watch during the week?

Speaker 2: I watch my favourite programmes – there's a game show I like on Wednesdays, and on Friday evenings there's a music programme I watch.

Speaker 1: Do you ever watch soap operas?

Speaker 2: No, never. I think they're boring.

Speaker 1: What about films?

Speaker 2: No, not really. Well, hardly ever, in fact.

Speaker 1: What about at weekends?

Speaker 2: I watch a lot of sports programmes at weekends. And sometimes I watch cartoons.

Speaker 1: Yeah, me too. Do you watch documentaries?

Speaker 2: No, I don't.

Speaker 1: What about the news?

Speaker 2: Sometimes, yes.

Speaker 1: OK – well, I think I watch the TV about as often as you do. But I like different programmes.

> **Answers**
>
> **Interview 1**
> chat shows: often
> soap operas: never
> drama series: usually
>
> **Interview 2**
> sports programmes: a lot at the weekend
> the news: sometimes
> game shows: On Wednesdays
> cartoons: sometimes

b Give students a few minutes to complete the *Me* column with their own information. Ask a few students to feedback to the class.

c Divide the class into pairs. Ask a stronger pair to demonstrate the example dialogue, drawing students' attention to the use of the question and answer forms. Give students time to ask and answer their questions and to complete the column for their partner. Monitor and check that students are taking turns to ask and answer, and that they are using the correct question forms and frequency expressions. Note down any repeated errors to go through as a class after the exercise. Ask pairs to feedback to the class the information they found out about their partner.

─────── ✳ OPTIONAL ACTIVITY ───────

In pairs, students can draw up the results of the questions in Exercise 7 as a graph.

8 Vocabulary

✳ What's the time?

Warm-up

Ask a stronger student the question *What's the time?* and elicit the response in English if possible. Ask students if they know how to express any other times in English. If so, draw a few clock faces on the board and ask them to come and write the time in words under them.

a ▶ **CD2 T6** Students look at the clocks and write their answers. Play the recording for students to check their answers.

Play the recording again, pausing after each time for students to repeat.

TAPESCRIPT/ANSWERS

1 12:00 (twelve o'clock)
2 8:45 (eight forty-five)
3 11:15 (eleven fifteen)
4 7:20 (seven twenty)
5 2:00 (two o'clock)
6 12:30 (twelve thirty)

> **Language note**
>
> Some students may produce times like *They are seven and twenty* or *They are seven twenty* because of the way their own language works. Remind students how we say times in English.

b ▶ **CD2 T7** Draw four clock faces on the board and elicit *o'clock, quarter past, half past* and *quarter to*. Play the recording while students look at the clocks in their books. Then play the recording again, pausing each time for students to repeat.

TAPESCRIPT

1 quarter past seven
2 half past seven
3 quarter to eight
4 twenty to six
5 five to seven
6 twenty-five past six

c ▶ **CD2 T8** Play the recording for students to listen only. Play the recording a second time for students to write the time they hear.

Check answers as a class.

TAPESCRIPT

1
Man: Excuse me. What's the time, please?
Woman: The time? Erm, it's six twenty.
2
Boy: There's a really good film on TV tonight.
Girl: Oh yeah? When?
Boy: Erm, nine o'clock, I think.
3
Boy: What time's the bus to Cambridge?
Woman: Half past ten.
4
Girl: Do you want to come to the cinema tonight?
Boy: Yeah, OK.
Girl: OK. Come to my house first.
Boy: What time?
Girl: Is quarter past seven OK?
Boy: Yeah, fine. See you then.
Girl: OK. Bye.

> **Answers**
> 1 6.20 2 9.00 3 10.30 4 7.15

Vocabulary notebook

Students should start a section called *Telling the time* and note down how to do this in English.

9 Speak

Students look at the information in the table. Give them a few minutes to complete the *Me* column with their own information. Divide the class into pairs. Students read through the example dialogue. Check any problems.

Ask a stronger pair to demonstrate the example question and answer, drawing students' attention to the use of the question *What time do you ...?* Give students a few minutes to ask and answer their questions and then to note down their partner's answers in the *My partner* column of the table. Ask pairs to feedback to the class about their partner.

Culture in mind

10 Read and listen

If you set the background information as a homework research task, ask students to tell the rest of the class what they found out.

Godalming is a town in Surrey, England. It is a prosperous part of the London commuter belt.

Britain's Got Talent is a British TV show. Singers, dancers, comedians, variety acts, and other performers compete against each other to win £100,000 and the opportunity to perform in front of the Royal Family.

Sheffield (population 534,500) is a city in South Yorkshire, England. During the 19th century, Sheffield became internationally famous for its steel production. Sheffield has more trees per person than any other city in Europe, estimated at more than 2 million; 61% of the city is green space.

a Students look at the pictures and read the questions. Give them a few minutes to read Claire's profile and to complete the table.

Weaker classes: Students can read the text silently or it can be read aloud. Go through the first item in the table in Exercise 10b for Claire as a class. Students complete the exercise. Remind them to refer back to the text on page 58 as necessary.

Check answers.

Answers
Age: 16
Programmes she doesn't like: sports programmes
Number of hours a week she watches TV: eight

b ▶ **CD2 T9** Play the recording while students listen and complete the table for Paul.

Weaker classes: Play the recording once for students to listen only. Play it a second time for students to complete their answers.

Check answers, playing and pausing the recording again as necessary.

TAPESCRIPT

Interviewer: Excuse me, can I ask you some questions, please?

Paul: Er, yes – what about?

Interviewer: About TV, actually. But first, what's your name and how old are you?

Paul: My name's Paul Evans and I'm 17.

Interviewer: Where do you live, Paul?

Paul: I live in Sheffield – in the north of England.

Interviewer: OK. Do you watch a lot of TV, Paul?

Paul: Um, yes, I do. Well, I watch something on TV every day.

Interviewer: What sort of programmes do you like?

Paul: Um, I like some of the drama series – my favourites are *CSI* and *Lost*. But I also love sports programmes. I watch football on TV, so I watch a lot of television on Saturdays and Sundays.

Interviewer: Do you like comedies?

Paul: No, not much.

Interviewer: What about soap operas?

Paul: No, I hate them! I think they're really stupid!

Interviewer: How many hours a week do you watch TV, Paul?

Paul: Hmm, about ten ... no, twelve hours a week, I think. Mostly at the weekend.

Interviewer: Thanks for talking to me, Paul.

Paul: No problem.

Answers
Age: 17
Programmes he doesn't like: comedies, soap operas
Favourite programme: *CSI*, *Lost*, sports programmes
Number of hours a week he watches TV: 12

c Students read through items 1 to 5. Check any problems. Go through the first item as an example, playing and pausing the recording after the answer.

Stronger classes: They can underline their answers and listen and check only.

Weaker classes: Play the recording once for students to listen only. Play the recording a second time for students to underline their answers.

Check answers, playing and pausing the recording again as necessary.

Answers
2 drama 3 football 4 12 5 at the weekend

d In small groups students discuss the questions. Ask groups to feedback to the class.

11 Write

a Ask students what Pavel's favourite programme is, what kind of programme it is and how often he watches it. Give them a few minutes to read Pavel's paragraph. Check answers.

Answers
His favourite programme is a game show called *The Jackpot*. He watches it once a week.

b This exercise can be set for homework. Go through the structure of Pavel's paragraph as a class, eliciting the type of information he has included. Students can draft their paragraph and swap with a partner to check before writing a final version.

Memo from Mario

I sometimes watch TV

1 Making the English words for the days of week feel real

▸ Dictate the day of the week backwards (*Saturday, Friday, Thursday*, etc.) to a student at the board who writes them from the bottom of the board up to the top in a vertical list.

▸ Ask the students to take the list down in their books and write 'Monday things' next to Monday, e.g.

Monday: school again ☹, too much homework, I go swimming

▸ Tell the students to jot down the things they associate with each day of the week.

▸ Be available to help them with new words.

▸ Put the students in groups of five. They read out their associations with the days of the week.

▸ Working alone again, the students write down their colour association with each day of the week and a fruit they associate with each day of the week. Ask several students to call out their associations and to explain why they think this way.

> **RATIONALE**
>
> In this activity the students 'fill' the English words with some of the primings they have for the equivalent mother tongue words. This makes the L2 words a lot easier to really take on board.

2 Creative revision of *Different places – different lives*

▸ Preparation: photocopy the text below.

▸ In class give out the photocopied text and teach these words: *banana, night, to bleach.*

▸ Ask the students to work in pairs to read through the text, and to correct it without looking at the original text.

▸ To round off the activity, ask the pairs to compare their corrected text with the original reading text on page 54.

> Calvin lives on Vatersay, a banana in the Outer Hebrides, China. The banana is very big, fifty kilometres long and fifty kilometres wide. There are less than a hundred snakes on the island. Calvin's father works as a policeman. He usually leaves the supermarket at 6 o'clock in the evening. His Mum spends the night at home. She often does the homework but this isn't the only work she does. She bleaches Calvin and his three sisters too. Vatersay hasn't got a supermarket so the children learn at home. Calvin and his dog sometimes watch TV in the morning but not very often because the picture is hardly ever bad.

> **RATIONALE**
>
> When low-level students have to correct a semantically fractured text, as above, it gives them a sense of power. A lot of students get a good deal of satisfaction from re-establishing order and ridding the text of annoying chaos.
>
> It is important, from early on, to establish the student's self image as that of a critical, independent reader.

Don't do that!

TOPIC: Feelings

TEXTS
Listening: a story about a relationship; a song
Reading: a personal email
Reading and listening: photostory: Kate looks great
Writing: an email about friends and school

SPEAKING
Describing how you feel

LANGUAGE
Grammar: negative imperatives
Vocabulary: adjectives to describe feelings
Pronunciation: linking sounds

1 Listen

Warm-up
Ask students if they have had an argument recently. If so, who with and what about? Ask them how they felt and how the other person involved felt. This can be done in L1.

a Look at the pictures with students. Ask students to work in pairs and decide on the order of the pictures. Listen to some of their ideas but do not give them the answers at this stage.

b ▶ **CD2 T10** Pre-teach necessary vocabulary, e.g. *confused, scared*. Play the recording while students listen and check answers.

TAPESCRIPT
Steve: This film's awful. I'm bored. Really bored.
Julie: Me too. And I'm confused – I mean, I don't understand the story [knocking sound] … What's that?
Steve: What?
Julie: That noise. What is it?
Steve: Hmm. I don't know. Stay here.
Julie: Don't go outside! I'm scared.
Steve: Don't worry, Julie. Everything's OK.
Julie: Steve? Where are you? Come back! Help!
Steve: Woooh!
Julie: Aagh!
Steve: It's me!
Julie: Oh Steve – you idiot! Don't do that!
Steve: Sorry, Julie. It's just a joke.

Julie: Oh Steve. Sometimes you're really, really stupid.
Steve: Don't be angry, Julie. And don't cry! I'm sorry, OK?
Julie: Bye Steve! Enjoy the rest of the film!
Steve: Julie! Julie, don't go away, please! Julie, I love you! Aagh! Why do I do these things? Now, where's my phone? I'll send her a message.

Answers
2 B 3 F 4 E 5 A 6 D

✳ OPTIONAL ACTIVITY

Play the recording again, pausing at times to draw students' attention to pronunciation and intonation. In pairs, students can act out the dialogue from Exercise 1. Circulate and help with pronunciation as necessary. Listen to some of the dialogues in open class as feedback.

2 Grammar

✳ Negative imperatives

a Students read through sentences 1 to 6.

Stronger classes: They can do this without listening again and can listen to check their answers only.

Weaker classes: Play the recording from Exercise 1 again for students to listen and match the names to the sentences.

Check answers, playing and pausing the recording again as necessary.

Answers
2 Steve 3 Julie 4 Julie 5 Julie 6 Steve

b Students look at the imperatives in Exercise 2a again. Elicit which ones are positive and which ones are negative, and elicit the rule for each. Give students a few minutes to read and complete the rule in the box.

Answer
Don't

✳ OPTIONAL ACTIVITY

To check understanding at this point, call out a verb, a student's name and the word *positive* or *negative*. The students must supply the positive or negative imperative of the verb. For example:
T: Juana, sit, positive.
S1: Sit!

T: Pietro, stand up, negative.
S2: Don't stand up!

c Give students a few minutes to look at the pictures and the words in the box. Go through the first item as an example, if necessary. Students complete the exercise. Check answers.

Answers
2 Don't go away.
3 Don't cry.
4 Don't open the window.
5 Don't touch it.
6 Don't laugh.

d Students read through sentences 1 to 6 and look at signs A to F. Go through the first item as an example. Students complete the exercise.

Weaker classes: This exercise can be completed in two stages. Students match the sentences and check answers. Students then match the completed sentences to the signs. Check answers.

Answers
2e B   3f A   4a E   5b F   6d D

Language note
Students may find it useful to translate some of these sentences into their own language to see the differences.

Grammar notebook
Remind students to note down the rules for negative imperatives and some examples from this section in their notebooks.

✱ OPTIONAL ACTIVITY

Stronger classes: They can draw their own signs and ask a partner to work out the imperative. Students could draw signs for the classroom to indicate classroom rules.

Weaker classes: As a class elicit some verbs and some imperative sentences. Students can then draw some signs based on those sentences.

3 Pronunciation

See notes on page 108.

4 Vocabulary

✱ *How do you feel?*

Warm-up
Books closed. Elicit any adjectives for feelings students know in English and write them on the board.

a ▶ **CD2 T13** Students open their books at page 62 and look at the adjectives in the box and pictures 1 to 8. Look at the example. Students complete the exercise. Play the recording for students to listen and check answers.

TAPESCRIPT/ANSWERS
1 confused   2 happy   3 excited   4 angry
5 worried   6 scared   7 sad   8 bored

b ▶ **CD2 T14** Play the recording, pausing after the first item. Go through the answer as a class, making sure students all agree.

Stronger classes: Play the recording once. Students complete the exercise using adjectives from Exercise 4a.

Weaker classes: Play the recording once for students to listen only. Play it a second time for students to listen and write an adjective. Remind them to use adjectives from Exercise 4a. Check answers, playing and pausing the recording again as necessary.

TAPESCRIPT
1 Stop it, will you. I said STOP!
2 Oh, no. Look! Ugh! A snake!
3 Oh, this film. It's awful!
4 Come on, yes, shoot! Yes, GOAL!
5 (somebody crying)
6 Oh no! I've got a test tomorrow – and I don't think I know the answers.

Answers
2 scared   3 bored   4 excited   5 sad
6 worried

Vocabulary bank Refer students to the vocabulary bank. Read through the words and phrases in open class and check understanding.

5 Speak

Divide the class into pairs. Students read through situations 1 to 6. Check any problems. Ask a stronger pair to demonstrate the example dialogue. Students take turns to ask and answer questions about each situation. Monitor and check students are taking turns and that they are responding using appropriate adjectives. Ask pairs to feedback to the class about their partner.

Vocabulary notebook
Encourage students to start a section called *Feelings* and to note down the words from this section and any translations which will help them.

In small groups (or as a whole-class activity), students choose an adjective from Exercise 4a and mime it for the rest of the group/class. The other students have one minute in which to guess the correct adjective. The student who guesses correctly chooses a different adjective and the game continues.

6 Read

a Ask students *Does Julie love Steve?* Give them a few minutes to read the email and find the answer (no).

b Students read through sentences 1 to 5. Check any problems.

Stronger classes: They can do this without reading the letter again and can then read and check their answers.

Weaker classes: Students can read the letter again. Go through the first item as an example before students complete the exercise.

Check answers, encouraging students to correct the false answers.

> **Answers**
> 1 F (She's angry and confused.)
> 2 T
> 3 T
> 4 F (She doesn't want him to visit, write or phone.)
> 5 T

Stronger classes: Students can write Steve's reply to Julie's email. Encourage them to think about how he is feeling and to use adjectives and imperatives from this unit.

Weaker classes: In small groups, they can discuss how they think Steve feels and feedback to the class. This could be done in L1.

7 Listen

If you set the background information as a homework research task, ask students to tell the rest of the class what they found out.

> **BACKGROUND INFORMATION**
> **Fleetwood Mac** are a British–American rock band formed in 1967 in London. They originally had success during the late 1960s British blues boom, when they were led by guitarist Peter Green, and had their UK number one hit *Albatross*. They had even more success between 1975 and 1987 with the release of the massive-selling albums *Rumours*, *Tusk* and *Tango in the Night*.

a ▶ **CD2 T15** Read through the options with students. Play the recording for students to listen and choose the best option. Check answers, playing and pausing the song again as necessary.

> **Answer**
> 3 The song says 'Think about tomorrow'.

b Students read through the underlined phrases. Check any problems. In pairs, students match the phrases to meanings a–f. Check answers.

> **Answers**
> b 2 c 6 d 1 e 5 f 3

c ▶ **CD2 T10** Play the recording again. In open class, students discuss the question. Encourage them to refer to lyrics in the song to support their arguments.

Vocabulary notebook

Remind students to note down any new vocabulary from the song.

Photostory: Kate looks great

8 Read and listen

Warm-up

Display some photos from magazines on the board. Ask students questions about the photos, e.g. *Do you like his hair? Do you like her shoes?* Then ask students to think of similar questions to ask the rest of the class.

a ▶ **CD2 T16** Read the instructions and question with students and ask students to guess the answer. Play the recording for students to listen and read to find the answers. Play the recording again, pausing as necessary for students to check their predictions.

> **Answers**
> Izzie wants to change her hair.

TAPESCRIPT

See the text on page 64 of the Student's Book.

b Read through questions 1–5 with students and check understanding. Students decide on the correct answers. Check answers in open class.

> **Answers**
> 2 b 3 a 4 a 5 b

9 Everyday English

a Read the expressions aloud with the class. In pairs, students find them in the photostory and decide who said them. Check answers. Students can then translate them into their own language.

Answers
1 Ray 2 Kate 3 Ray 4 Jo

b Discuss the expressions in Exercise 9a as a class and ask students how they would say these things in their own language. Are there any similarities with English?

c ▶ CD2 T17 Read through the sentences with students and clarify any problems with understanding. In pairs, students decide on the correct order for the dialogue. Check answers and ask students to practise the correct dialogue.

TAPESCRIPT/ANSWERS

Polly: Hi Kevin. How are you?

Kevin: I'm fine thanks, Polly. But what about you? I think you're sad. What's wrong?

Polly: Nothing really. Well, the thing is, my cat's ill. She's old too, and I'm a bit worried.

Kevin: Oh, that's sad. But don't worry. I'm sure she'll be OK.

Polly: Yes, perhaps. Anyway, let's go – I don't want to be late for school.

Kevin: Oh, you're right – it is late. Let's go!

d Students read the dialogues. Check any problems. Go through the first dialogue as an example, if necessary. Students complete the exercise. Check answers.

Answers
1 I think 2 What's wrong? 3 anyway
4 the thing is

✳ OPTIONAL ACTIVITY

Divide the class into pairs and ask them to practise the dialogues. You may like to read through the dialogues yourself first to give an example of correct pronunciation and intonation. When students have practised the dialogue, they take it in turns to close their book and try to remember their part. Their partner can give them prompts to help them remember. Encourage students to say the whole dialogue without looking at their books.

Vocabulary notebook

Encourage students to add these expressions to the *Everyday English* section in their vocabulary notebooks.

10 Improvisation

Divide the class into pairs. Tell students they are going to create a role play between Izzie and Jo. Read through the instructions with students. Give students two minutes to plan their dialogue. Circulate and help with vocabulary as necessary. Encourage students to use expressions from Exercise 9. Students practise their conversation in pairs. Listen to some of the best conversations in open class.

11 Free Time ⊙ DVD Episode 4

a Look at the photo with students and ask them to describe what is happening and answer the questions. Divide the class into pairs and ask students to create a short dialogue for the people in the photo. Circulate and help with vocabulary as necessary. Listen to some of the dialogues in open class.

Answers
Mark and his little brother. Students' own answers.

b Divide the class into pairs. Read the instructions with students and check understanding of difficult vocabulary, e.g. *babysitting*. Ask them to work with their partner and write a story. You may prefer students to do this individually. Circulate to check students are on track and to help with vocabulary. Students write their stories and read them out to the class as feedback. Hold a class vote to decide on the best story.

c Play Episode 4 of the DVD for students to find out what happens.

12 Write

If you set the background information as a homework research task, ask students to tell the rest of the class what they found out.

> **BACKGROUND INFORMATION**
> **San Francisco** is a large US city situated on the west coast of California between the Pacific Ocean and San Francisco Bay. These are connected by a strait called The Golden Gate. It is the USA's largest port on the west coast and a lot of trade is done with Asia, Alaska and Hawaii. The city was founded in 1776 by the Spanish and they named it Yerba Buena but it was taken by the Americans in 1846. In 1848 the California Gold Rush meant that many people came to California in search of their fortune. The city has suffered several major earthquakes.

a Students read the email and answer the questions.

> **Answer**
> There's a new boy called Brad in her class and a new English teacher. She asks about school, friends, teachers and whether her friend is happy.

b This task can be set for homework. Students read through the points they must include in their email reply.

Stronger classes: They can draft their emails and then write a final version for homework.

Weaker classes: Go through each point as a class and elicit examples. Students then draft their email and swap with a partner to check. They can then produce a final version.

13 Last but not least: more speaking

Tell students they are going to play a game called *Simon says*. The simplest way to explain the game is to play it, so give students an example and ask them to follow your instructions. Explain students get a black point if they make a mistake and that using sentences with *Don't* makes the game more difficult.

Divide the class into groups of four. Students play the game. Circulate to ensure they are using language correctly.

Check your progress

1 Grammar

a 2 goes 3 plays 4 eat 5 asks 6 read

b 2 We usually eat chicken on Mondays.
3 I always go shopping at the weekend.
4 I am usually tired in the mornings.
5 The teacher often smiles at us.
6 I hardly ever eat fruit.

c 2 Come 3 Don't watch 4 Write 5 Don't eat

2 Vocabulary

a 2 Sunday 3 Monday 4 Wednesday 5 Tuesday
6 Saturday 7 Friday

b 2 7.00 3 11.30 4 6.20 5 11.45

c 2 angry 3 excited 4 bored 5 unhappy

How did you do?

Check that students are marking their scores. Collect these in, check them as necessary and discuss any further work needed with specific students.

Memo from Mario

Don't do that!

① Kinaesthetic practice of positive and negative imperatives

▶ Ask the students to stand up. Explain that when *you* give them an order they must not move a muscle; if they move, they are out of the game.

▶ Explain that when *Simon* gives an order they are to obey.

▶ Explain that when *O'Grady* gives an order they are to do the opposite of what he says.

▶ Here are some possible commands:

Simon says sit down!

Stand up!

Simon says touch your nose!

O'Grady says don't touch your hair!

O'Grady says don't touch your knee!

Sit down!

Simon says sit down!

O'Grady says don't touch your head!

O'Grady says don't sing!

▶ Once the students have got the hang of the game, get students to come up and give the orders.

> **RATIONALE**
>
> Some people associate this kind of movement activity with primary school. However, I have used variations of 'Simon says' with all age groups.
>
> The fun of this particular version is disobeying O'Grady. There is something mildly surreal and 'naughty' about it.

② A different way to introduce Julie's email (page 63)

▶ Preparation: make one photocopy of the snippets from Julie's email below and enlarge them as much as possible. Cut them up. Have a small prize ready.

▶ Before doing the activity, stick the snippets round the classroom on chairs, on walls, on the floor and on objects. Make sure the snippets are positioned out of order.

▶ Pair the students and ask them to go round the room with pen and paper and copy the snippets in the right order. Offer a small prize for the first pair able to read out Julie's email in the correct order (Do not help them with their game strategy!).

▶ When the first pair reports that they have finished, ask them to read the email as they have pieced it together. Give the prize to the first pair who have the text as it is on the page.

▶ All the students now read the email on page 63 of the Student's Book and compare it to their version.

I'm confused and I'm angry

very angry about yesterday

It isn't the first time, is it?

Sometimes you do

really stupid things

and then I get scared or angry

Your text message today

says that you still love me

Well, sorry but it's too late

I don't love you anymore

Don't visit me again

Don't write and don't phone

I've got a new boyfriend

so leave me alone

It's all over for us

> **RATIONALE**
>
> One good way of getting the students into a reading text is to give them a kind of editing exercise like this one. It brings them into active engagement with the text.
>
> A physically boisterous class will not do this activity in silence, so it may be good to let your colleagues in nearby classrooms know that there will be some noise coming from your room. What a relief for the students to be allowed to learn language actively without being nailed to their seats!

Yes, I can

Unit overview

TOPIC: Sport

TEXTS

Reading and listening: a text about a disabled athlete
Listening: information about abilities of people and animals
Listening: a conversation about sport
Reading: a text about sport in British schools
Writing: an email about sport

SPEAKING AND FUNCTIONS

Asking and answering questions about ability
Talking about what you like and don't like doing

LANGUAGE

Grammar: *can/can't* (ability); *like / don't like + -ing*
Vocabulary: sports
Pronunciation: *can/can't*

1 Read and listen

If you set the background information as a homework research task, ask students to tell the rest of the class what they found out.

BACKGROUND INFORMATION

Cerebral palsy is a term used to describe a group of chronic conditions affecting body movements and muscle coordination. It is caused by damage to one or more specific areas of the brain.

Boston (population c.609,023) is the capital of the state of Massachusetts, and one of the oldest cities in the United States. Its rich history attracts 16.3 million visitors annually.

A triathlon is a multi-sport endurance event consisting of swimming, cycling, and running. The most popular Ultra Distance triathlon is called the Ironman.

Warm-up

Books closed. Ask students if they know anyone who has won any sporting competitions and discuss this in open class. If not, ask them what kind of sport they like watching live or on television.

a Give students a few minutes to look at the pictures and read the questions. Pre-teach any necessary vocabulary, e.g. *wheelchair, cerebral palsy, triathlon, take part, lie.*

Stronger classes: They can read the article silently and check their answers.

Weaker classes: Read the article aloud as a class and then ask students to check their answers.

Answers

The man in the wheelchair is Rick Hoyt.
The other man is his father. They are doing a triathlon.

b ▶ **CD2 T18** Students read through questions 1 to 6. Check any problems. Go through the first item as an example, if necessary.

Stronger classes: They can answer the questions and then listen and check.

Weaker classes: Play the recording while students read and listen. Students complete the exercise.

Check answers, playing and pausing the recording as necessary.

TAPESCRIPT

See reading text on page 68 of the Student's Book.

Answers

1 He uses a computer.
2 They swim four kilometres, cycle 180 kilometres and run 42 kilometres.
3 His father pushes him in his wheelchair in the running, he swims and pulls Rick in a boat in the swimming, and Rick sits in a seat on the front of his father's bike in the cycling.
4 Team Hoyt.
5 They take about 15 or 16 hours.
6 Students' own answers; discuss in L1 if necessary.

✳ OPTIONAL ACTIVITY

Give students this True/False exercise on the reading text. Encourage students to correct the false information.

1 Rick is Australian. (False. He's American.)
2 He loves sport. (True)
3 A triathlon winner usually finishes in about nine hours. (True)
4 Team Hoyt usually take ten hours to complete a triathlon. (False. They take 15 or 16 hours.)

2 Grammar

✱ can/can't (ability)

a **Stronger classes:** Students read through the examples from the article and translate them into their own language. Are there similarities or differences? Ask students to identify the positive (*can*) and negative (*can't*) form of the verb in each sentence. Ask students to give an example of something they can/can't do.

Weaker classes: Books closed. Write the following example sentences (or two of your own) on the board: *I can speak English. They can't speak Russian.*

Ask students to think about how they would say these sentences in their own language. Then ask them to identify the positive (*can*) and negative (*can't*) form of the verb in each sentence. Students open their books at page 69 and look at the examples from the reading text. Encourage students to give an example of their own using *can/can't*.

b Students go through the reading text and underline examples of *can/can't*. They can compare answers in pairs before a whole-class check.

> **Answers**
> Rick can't run, cycle or swim …
> Rick can take part …

c Students read through the table. Check any problems. Students complete the exercise. Check answers.

> **Answers**
> Negative: can't
> Question: Can
> Short answer negative: can't

Language notes

1 Students may produce sentences like *I don't know speak English* because of the way their own language works. Remind them of the function of *can* in English, if necessary.

2 Remind students that we never use the auxiliary verbs *do/does* with *can*.

3 *Can* is the same for all persons, singular and plural.

4 *Can/can't* are followed by the infinitive without *to*, e.g. *I can sing.* NOT ~~*I can to sing.*~~

---

d Students read through prompts 1 to 8. Check any problems. Go through the example as a class, drawing students' attention to the use of *but* to introduce the negative part of the sentence. Students complete the exercise. Check answers.

> **Answers**
> 2 Claire can ride a bike but she can't swim.
> 3 They can learn to count but they can't learn to speak English.
> 4 I can use a computer but I can't draw pictures with it.
> 5 She can play the guitar but she can't play the violin.
> 6 My sister can play the piano but she can't sing.
> 7 Uncle Jim can fly a plane but he can't ride a bike!
> 8 My mum can sing but she can't play the guitar.

Grammar notebook

Students should start a section called *can/can't* and make a note of the forms and any translations to help them.

3 Listen

 CD2 T19 Students read through statements 1 to 5. Check any problems.

Stronger classes: They can predict whether the statements are true or false and then listen and check their answers.

Weaker classes: Play the recording for students to listen only. Students complete the exercise.

Check answers, playing and pausing the recording again as necessary.

TAPESCRIPT

Camels are amazing animals. They can live for up to six months in the desert without water.

Did you know, the human eye can see over one million different colours?

Kangaroos don't run. They hop. They have very strong back legs. A kangaroo can hop ten metres in one go.

In the USA, a man called Mark Hogg can eat 94 worms in 30 seconds.

This is true. There is a man in Cuba who can dive without oxygen and can go to a depth of 162 metres.

> **Answers**
> 1 F (They can live without water for six months.)
> 2 T
> 3 F (They can hop ten metres.)
> 4 T
> 5 T

✱ OPTIONAL ACTIVITY

This can be set for homework. Students can make up their own quiz based on animals, nature, etc. and can write quiz questions using *can/can't*.

Pronunciation

See notes on page 108.

 Speak

Before students begin Exercise 5, ask them to read through the information in the Look! box. They can translate *but not very well* if it helps.

Divide the class into pairs. Students read through the words in the box and the example dialogue. Ask a stronger pair to demonstrate the example dialogue, drawing students' attention to the expression *but not very well* which they have just seen in the Look! box. Students complete the exercise. Monitor and check students are taking turns to ask and answer, and that they are adding two more questions of their own. Ask pairs to feedback to the class with information about their partner.

Ask students who can do the things in Exercise 5 to give a short demonstration to the rest of the class.

 Vocabulary

✻ Sports

Warm-up

Books closed. Ask students if they know the English words for any sports. Elicit the words they know and write them on the board. Ask students to compare those words with the words in their own language. Are there any similarities?

Students open their books at page 72, read through the words in the box, and look at the pictures. Look at the example as a class.

Stronger classes: They can match the words in the box with the pictures.

Weaker classes: See if any of the elicited words on the board match the pictures first. Then students can work their way through the words in the box, matching them to the pictures.

▶ **CD2 T22** Play the recording for students to listen and check answers.

TAPESCRIPT/ANSWERS

1 play volleyball
2 ski
3 play football
4 snowboard
5 play tennis
6 ride a horse
7 play basketball
8 do gymnastics
9 rollerblade

10 cycle
11 play rugby
12 skateboard

Vocabulary bank Refer students to the vocabulary bank. Read through the words and phrases in open class and check understanding.

Vocabulary notebook

Encourage students to start a section called *Sports* and to note down any new words from this section.

✻ OPTIONAL ACTIVITY

Whole class or small groups. Students choose a sport and mime it. The first student who guesses correctly takes the next turn.

 Listen

a ▶ **CD2 T23** Students read through the list of sports. Check any problems.

Stronger classes: Ask students to predict which sports they think Hannah and Sam will talk about. Students listen to check their ideas.

Weaker classes: Play the recording for students to listen only. Students complete the exercise.

Check answers, playing and pausing the recording again as necessary. Ask students who mentioned which sport.

TAPESCRIPT

Sam: Do you like sport, Hannah?

Hannah: Oh, yeah. In New York, I go rollerblading every week. I just love it. And I play tennis sometimes.

Sam: Oh, tennis. Really?

Hannah: Oh, don't you like tennis?

Sam: Well, I like watching it on TV sometimes, you know, Wimbledon and things, but I don't really like playing it myself. Swimming's my sport. And football, of course.

Hannah: Oh, yeah, football. Me, too. The New York Giants, they're my favourite football team. I love going to the games.

Sam: Oh, right. You mean American football.

Hannah: Oh, yeah, you're right, sorry. When you say football here in England, you mean soccer, don't you? Do you play soccer, Sam? I mean, football?

Sam: Yes, I do. There's a team at our school. We're really good. We usually win.

Hannah: Ah, maybe I can come ...

Answers
They talk about American football, swimming, tennis, football (soccer) and rollerblading.

b ▶ CD2 T23 Students read through statements 1 to 4. Check any problems. Go through the first item as an example, if necessary.

Stronger classes: They can answer the questions and then listen and check only.

Weaker classes: Play the recording again while students listen only. Students complete the exercise.

Check answers, playing and pausing the recording as necessary to clarify any problems.

> **Answers**
> 1 F (She goes rollerblading every week.)
> 2 F (He doesn't like playing tennis, but he enjoys watching it on TV.)
> 3 T
> 4 T

8 Grammar

✱ *like / don't like + -ing*

a **Stronger classes:** Students read through the examples. Elicit which verb form follows *like / don't like* and *love (-ing)* and ask students to give you an example of their own of something they *like / don't like / love* doing. Students then read through the table and complete the rule.

Weaker classes: Books closed. Write the following examples (or some of your own) on the board: *I like learning English. I don't like doing homework. I love going to the cinema.* Ask students to identify which verb form follows *like / don't like* and *love* and elicit or explain that these verbs are always followed by the *-ing* form. Students then open their books at page 71 and read the examples and the table. Ask students to give an example of their own for the verbs. Students then complete the rule.

Check answers.

> **Answer**
> like, love, hate

> **Language note**
>
> Some students may produce statements like *I am liking watching TV* or *TV is liking to me* because of the way their own language works. Remind them that these verbs are always followed by *-ing* in English and that the person is always the subject.

b Students read through prompts 1 to 5. Go through the example, if necessary. Students complete the exercise. Check answers.

> **Answers**
> 2 She doesn't like going to the cinema.
> 3 Do your parents like going on holiday?
> 4 His brother really likes watching soccer.
> 5 I hate swimming in the sea.

c This exercise could be set for homework. Students complete the questions with the correct verbs. Let students compare answers with a partner before checking in open class.

> **Answers**
> 2 watch 3 get up 4 getting up 5 go
> 6 going

Get it right! Refer students to the Get it right! section. These exercises can be used as homework or for fast-finishers.

Grammar notebook

Students should start a section called *like / don't like + -ing* and make a note of the rules, adding some example sentences of their own.

9 Speak

a Divide the class into pairs. Tell them to ask each other the questions in Exercise 8c and to make a note of their partner's answers.

Stronger classes: They can ask the same questions as in Exercise 8c and then ask some more of their own.

Weaker classes: Elicit some questions (or prompts) they want to ask their partner (putting them on the board if necessary) and give them a few minutes to ask and answer.

Monitor and check students are taking turns to ask and answer questions and that they are using the correct forms of the verb in the box and using some time expressions. Make a note of any repeated errors to go through as a class after the exercise.

b Ask a stronger pair to demonstrate the example sentence, drawing students' attention to the use of the *-ing* forms and the use of the time expressions. Ask pairs to feedback what they found out about their partner.

Culture in mind

10 Read and listen

If you set the background information as a homework research task, ask students to tell the rest of the class what they found out.

Warm-up

Ask students which sports they participate in and which sports they like watching live or on television. Does anyone play for a team? If so, in what sport and how often do they practise, play, etc.?

a Students look at the photos and read the list of sports. Give them a few minutes to match the sports to the photos. Check answers.

Answers
2 E 3 A 4 F 5 B 6 C

b ▶ **CD2 T24** Students read the instructions. Check any problems.

Stronger classes: They can read the text silently and complete the exercise.

Weaker classes: The text can be read aloud and then students can complete the exercise.

Check answers.

Answers
Craig: cricket, rugby, rowing
Julia: netball, orienteering

c Students read through sentences 1 to 6. Check any problems. Go through the first item as an example, if necessary. Students read the text again and complete the exercise. Students can compare answers in pairs before a whole-class check.

Answers
2 Craig 3 Craig 4 Julia 5 Craig 6 Julia

d Divide the class into pairs or small groups. Students read through the questions and the Fact box and then discuss the questions. Ask pairs/groups to feedback to the rest of the class. Are there any major differences between school sports in Britain and the students' own country? If so, discuss these in more detail as a class.

Weaker classes: This can be discussed as a whole class.

11 **Write**

If you set the background information as a homework research task, ask students to tell the rest of the class what they found out.

a Students read the question and find the answer in the email.

Answer
Manchester City

b This exercise can be set for homework. Students read through the prompts they must include in their email. Remind them of the conventions of writing emails:

- Openings: Can be informal, e.g. *Hello/Hi*
- Main body: Does not need to be divided up into paragraphs
- Closings: Can be signed off informally, e.g. *Write soon, Best wishes*, etc.

Stronger classes: They can draft, check and write a final version for homework.

Weaker classes: They can draft their emails in class and then swap with a partner to check. They can produce their final versions for homework.

Memo from Mario

Yes, I can

1 Extra practice of *can*

▶ Pre-teach any of the verbs in the dictation below that your students do not yet know.

▶ Also pre-teach the phrases *at birth, at 8 days, at three months, at two.*

▶ Tell them to write the sentences you dictate and then decide at what age a person can first do certain things, e.g.

You dictate: *A child can talk*

▶ The students write these words and put down the age at which they think this happens, e.g. *at 5 days, at 20 months, at three.*

▶ Dictate these *can do* sentences. You need to keep reminding the students to put down their guess at the correct age.

A baby can walk

A baby can cry

A baby can smile

A child can swim

A baby can walk

A baby can breathe

A child can run

A child can talk

A child can read

A child can play football

A child can ski

A child can skateboard

▶ Put the learners in groups of five to compare the ages by which they reckon people can do various things.

> **RATIONALE**
> The idea of this very simple exercise is to help students meet the *can* structure in a powerful and basic context. Many of the *cans* above are life-necessary and central to human existence.

2 Extra practice of *like/hate/not like + -ing*

▶ Write this 'action portrait' of a character up on the board:

He doesn't like playing tennis.

His dad likes him playing tennis.

He hates practising his serve.

He is very strong.

He hates losing.

He loves winning.

▶ Tell the students to work on their own and write three sentences about the type of person they imagine. Then put them in groups of five to read out their sentences to each other.

▶ Repeat the exercise with the following 'action portrait'.

She doesn't like school.

She loves skateboarding.

She is very brave.

She loves danger.

She hates staying at home.

> **RATIONALE**
> The exercise asks the students to imagine the two people rather than to think about the new grammar. Our hope is that this re-focusing will help the students assimilate the structural patterns.

Unit overview

TOPIC: present activities

TEXTS

Reading and listening: a text about someone sailing around the world; photostory: A kickabout
Listening: sounds; saying what people are doing
Writing: a holiday postcard

SPEAKING AND FUNCTIONS

Talking about what people are doing
Describing your house or flat

LANGUAGE

Grammar: present continuous
Vocabulary: house and furniture
Pronunciation: /h/ *have*

1 Read and listen

Warm-up

Ask students what kinds of holidays they like going on. Have any of them ever been on a sailing holiday? If so, where? Did they enjoy it? If not, would they like to go on one? This can be discussed in L1.

a Students look at the pictures and read the questions. Check any problems. Elicit suggestions. Pre-teach any necessary vocabulary before students read the text, e.g. *journey, dolphins, whales, tropical.*

Stronger classes: They read the text and check their answers.

Weaker classes: Ask students to read the text aloud to the class while students check their answers.

Did students predict correctly?

> **Answers**
> He is a bus driver. He is sailing around the world.

b ▶ **CD2 T25** Students read through sentences 1 to 4. Check any problems. Go through the example as a class.

Stronger classes: They can do this as a listening exercise only, without reading the text.

Weaker classes: Play the recording for students to read and listen. Students complete the exercise. Check answers, playing and pausing the recording again as necessary to clarify any problems.

Encourage students to correct the false statements.

TAPESCRIPT

See reading text on page 74 of the Student's Book.

> **Answers**
> 1 F (He normally just goes on a short journey.)
> 2 T
> 3 F (He's doing it alone.)
> 4 F (Sometimes the weather gets bad and he has problems.)

2 Listen

a ▶ **CD2 T26** Tell the students they are going to listen to a conversation between John and his wife Pauline. Ask students to predict what they will talk about, and write any interesting ideas on the board. Read through the dialogue with students and check understanding of difficult words: *upstairs, progress, outside.* Play the recording for students to listen and complete the dialogue. Let them check answers with a partner before feedback in open class.

TAPESCRIPT

Pauline: Hi, John. How are you?

John: Fine, yeah, I'm fine. How are you? What are you doing?

Pauline: Oh, I'm eating breakfast in the kitchen. Andy's upstairs in the bathroom – he's having a shower. So, are you OK?

John: Yes, I'm making good progress. And I'm getting very close to South Africa.

Pauline: Great!

John: Yes, and guess what? I can see dolphins outside! They're swimming next to the boat.

Pauline: Oh, how lovely.

John: It is! But I'm worried. The weather's changing. There's a strong wind now and it's starting to rain. A bad storm's coming, I think. Sorry, Pauline, I can't talk any more. I have to go outside.

Pauline: John? Can you hear me, John?

> **Answers**
> 2 d 3 f 4 e 5 b 6 a

b Students match the beginnings and endings of the sentences. Check answers.

Answers
2 e 3 d 4 a 5 b

 # Grammar
✻ Present continuous

a **Stronger classes:** Students read through the examples from the text. Then they read the dialogue again on page 74 and underline further examples. Ask them what they notice about how the present continuous tense is formed, and elicit that it is formed with the present tense of the verb *be* and the *-ing* form of the verb. At this point, elicit the negative, question and short answer forms. Students then complete the table. Check answers before students complete the rule. Then ask students to give you an example of their own using the present continuous, making sure they are clear that the tense is used to talk about something happening at the time of speaking.

Weaker classes: Books closed. Write the following examples (or some of your own) on the board: *I am speaking English. You are sitting in the classroom.* Ask students to work out how the present continuous is formed and elicit or explain that it is formed using the present tense of the verb *be* and then the *-ing* form of the following verb. Students now open their books at page 75 and look at the examples from the dialogue. They then underline further examples of this tense in the dialogue. Elicit the other forms of the tense, and then students complete the table and the rule.

Answers
Positive: 're; 's
Negative: -ing; aren't/-ing; isn't/-ing
Question: Am/-ing; Are/-ing; Is/-ing
Short answer: am/'m not; are; aren't; is; isn't
Rule: present continuous, *be*

> **Language notes**
> 1 Remind students that we do not repeat the main verb in short answers in the present continuous. Students may find it useful to know that in the question form we only invert the verb *be* and the subject.
> 2 Students may have problems with the use of this tense rather than the form. Make sure they are clear about the difference between this tense and the present simple.

LOOK! ⌕

Draw students' attention to the verbs in the box and explain that some verbs have a spelling change in the *-ing* form. Give them the following rules:

1 Verbs which end in an *e* in the base form: drop the *e* and add *-ing*.
2 Verbs of one or two syllables which end in a vowel plus a consonant: double the final consonant and add *-ing*.

✻ OPTIONAL ACTIVITY

Give students the following base forms and ask them to spell out the *-ing* form based on the spelling rules in the Look! box:

1 travel – travelling
2 write – writing
3 eat – eating
4 drop – dropping
5 see – seeing

b Students read the dialogues. Check any problems. Go through the first dialogue as an example, making sure students are clear about the use and form of the present continuous. Students complete the exercise. Remind them to use short forms.

Weaker classes: Put the base forms of the verbs in Exercise 2b on the board and elicit the present continuous forms. Students then use these to help them complete the exercise.

Check answers. Clarify any spelling problems.

Answers
2 's having 3 's playing 4 'm having
5 'm buying

c Students read through prompts 1 to 4. Go through the example as a class, drawing students' attention to the short answer and the explanation following the short answer. Students complete the exercise. Remind them to think carefully about the spelling of each verb. Check answers.

Answers
2 Are they eating ice creams? No, they aren't. They're drinking milkshakes.
3 Is she reading a book? No, she isn't. She's listening to a CD.
4 Is your father working today? No, he isn't. He's having a day off.

Grammar notebook

Encourage students to make a note of the rule with some examples and translations of their own.

Whole class or small groups. Students can choose an activity from Exercise 2 (or one of their own choice if they are a stronger class) and mime it to the rest of the class/group. The others must guess what they are doing, using the present continuous tense. The student who guesses correctly takes the next turn.

Listen

 CD2 T27 Play the recording, pausing after the first item. Go through the example as a class, explaining to students that they must write a present continuous sentence to describe what they think the person on the recording is doing. Play the rest of the recording while students listen. If necessary, play the recording again. Check answers.

Answers
2 He's having a shower.
3 They're playing football.
4 She's swimming.
5 He's drinking.
6 They're singing.

Speak and write

a Give students a few minutes to look at the pictures and, in their notebooks, write present continuous sentences about the people. Remind them about spelling rules for -ing forms, if necessary.

Do not check answers at this stage.

Divide the class into pairs. Students read their sentences to each other and see if they are both the same or if they have written different sentences. Ask pairs to feedback to the class. Does everyone agree on the sentences?

Answers
B Daisy's riding a bike and talking on the phone.
C Ben and Liz are eating and watching TV.
D Max is using a computer and drinking.
E Tom and Amy are eating and talking.
F Sam is playing football.

b Ask a stronger pair to demonstrate the example dialogue. Students cover the sentences they wrote in Exercise 5a and ask and answer questions about the pictures. Monitor and check students are taking turns to ask and answer, and that they are using the correct present continuous forms. Make a note of any repeated errors to go through as a class after the exercise.

c Students can work in the same pairs as Exercise 5b or with a different partner. Ask a stronger pair to demonstrate the example sentences, drawing students' attention to the use of the present continuous forms and the use of I think. Students ask and answer about their family. Monitor and check students are taking turns to speak, and that they are using the correct present continuous forms. Make a note of any repeated errors to go through as a class after the exercise. Ask a few pairs to feedback to the rest of the class.

Pronunciation

See notes on page 109.

Vocabulary

✳ House and furniture

Warm-up

Books closed. Pre-teach the words *room* and *furniture*, then ask students if they know the names of any rooms or furniture in English. Elicit the words they know and write them on the board (or ask students to come and write them).

▶ **CD2 T29** Students open their books at page 77 and look at the picture and the words in the boxes. If they have given any of the words already in the Warm-up they can fill those in. Go through the example as a class, if necessary. Students then match the other words. Play the recording while students listen and check answers.

TAPESCRIPT/ANSWERS

1 kitchen   2 bathroom   3 bedroom
4 living room   5 hall   6 garden   7 garage
a window   b door   c bed   d sofa   e chairs
f armchair   g table   h toilet   i shower
j bath   k fridge   l cooker

Vocabulary bank Refer students to the vocabulary bank. Read through the words and phrases in open class and check understanding.

Vocabulary notebook

Encourage students to start a section called *House and furniture*, to note down any new words from this section, and to illustrate or write translations to help them remember the new items.

Speak

Divide the class into pairs. Ask a stronger student to read out the example sentences, drawing students' attention to the use of the house and furniture vocabulary and the prepositions. Give students time to ask and answer about their houses/flats. Monitor and check students are taking turns to describe where they live and make a note of any repeated errors in vocabulary or pronunciation to go over as a class after the exercise. Ask students to feedback about their partner's house/flat.

Students look at the pictures and the words. Ask them to say where things are, using the three prepositions. For example:
T: Bea, where is your bag?
S1: It's under my desk.

Students work in pairs. Students draw a plan of their bedroom for a partner. The partner must use furniture vocabulary and prepositions to guess where the furniture is in the bedroom.

Photostory: A kickabout

9 Read and Listen

Warm-up

Ask students if they play football. If so, how often do they play, and where? If not, ask students which sports they do. Listen to some of their answers in open class.

a ▶ CD2 T30 Students read the title of the photostory and answer the question. Play the recording for students to check their answers. Explain that *a kickabout* is an informal game of football.

> **Answers**
> Darren wants to play football.

b Read through items 1–4 with students and do the first one as an example, if necessary. Students answer the questions. Check answers.

> **Possible answers**
> 1 She's studying.
> 2 He's making something.
> 3 He's working.
> 4 Because he's losing.

10 Everyday English

a Read the expressions aloud with the class. Ask students to try to remember who said them without looking back at the text. In pairs, students find them in the text of the photo story and discover who said them. Check answers. Students can then translate the expressions into their own language.

> **Answers**
> 1 Darren 2 Mark 3 Ray 4 Ray

b Ask students to look at the expressions in the dialogue and, in L1, discuss what they think they mean. Is a direct translation possible in their language? If not, discuss how they might express a similar meaning.

c ▶ CD2 T31 Read through the sentences with students and clarify any problems with understanding. In pairs, students decide on the correct order for the dialogue. Check answers and ask students to practise the correct dialogue.

TAPESCRIPT/ANSWERS

Millie: Dad? I'm going out now, OK?

Dad: What? But Millie, you've got lots of homework.

Millie: But I'm almost finished, Dad. I can finish tomorrow morning. I've got a bit of time before the English lesson.

Dad: Well, Millie – why don't you finish it now? Then you can go out and have fun, and not worry about it any more.

Millie: Oh, all right Dad. Maybe you're right.

Dad: Good girl.

d Ask students to read through the dialogues and check they understand them. Check any vocabulary problems. Go through the first item as an example. Students complete the exercise and compare answers in pairs before a whole class check.

> **Answers**
> 1 Why don't you 2 all right 3 a bit of
> 4 Lots of

Vocabulary notebook

Encourage students to add the expressions to the *Everyday English* section in their vocabulary notebooks and, if necessary, to add translations to help them remember the meanings.

11 Improvisation

Divide the class into groups of four. Tell students they are going to create a role play. Read through the instructions with students. Give students two minutes to plan their role play. Circulate and help with vocabulary as necessary. Encourage students to use expressions from Exercise 10, but do not let them write down the text. Students practise their role plays. Listen to some of the best role plays in open class.

12 Free Time

a Ask students to look at the photo and answer the questions.

> **Answers**
> It is Darren's birthday. Students' own answers.

b Read through the instructions with students and ask them to write answers to the questions. With weaker classes, you may like to ask students to work in pairs. Circulate and help with vocabulary as necessary. As feedback, listen to some of their ideas in open class.

b Play Episode 5 of the DVD for students to find out what happens.

13 Write

If you set the background information as a homework research task, ask students to tell the rest of the class what they found out.

> **BACKGROUND INFORMATION**
> **Portugal** (population c.10,707,000), officially the Portuguese Republic, is a country in southwestern Europe on the Iberian Peninsula. During the 15th and 16th centuries, Portugal was one of the world's major economic, political and military powers and had a global empire reaching areas of Africa, Asia, and South America. It is a member of the European Union and the United Nations.

You may want to bring in blank postcards for students to do this exercise.

Warm-up

Ask students if they send postcards to people when they go on holiday. If so, who do they send them to and what sort of news do they write on postcards?

a Students read through questions 1 to 5. Check any problems. Students then read the postcard and answer the questions. Go through the first item as an example, if necessary. Check answers.

> **Answers**
> 1 It's near the beach.
> 2 Because it's got a swimming pool.
> 3 They're doing some shopping in the town.
> 4 She's having breakfast.
> 5 It's fantastic, sunny and warm.

b This part of the exercise can be set for homework. Students read through the questions. Check any problems. Elicit or explain the conventions of postcard writing:

- Layout: Always write on the left-hand side and put the address on the right.
- Opening: This can be quite informal, e.g. *Hello, Hi* or *Dear* can be used.
- Main body of letter: Complete sentences do not have to be used and it does not have to be divided up into paragraphs.
- Closing: Informal signing off: *Love, See you soon, Hope you're OK*, etc.

Students choose a holiday destination and imagine what they will tell their friend.

Stronger students: They can draft and write their final versions.

Weaker classes: Go through a draft postcard on the board. Students then draft their own versions and check them with a partner. They can produce their final versions for homework.

> ✱ OPTIONAL ACTIVITY
>
> If you have provided blank postcards for students, they could illustrate the fronts or stick photos from magazines. All the postcards could be displayed round the class and the class can vote for the best one.

LOOK!

Students look at the pictures and the words in the Look box. Ask a question about today. For example:
T: Janek, what's the weather like today?
S: It's sunny.

14 Last but not least: more speaking

a In pairs, students imagine they are on holiday in a place of their choice, and take two minutes to answer the questions. Make sure they both make a note of the answers in preparation for the next exercise.

b Students sit back to back and act out a phone conversation about their holiday. Circulate and help with vocabulary as necessary. Students could repeat the activity with a different partner. Listen to a few of the dialogues in open class as feedback.

Check your progress

1 Grammar

a
2 Do you like watching soap operas on TV?
3 My brother likes swimming in the sea.
4 Her cat doesn't like drinking milk.

b
2 My Dad can stand on his head and he can walk on his hands.
3 Tessa can play football but she can't rollerblade.
4 Kylie and Annie can't sing but they can dance.

c
1 'm reading a book
2 's having a shower
3 're watching TV
4 's looking for a CD
5 's dancing

2 Vocabulary

a
2 volleyball 3 rugby 4 skateboard 5 basketball
6 cycling 7 gymnastics

b
2 fridge 3 living room 4 table 5 bathroom
6 shower 7 sofa 8 bedroom 9 cooker

How did you do?

Check that students are marking their scores.
Collect these in, check them as necessary and
discuss any further work needed with specific
students.

Memo from Mario

A bad storm's coming

① Revision of Exercise 2a (Listen)

▶ Preparation: photocopy the text below.

▶ Give out the text. Ask the students to read it through and to cross out any of the questions they do not find interesting or relevant. Ask them to add any questions they would like to have answered.

▶ Pair the students. Tell them to ask their partner the questions they kept and any new ones they added. Tell them to work through all of one person's questions at a time.

Pauline: Hi, John. How are you?

Is she ringing him or is he ringing her?
Is it the same time in her house and on his boat?
How does she feel when she hears his voice?
Do you think it's summer or winter?

John: Fine, yeah, I'm fine. How are you? What are you doing?

Is John really feeling fine?
Does he actually want to know what Pauline is doing?
Is he feeling homesick?

Pauline: Oh, I'm eating breakfast in the kitchen. And Andy's upstairs in the bathroom - he's having a shower. So, are you OK?

Why is she telling him all these things about the house?
What is she really thinking about?

John: Yes, I'm making good progress. And I'm getting very close to South Africa.

Is John sailing to South Africa from Australia, from Europe or from South America?
Is he sailing west or east or south?
How big is his boat?

Pauline: Great!

What is Pauline really thinking?
Is she proud of him?
What is John thinking when she says 'Great'?

John: Yes, and guess what? I can see dolphins outside! They're swimming next to the boat.

Is John really interested in the dolphins?
Is the sea calm?
What is happening outside?

Pauline: Oh, how lovely!

Are the dolphins important to her?
Is Pauline happy for John?
Does she love him?

John: It is! But I'm worried. The weather's changing. There's a strong wind now and its starting to rain. A bad storm's coming, I think. Sorry Pauline, I can't talk any more. I have to go outside.

How is John feeling?
How is Pauline feeling?
Does John like danger?
Do you like danger?

Pauline: John? Can you hear me, John?

Why is he sailing round the world?
Is John a hero?
Is John running away from his home?

▶ Round off with a whole-class discussion on exciting, hazardous ventures like sailing round the world.

> **RATIONALE**
>
> Inviting students to cross out questions that do not appeal to them is a way of promoting critical thinking and gives students a sense of power.
>
> This telephone conversation is very humanly rich and the work suggested above aims to make sure the learners notice the richness.

② A fun way of drilling present continuous forms

▶ Get the students up and standing in a large circle. Join the circle yourself.

▶ Mime a simple action, e.g. touching your nose. Then ask the student to your right to mime a new action, e.g. touching her ear, but saying *I'm touching my nose.*

▶ The whole circle then choruses *Oh no you're not, you're touching your ear!*

▶ The activity carries on round the circle. The fun starts when the chorusing students misunderstand the mime they have just seen and get corrected by the miming student!

11 Special days

Unit overview

TOPIC: Clothes and special days

TEXTS
Reading and listening: special days in Scotland
Listening: descriptions of clothes
Reading: an article about the Edinburgh Festival
Writing: an email about a festival in your country

SPEAKING AND FUNCTIONS
Asking and answering about clothes and shopping

LANGUAGE
Grammar: prepositions: *at, in, on*; *can/can't*
(asking for permission); *one/ones*
Vocabulary: months of the year and seasons;
clothes
Pronunciation: /æ/ and /e/

1 Read and listen

If you set the background information as a homework research task, ask students to tell the rest of the class what they found out.

BACKGROUND INFORMATION

Scotland see Background Information Unit 6, Exercise 1.

Robert Burns (25 January 1759 – 21 July 1796), also known as Rabbie Burns, Scotland's favourite son and The Bard, was a Scottish poet and lyricist. He is widely regarded as the national poet of Scotland, and is celebrated worldwide. His poem (and song) *Auld Lang Syne* is often sung at Hogmanay and *Scots Wha Hae* served for a long time as an unofficial national anthem of the country.

Haggis is a dish containing sheep's heart, liver and lungs, minced with onion, oatmeal, suet, spices, salt and stock, and traditionally boiled in the animal's stomach for approximately three hours. Most modern haggis is prepared in a casing rather than an actual stomach. There are also meat-free recipes for vegetarians. Haggis is traditionally served with 'neeps and tatties' (swede, yellow turnip and potatoes, boiled and mashed separately) and a 'dram' (i.e. a glass of Scotch whisky), especially as the main course of a Burns supper.

A **kilt** is a knee-length garment with pleats at the rear, originating in the traditional dress of men and boys in the Scottish Highlands of the sixteenth century. It is usually made of woollen cloth in a tartan pattern. It is worn mainly on formal occasions or at Highland Games and sports events.

Tartan is a pattern, particularly associated with Scotland, consisting of criss-crossed horizontal and vertical bands in multiple colours. Tartans originated in woven cloth, but now many other materials are used. Until the middle of the nineteenth century, the highland tartans were associated with regions, as cloth weavers used natural dyes from their own area. In the mid-nineteenth century specific tartans became associated with specific Scottish clans or families.

Tossing the caber is a traditional Scottish event involving the tossing of a large wooden pole called a caber. The object is not the distance of the throw, but rather to have the caber fall directly away from the thrower after landing. A perfect throw ends with the 'top' end nearest to the thrower and the 'bottom' end pointing exactly away.

Warm-up

Ask students if they have any special festivals in their town/country. Ask students when the festivals are celebrated and ask them to describe what happens during the festivals. This can be done in L1 if necessary.

a Ask students to look at the pictures on page 82 and describe what they can see.

b Students read the text and match the photos to the names of the three festivals listed in the article.

Weaker classes: You may want to pre-teach some vocabulary, e.g. *poet, haggis, coal, warmth, kilts, tartan, trunk.*

> **Answers**
> 1 Burns Night = Photo B
> 2 Hogmanay = Photo C
> 3 Highland Games = Photo A

c ▶ **CD2 T32** Students read through sentences 1 to 3. Check any problems. Play the recording for students to read and listen. Go through the first item as an example, if necessary. Students complete the exercise. Check answers, playing and pausing the recording again as necessary.

See reading text on page 82 of the Student's Book.

> **Answers**
> 1 Hogmanay
> 2 Burns Night
> 3 Highland Games

✱ OPTIONAL ACTIVITY

In pairs or small groups, students can choose which festival they would like to go to and the reasons why. They can then feedback to the rest of the class.

Or, you could ask students these True/False questions about the reading text. Encourage students to correct the false information:

1 Burns Night is in February. (False. It is in January.)
2 Burns was a famous singer. (False. He was a poet.)
3 Hogmanay is on the last day of the year. (True)
4 For Hogmanay, people stay at home. (False. They visit their friends.)
5 Men always wear trousers at the Highland Games. (False. They wear kilts.)
6 There is music and sport at the Highland Games. (True)

② Vocabulary

✱ Months of the year and seasons

Warm-up

Stronger classes: Books closed. Write the date in full on the board and draw students' attention to the month. Elicit any other months of the year they may know in English and put them on the board. You can ask a few students to come up and try to put the months in order at this stage if students have come up with a significant number.

Weaker classes: Put all the months on the board in English in jumbled order. Ask students to come up and write them in the correct order.

a ▶ **CD2 T33** Students open their books at page 83 and look at the months in Exercise 2a. Students read through the months quickly.

Stronger classes: Play the recording for students to listen and underline the main stress.

Weaker classes: It may be useful to write all the months on the board before you play the recording if you did not do this in the Warm-up. Play the recording, pausing after January. Elicit where the stress falls and mark it on the board, as in the example. Play the rest of the recording for students to listen and underline the stress.

Play the recording for students to check their answers, pausing as necessary to clarify any problems.

See page 83 of the Student's Book.

b Students go back through the text on page 82 and underline the months in it. Check answers.

> **Answers**
> Burns Night text: January
> Hogmanay: December, January

> **Language note**
> Make sure students are pronouncing February correctly /februri/. Students may also find it useful to compare how the months of the year are said in their own language and to compare them with English.

Vocabulary notebook

Encourage students to start a section called *Months of the year* and to note down the months from this section.

✱ OPTIONAL ACTIVITY

Stronger classes: In pairs, students can discuss what their favourite month is and why, e.g. the month their birthday falls in, the month they have holidays, etc.

Weaker classes: Call out a student's name and give them a month of the year in random order. The student then supplies you with the month which follows. Continue in this way until all 12 months have been practised. For example:
T: Laura, August.
S1: September. Marc.
S2: October. Katerina …

c ▶ **CD2 T34** Students read through the words in the box. Check students know how to pronounce each season: /ˈsʌmə/ /ˈɔːtəm/ /ˈwɪntə/ /sprɪŋ/. Go through the first item as a class, if necessary. Students complete the exercise. Play the recording once for students to listen and check. Play the recording a second time, pausing for students to repeat.

TAPESCRIPT/ANSWERS

A summer B autumn C winter D spring

d Divide the class into pairs. Give students a few minutes to discuss the questions and then feedback to the class.

> **Language note**
> Students may find it useful to compare how the seasons are said in their own language and how they are said in English.

Vocabulary notebook

Encourage students to make a note of the seasons in English.

Grammar and speaking

Prepositions

a Students read through the examples in the table. Ask students if they can see any patterns in when we use each preposition and elicit that *at* is usually used with times, *in* with months and seasons and *on* with days of the week. To check understanding at this point, ask a few students to give you some examples of their own using the prepositions from the table.

b Students read through sentences 1 to 4. Check any problems. Go through the first item as an example, if necessary. Students complete the exercise. Check answers.

> **Answers**
> 1 at 2 on 3 in 4 in

c Divide the class into pairs. Ask a stronger student to read out the example sentences, drawing students' attention to the preposition in each. Ask students to explain why each preposition is used to make sure they understand. Students exchange information about themselves. Monitor and check students are taking turns to give information and that they are using the correct prepositions and the correct pronunciation of the months of the year. Ask a few pairs to feedback to the rest of the class.

> **Get it right!** Refer students to the Get it right! section. These exercises can be used as homework or for fast-finishers.

Grammar notebook

Encourage students to copy the table from Exercise 3a into their notebook and to write translations if necessary.

* **OPTIONAL ACTIVITY**

Call out a time, season or month and a student's name. The student must supply you with the correct preposition to go with the word you have called out. Continue until you feel students are clear about the use of these prepositions.

Vocabulary

* Clothes

a ▶ **CD2 T35** Books closed. Elicit the names of any clothes students know already in English and write them on the board. Check students know how to pronounce each word. Students then open their books at page 84 and look at the picture. They match the names of the clothes in the box with the picture. Go through the first item as an example, if necessary. Then play the recording for students to listen and check. Play the recording a second time, pausing after each item for students to repeat.

1 E T shirt   2 F scarf   3 C shirt   4 A dress
5 G trousers   6 I jumper   7 H socks   8 J jacket
9 D top   10 B jeans   11 K shoes   12 L trainers

b Students go back through the text on page 82 and underline examples of clothes. They can compare answers in pairs before a whole-class check.

> **Answers**
> Hogmanay: coats
> Highland games text: kilts, socks, skirts, blouses, scarves

> **Language notes**
> 1 Remind students that we use the verb *wear* with clothes in English.
> 2 The word *trousers* is always plural in English.

Vocabulary bank Refer students to the vocabulary bank. Read through the words and phrases in open class and check understanding.

Vocabulary notebook

Encourage students to start a section called *Clothes* and to note down the words for clothes from this section and illustrate or translate the items to help remember them.

* **OPTIONAL ACTIVITY**

Students take a few minutes to look at what their partner is wearing. They then stand back to back and describe the clothes and the colours of each item to the rest of the class. The rest of the class must decide if the student has given an accurate description of their partner.

Listen

▶ **CD2 T36** Students look at the pictures.

Stronger classes: Play the recording for students to listen and number the pictures in the correct order.

Weaker classes: Elicit and write on the board what each model is wearing so students know what they are listening for. Play the recording, pausing after the first item and go through this as an example. Play the rest of the recording for students to listen and mark the order. Check answers. Play the recording again to clarify any problems, if necessary.

TAPESCRIPT

1 OK, and here comes our first model, Jonathan. He's looking good in his blue jeans, his grey trainers and his white T-shirt. And what a lovely leather jacket too! Let's give him a big hand.

2 And here comes Samantha. Isn't she elegant in her blue dress, black shoes and her wonderful

white scarf? Thank you very much, Samantha. And can I ask for a round of applause for Samantha, please.

3 And now, George. Well, how do you like these grey trousers, with the green shirt and the black jumper? Isn't that a great combination? A big hand for George, please. Thank you.

4 All right, and here we have Natalie. And Natalie's wearing a grey skirt with a pink top and beautiful black shoes. Let's give her a big hand too.

Answers
A 2 B 4 C 1 D 3

✱ OPTIONAL ACTIVITY

Ask a student to choose another person in the class and to describe what they are wearing without giving the name. The rest of the class must guess who is being described. The student who guesses correctly then describes someone else. Set a time limit for this.

6 Speak

a Divide the class into pairs. Ask a stronger pair to read out the example dialogue. Students exchange information in their pairs. Remind them to choose people from different pages and not to show their partner which page they are looking at. Monitor and check students are taking turns to ask and answer.

b Students can work with the same partner from Exercise 6a or swap pairs so they have a new partner. Give students a few minutes to read through the prompt questions. Check any problems. Ask a stronger pair to demonstrate asking and answering the first question. Give students a few minutes to ask and answer questions. Monitor and check students are taking turns to ask and answer and that they are answering appropriately.

✱ OPTIONAL ACTIVITY

Put pairs into groups and ask a stronger student to feedback to the class on what they found out about their partner. For example: *Tomas goes shopping for clothes about once a month. He usually goes shopping alone, but sometimes he goes with his family.*

7 Pronunciation

See notes on page 109.

8 Grammar

✱ *can/can't* (asking for permission)

a Students read the question and then the two dialogues and find the answer.

Weaker classes: You may want to read the dialogues aloud as a class.

Answers
1 He wants to buy trainers.
2 She wants to buy a shirt.

b Students read the example.

Stronger classes: Elicit when *Can I ...?* is used.

Weaker classes: They may find it helpful to refer back to Exercise 8a and locate the expression *Can I ...?* in each conversation. Then they can explain when it is used.

Answer
When we ask for permission to do or have something.

c Students now go back through the conversation in Exercise 8a and underline examples of the expression.

Answers
1 Can I try them on?
2 Can I have that green shirt please? Can I try on a medium?

d ▶ CD2 T39 Students look at the pictures. Play the recording, pausing after the first dialogue, and go through this as an example. Play the rest of the recording for students to listen and match. Students can compare answers in pairs before a whole-class check.

TAPESCRIPT
1
Boy: Can I use your MP4 player?
Girl: No, sorry James, you can't. I'm using it.
Boy: OK.
2
Girl: Is that magazine good?
Boy: Yes, it's great.
Girl: Can I read it?
Boy: Yes, of course you can! Here you are!
3
Man: Can I try this shirt on, please?
Woman: Yes, of course you can.
4
Girl: Dad, can I watch my programme now?
Man: No, sorry, you can't. I'm watching the football.

Answers
1C   2D   3A   4B

e ▶ CD2 T40 Students read through dialogues 1 and 2.

Stronger classes: They can predict the missing words and then listen and check only.

Weaker classes: Play the recording while students listen. Then give students time to fill in the gaps.

Check answers, playing and pausing the recording as necessary to clarify any problems.

Play the recording again, pausing after each dialogue for long enough for students to repeat.

TAPESCRIPT
See dialogues 1 and 2 for Exercise 8d.

> **Answers**
> Dialogue 1: Can; you can't
> Dialogue 2: Can; you can

Weaker classes: Ask pairs to act out the dialogues from Exercise 8e.

f Divide the class into pairs. Students look at the pictures. Ask a stronger pair to demonstrate an example dialogue for the first picture. Remind them to use expressions with *Can I ...?*. Students complete the dialogues for each picture. Monitor and check students are taking turns to ask and answer questions and that they are using appropriate expressions for each picture. Ask pairs to read out or act out their dialogues to the rest of the class.

> **Possible answers**
> Can I borrow your bike, please? Yes, of course you can. / No, sorry, you can't.
> Can I try on those shoes, please? Yes, of course you can.
> Can I have an ice cream, please? Yes, OK. / Sorry, you can't.
> Can I watch my programme now? Yes, all right. / No, not now.

✳ one/ones

9 Students read through the examples.

Stronger classes: Elicit or explain when *one/ones* is used (*one* is used to replace a singular countable noun that has already been mentioned; *ones* replaces a plural countable noun that has already been mentioned).

Weaker classes: Ask them to look at each sentence and to find a noun in the first part (trainers/shirt). Ask them what they can tell you about each noun and elicit that *trainers* is plural and countable and *shirt* is singular and countable. Follow the stronger classes procedure from this point.

h Students read through the two dialogues. Go through the example as a class, drawing students' attention to the noun which *ones* replaces (trousers). Students complete the exercise. Students can compare answers in pairs before a whole-class check.

> **Answers**
> 1 ones
> 2 one; one; one

Stronger classes: They can write and act out their own dialogues asking and giving permission and including *one/ones*.

Weaker classes: They can act out their completed dialogues from Exercise 8h.

Culture in mind

9 Read and listen

If you set the background information as a homework research task, ask students to tell the rest of the class what they found out.

> **BACKGROUND INFORMATION**
> **Edinburgh** (population c.471,650) is the capital city of Scotland. It is the second-largest city in Scotland and the seventh most populous in the United Kingdom. Edinburgh has a spectacular setting. The Old Town and New Town districts of Edinburgh were listed as a UNESCO World Heritage Site in 1995. There are over 4,500 listed buildings within the city. The city attracts 1 million overseas visitors a year, making it the second most visited tourist destination in the United Kingdom, after London. In 2009, Edinburgh was voted the 'most desirable city in which to live in the UK'.
>
> **Edinburgh Festival** is a collective term for several simultaneous arts and cultural festivals that take place during August each year in Edinburgh, Scotland. The festival began in 1947 and is now the largest cultural event in the world. The number of visitors who go to Edinburgh for the festival is roughly equal to the settled population of the city.
>
> **The Edinburgh Military Tattoo** is a military display performed by British Armed Forces, Commonwealth and international military bands and display teams.
>
> **Edinburgh Castle** is a fortress which dominates the skyline of Edinburgh, Scotland, from its position on the volcanic Castle Rock. There has been a royal castle here since the twelfth century, and the site was a royal residence until 1603. The castle is Scotland's second-most-visited tourist attraction and houses the Scottish National War Memorial, and National War Museum of Scotland.

Bagpipes are a musical instrument, where the player blows into a bag and then expels the air through some pipes. The Scottish bagpipes are the most common, but bagpipes are also found in Ireland and throughout Europe, Northern Africa, the Persian Gulf, and the Caucasus.

Warm-up

Books closed. Ask students if they have heard of the Edinburgh Festival. Ask them where Edinburgh is (Scotland) and if they know when the festival takes place (in summer). Students then open their books at page 86 and read the text quickly and find the answers.

a Pre-teach any difficult vocabulary, e.g. *laughing, bagpipes*. Students read through sentences 1 to 5. Check any problems. Give students a few minutes to look at the pictures and guess the answers to the questions before reading the text to check their ideas. Ask students to correct the false sentences. Check answers.

Answers
1 T
2 F (There is a festival every year.)
3 F (There is a film festival, theatre festival, book festival and more.)
4 F (Actors and artists come from around the world.)
5 T

b ▶ **CD2 T41** Students read through questions 1 to 5. Go through the first item as an example, if necessary. Give students time to read the text again and answer the questions. Check answers.

Answers
1 In 1947.
2 It is many events.
3 Army bands play music and there is Scottish country dancing.
4 Over 200,000.
5 Because hotels and guest houses are always full.

c Divide the class into pairs or small groups. Give students time to discuss the questions and then ask them to feedback to the class.

10 Write

If you set the background information as a homework research task, ask students to tell the rest of the class what they found out.

BACKGROUND INFORMATION

Halloween is traditionally celebrated on 31 October, the eve of All Saints' Day. The name was originally known in medieval England as All Hallows. Children nowadays dress up and go round houses in their neighbourhood asking for treats and if they don't receive a treat they may play a trick on the person.

Trick or Treat is what children say on Halloween. Treats can be sweets or money. If people do not provide a treat, then children play a trick on the person. It was originally an American custom but is becoming more popular in the UK.

Warm-up

Ask students to look at the pictures and suggest what this festival is called and when this festival happens.

a Pre-teach any difficult vocabulary, e.g. *witches, ghosts*. Students read the question. Give them a few minutes to read the email to check their predictions to the Warm-up and to find the answer.

Answers
Young people knock on people's doors and get treats, or they play tricks on people who don't give them treats.

b This exercise can be set for homework. Students read the prompt questions.

Stronger classes: They can draft their own answers to the questions and make their own notes. They can then write a final version, checking that they have answered all the questions.

Weaker classes: Go through each question as a class, eliciting and putting the suggestions on the board. Students can then use the information on the board to draft their email. They can then swap with a partner and check the drafts before producing their final version.

✳ OPTIONAL ACTIVITY

Students can bring in photos or illustrate their emails with pictures of the festivals they have written about.

Memo from Mario

Special days
Three activities with months

Activity 1

▶ Teach these forms: *on the first/second/third/fourth/ fifth/sixth/twenty-first/twenty-second/twenty-third/ thirty-first of ...*

▶ Go round the room asking *When is your birthday?* Students reply with the day and month, e.g. *on the sixth of May.*

▶ Tell the students to line up in birthday order. Ask the first student *When's your birthday?* They answer *on the ...th of ...* . The first student then turns to the second student and asks the same question, and so on down the line.

▶ Then tell the students to line up in the order of their mothers' birthdays. Ask the first student *When's your Mum's birthday?* Then repeat the activity above using this question.

Activity 2

▶ Ask the students to work on their own and think of one good or bad thing about each month of the year. Give them these stems to complete:

I love ...

I don't like ...

I like January 'cos ...

I quite like ...

I hate ...

▶ The students may be short of vocabulary in this writing exercise, so try to be everywhere to help!

▶ Put the students into groups of four to share the sentences they have written.

Activity 3

▶ Demonstrate the exercise with a volunteer student.

You: January plus one

Student: February
   June minus three

You: March
   April plus eleven

Student: March

▶ Pair the students and ask them to play 'month' tennis. Monitor pronunciation.

▶ Ask them to play the game again with a new partner.

12   He was only 22

Unit overview

TOPIC: Famous pop stars from the past

TEXTS

Reading and listening: an article about the death of three musicians; photostory: An accident in the park
Listening: a dialogue about the Beatles; dates
Writing: an email to a friend about a holiday

SPEAKING AND FUNCTIONS

Using time expressions to talk about the previous day
Talking about dates and birthdays

LANGUAGE

Grammar: past simple: *was/wasn't*; *were/weren't*
Vocabulary: time expressions; ordinal numbers and dates
Pronunciation: *was/wasn't* and *were/weren't*

① Read and listen

If you set the background information as a homework research task, ask students to tell the rest of the class what they found out.

> **BACKGROUND INFORMATION**
>
> **Buddy Holly** (born Charles Hardin Holley, 7 September 1936 – 3 February 3 1959) was an American singer-songwriter and a pioneer of rock and roll. Although his success lasted only a year and a half, his works and innovations inspired a number of great pop musicians, notably The Beatles, The Beach Boys, The Rolling Stones, and Bob Dylan.
>
> **Iowa** is a state in the Midwestern region of the USA. It gets its name from the Ioway people, one of the many American Indian tribes that occupied the state at the time of European exploration. Iowa has been listed as one of the safest states in which to live. Des Moines is Iowa's capital and largest city.
>
> **Ritchie Valens** (born Richard Steven Valenzuela, 13 May 1941 – 3 February 1959) was an American singer, songwriter and guitarist. His recording career lasted only eight months. His most famous hit is *La Bamba*, which became a hit in 1958.
>
> **The Big Bopper** (born J. P. Richardson, 24 October 1930 – 3 February 1959) was an American disc jockey, singer, and songwriter. He is best known for his recording of *Chantilly Lace*.

> *Peggy Sue* is a rock and roll song originally released as a single by Buddy Holly and the Crickets in 1957. The song went to No. 3 on the Billboard Hot 100 in 1957. It is ranked No. 194 on the *Rolling Stone* magazine's list of The 500 Greatest Songs of All Time.
>
> *That'll Be the Day* is a song written by Buddy Holly and Jerry Allison and originally recorded by Buddy Holly and The Crickets. The song went to No. 3 on the *Billboard* Hot 100 in 1957.
>
> **Don McLean** (born 2 October 1945, New York) is an American singer-songwriter. He is most famous for the 1971 album *American Pie*, containing the renowned songs *American Pie* and *Vincent*.
>
> *American Pie* is a folk rock song by singer-songwriter Don McLean which was a No. 1 USA hit for four weeks in 1972. The song is an abstract story surrounding 'The Day the Music Died': the 1959 plane crash that killed Buddy Holly, Ritchie Valens, The Big Bopper (Jiles Perry Richardson, Jr.), as well as the pilot, Roger Peterson.

Warm-up

Ask students if they know of any famous pop stars who have died young. Do they know how old they were when they died? Put suggestions on the board.

a Students read the questions and look at the pictures. Elicit suggestions. Students then read the article quickly and check their answers.

Weaker classes: You may want to pre-teach some vocabulary, e.g. *successful*, *wind*, *crashed*, *pilot*.

> **Answers**
> The text is about three men who died in 1959. The three men were pop stars (Buddy Holly, Richie Valens and the Big Bopper).

b ▶ **CD2 T42**   Students quickly read through statements 1 to 5. Check any problems. Go through the first item as an example, if necessary.

Stronger classes: They can complete the exercise and listen and check only.

Weaker classes: Play the recording once for students to listen and read. Students complete the exercise. Play the recording again, pausing after each answer for students to check answers. Encourage students to correct the false answers.

TAPESCRIPT

See reading text on page 88 of the Student's Book.

2 Grammar

✱ Past simple: *was/wasn't*; *were/weren't*

a **Stronger classes:** Students read through the examples from the reading text. Elicit which verbs are singular (*was/wasn't*) and plural (*were*). Also elicit how the negative is formed (*was + not*). Ask them to give you an example using the negative plural form. Ask a few students to volunteer examples of their own using the different forms. Students then read and complete the table.

Weaker classes: Books closed. Write the following examples (or some of your own) on the board: *You were in Class X last year. I was in Scotland last summer. Tom wasn't at school yesterday.* Ask them to identify which are the singular (*was*), plural (*were*), and negative forms (*wasn't*). Then ask them to work out how the negative plural form is made (*were + not*). Ask a few students to give you an example of their own using *was/wasn't* or *were/weren't*. Students open their books at page 89 and look at the examples from the reading text. Give them a few minutes to complete the table.

Answers
Positive: was
Negative: was not; weren't
Question: Were
Short answer: wasn't

b Students quickly look through the text again and underline all the other examples of the verb *be*.

Answers
They were Buddy...; The three men were...;
Holly was...; Bopper were...; It was...;
there was...; there was...; pilot, were...;
Valens was...; Bopper was...; It was...

c Students read through questions 1 to 6. Go through the example as a class, if necessary. Students complete the exercise. Check answers.

Answers
2 was 3 was 4 weren't 5 weren't 6 was

d This exercise can be set for homework. Students complete the sentences with *was* or *were*. Let them compare answers with a partner before open class feedback.

Answers
2 Were 3 Were 4 Was 5 Was 6 Were
7 Was

Grammar notebook

Remind students to start a section called *Past simple: was/were and were/weren't* and to note down the completed table and some examples of their own from this exercise.

3 Pronunciation

See notes on page 109.

4 Vocabulary and speaking

✱ Time expressions

a Students read through the words in the box and the table. Go through the examples in the table and then give students a few minutes to complete the exercise. Check answers. Ask students to give you some examples of their own for the time expressions. Remind them that they are all past time expressions and that they should use *was/wasn't*, *were/weren't* in their examples.

Answers
Last: month, weekend
Yesterday: evening, afternoon

b Ask students to look at the table and write where they were at different times in the *Me* column. You may like to give your own example to get them started. Circulate and help with vocabulary as necessary.

c Divide the class into pairs. Ask a stronger pair to demonstrate the example dialogue, drawing students' attention to the use of the time from the box and a time expression from Exercise 4a. Students ask and answer questions. Monitor and check students are taking turns to ask and answer, and that they are using the times and time expressions correctly.

Make a note of any repeated errors to go through as a class after the exercise. Ask a few pairs to tell the rest of the class what they found out about their partner.

d Read through the example sentences with the class. Students take it in turns to tell the class about their partner's day. Pay attention to pronunciation and correct use of time expressions.

5 Read and listen

If you set the background information as a homework research task, ask students to tell the rest of the class what they found out.

> **BACKGROUND INFORMATION**
>
> **The Beatles** were an English rock group of the 1960s who are said to influence music to this day. The group were from Liverpool and were John Lennon (1940–1980), Paul McCartney (1942–), George Harrison (1943–2002) and Ringo Starr (Richard Starkey) (1940–). Lennon and McCartney wrote most of the songs and music. The group had their first No. 1 hit single in 1963 with the song *Please Please Me*. By 1966 they had had eight more No. 1 singles and five No. 1 albums.
>
> *Miss You* is a song performed by the Rolling Stones and included on their 1978 album *Some Girls*. It was the Stones eighth US No. 1.
>
> **John Lennon** (born 9 October 1940 in Liverpool), was a rhythm guitarist, a keyboard player and a vocalist. He met the musician Paul McCartney in 1957 and they formed the Beatles in 1960. In 1962, Lennon married Cynthia Powell and they had a son, John Julian Lennon. They divorced in 1968. In 1969 he met and married the Japanese artist and musician, Yoko Ono. They had a son, Sean Lennon, in 1975. John Lennon was murdered in October 1980. The airport in Liverpool is named after him.

a Read through the questions in open class. Students read the text quickly to find the answers. Check answers.

> **Answers**
> 1 The Beatles   2 It was their last concert.

b Divide the class into pairs. Students try to answer the questions. Do not give answers at this stage.

c ▶ **CD2 T45** Play the recording for students to listen and check their answers to Exercise 5b. Play it a second time, pausing as necessary to clarify any problems.

TAPESCRIPT

Alan: What kind of music do you like Gran?

Gran: Well, my favourite group were the Beatles.

Alan: Oh, right. Were they from London?

Gran: No they weren't! They were from Liverpool. Oh, they were fantastic, just wonderful.

Alan: How many of them were there – in the Beatles, I mean?

Gran: There were four of them – John Lennon, Paul McCartney, George Harrison and Ringo Starr. They were very young – and I was very young too! John was my favourite, but they were all great. All the girls in my school were crazy about them!

Alan: Right! Are their songs still on the radio?

Gran: Yes, they are. That song *Yesterday*, for example – that's a really famous Beatles song, they play that on the radio a lot.

Alan: Oh yeah, I know that one. There was a really good song on the radio last week, it was called *Miss You* – I think that was the Beatles too.

Gran: No, Alan, I don't think so. *Miss You* was the Rolling Stones, not the Beatles.

Alan: OK, if you say so, Gran. Anyway, when did the Beatles break up – when did they stop?

Gran: 1970. John Lennon just said 'I want to stop', and they stopped.

Alan: John Lennon – hmm. He died, I think.

Gran: Yes, in 1980. December 1980. He wasn't very old – he was only 40. I remember the day he was shot – I was really sad.

Alan: Yeah, sorry Gran. But tell me some more about the Beatles.

Gran: Well, ...

> **Answers**
> 1 Liverpool
> 2 Four
> 3 John, Paul, George and Ringo

c ▶ **CD2 T45** Students read the questions. Elicit their responses, then play the recording again while students listen and check their answers.

> **Answers**
> 1 T
> 2 F (Some Beatles songs are on the radio a lot.)
> 3 F (*Miss You* was a Rolling Stones song.)
> 4 T
> 5 F (He was 40.)

Vocabulary

✳ Ordinal numbers and dates

a ▶ **CD2 T46** Students quickly read the list of numbers. Explain that this list of numbers is written the way dates are said (refer students to the Look! box if necessary). Play the recording, pausing after each number for students to repeat.

TAPESCRIPT

See page 91 of the Student's Book.

✳ **OPTIONAL ACTIVITY**

Ask a student to tell the rest of the class today's date and then ask some others to give a few other significant dates of festivals to make sure they have all understood.

b ▶ **CD2 T47** Play the recording, pausing after the first item and going through this as an example. Play the rest of the recording for students to listen and write down the numbers they hear. Students can compare answers in pairs before a whole-class check. Play the recording again if necessary to clarify any problems.

TAPESCRIPT/ANSWERS

1 third   2 seventh   3 tenth   4 eleventh
5 nineteenth   6 twentieth   7 twenty-third
8 thirtieth

c Divide the class into pairs, or if students checked answers in pairs for Exercise 6b, they can stay in those pairs. Ask a stronger pair to demonstrate the example question and answer. Students then continue asking and answering questions about the other months. Monitor and check students are taking turns to ask and answer, and that they are using ordinal numbers correctly. Make a note of any repeated errors to go through as a class after the exercise.

d ▶ **CD2 T48** Students read through items 1 to 4. Play the recording, pausing after the first item and go through this as an example. Play the recording for students to listen and complete the exercise. Check answers, playing and pausing the recording as necessary to clarify any problems.

TAPESCRIPT

1

Boy: When's your birthday, Jane?

Girl: The sixth of December.

Boy: The sixth of December?

Girl: Yes, that's right.

2

Girl: When's Emma's birthday?

Boy: Oh, um, let me think. Erm, oh, yes. The thirteenth of June.

Girl: The thirteenth of June? Really? That's the same day as my grandmother's.

3

Boy: Is there a concert in January?

Girl: Yeah. It's on the fourth.

Boy: Great. Erm, let me write it down. Fourth of January.

4

Girl: Bye, Peter. Have a good holiday in Paris.

Boy: Oh, thanks.

Girl: When are you coming back?

Boy: Oh, the twenty-third of April.

Answers
1 b   2 a   3 a   4 b

e Students read through dates 1 to 5. Go through the example as a class, making sure students are clear about the differences between the written and spoken forms. Students can complete this exercise in pairs or you can ask individual students to give you the dates.

Answers
2 The thirtieth of November, nineteen seventy-eight
3 The sixteenth of January, nineteen eighty-five
4 The seventeenth of October, nineteen seventy-four
5 The second of February, two thousand and three
6 The first of March, nineteen ninety nine

f Divide the class into pairs. Students read through questions 1 to 4. Ask a stronger pair to demonstrate the question and answer for item 1. Draw students' attention to the use of ordinal numbers and dates and months in the answer. Students complete the exercise. Ask a few pairs to feedback on the information they found out about their partner.

LOOK! 🔍

It may be useful to draw students' attention to the information in this box at this point. Students should be aware that dates in English are written differently from the way they are said.

Vocabulary notebook

Encourage students to start a section called *Ordinal numbers and dates* and to note down some examples of their own.

✳ **OPTIONAL ACTIVITY**

Call out some numbers and ask students to give you the relevant ordinal numbers.

Photostory:
An accident in the park

7 Read and Listen

Warm-up

Ask students, in L1 if necessary, if they have ever broken a bone or been injured, for example by falling off their bike, or in a football game. If not, ask if they know anyone who has broken a bone.

a ▶ CD2 T49 Students look at the title of the story and the pictures and answer the question. Play the recording for students to read and listen to check their answers. If students ask questions about vocabulary, write the words on the board, but do not explain the meaning at this stage.

> **Answers**
> She was knocked over in the park while she was skateboarding.

b Read through sentences 1–6 with students and check understanding of difficult vocabulary: *ground, helmet*. In pairs, students complete the exercise. Encourage them to find the mistakes in the sentences without looking back at the text. Check answers in open class.

> **Answers**
> 1 ~~running~~ skateboarding
> 2 ~~skateboard~~ bike
> 3 ~~leg~~ head
> 4 ~~head~~ arm
> 5 ~~the boy's~~ her
> 6 ~~Mark~~ Kate

8 Everyday English

a Ask students to find the expressions 1 to 4 in the text on page 92 and decide who says them. Ask students to translate the expressions into their own language. Check answers.

> **Answers**
> 1 Mark   2 Izzie   3 Izzie   4 Izzie

b Discuss the expressions in Exercise 8a as a class and ask students to try and work out how they would say these things in their own language. Are there any similarities with English?

c ▶ CD2 T50 Read through the sentences with students and clarify any problems with understanding. In pairs, students decide on the correct order for the dialogue. Check answers and ask students to practise the correct dialogue.

TAPESCRIPT/ANSWERS

Liz: Hey Dave. Are you OK?

Dave: No, I'm not. My little sister's in hospital. Her arm's broken.

Liz: Oh no! Poor her! What happened?

Dave: Well, I opened the door of our living room. She was on the floor, you know, playing with her toys. The door hit her arm. It was awful! And it was my fault!

Liz: Oh, Dave, come on. It's not really your fault, you know. Accidents happen – especially at home.

Dave: I know. But I feel terrible now. Poor Jenny – she's only seven!

d Ask students to read through the dialogues and check they understand them. Check any vocabulary problems. Go through the first item as an example. Students complete the exercise and compare answers in pairs before a whole class check.

> **Answers**
> 1 suddenly   2 my fault   3 Poor   4 you know

✳ OPTIONAL ACTIVITY

Weaker classes: Students can act out the dialogues. Make sure they are saying them with the correct intonation and expression and in the right context.

Stronger classes: Students can write their own short dialogues using the expressions. They can then act them out in front of the class. Make sure they are saying them with the correct intonation and expression and in the right context.

Vocabulary notebook

Encourage students to add the expressions to the *Everyday English* section in their vocabulary notebooks and to add translations to help them remember the meanings.

9 Improvisation

Divide the class into groups of four. Tell students they are going to create a role play. Read through the instructions with students. Give students two minutes to plan their role play. Circulate and help with vocabulary as necessary. Encourage students to use expressions from Exercise 8, but do not let them write down the text. Students practice their role plays. Listen to some of the best role plays in open class.

10 Free Time ⊙ DVD Episode 6

a Divide the class into pairs or small groups. Ask students to look at the photos and imagine possible accidents. Students mime their accidents for the rest of the group.

b Look at the photo and tell students it is taken from the DVD. Students imagine what accidents might happen.

c Play Episode 6 of the DVD for students to check their answers.

11 Write

If you set the background information as a homework research task, ask students to tell the rest of the class what they found out.

> **BACKGROUND INFORMATION**
> **Spain** (population c.46 million) is a country in Southern Europe, bordering Portugal and France. Since becoming a democracy in 1973, Spain has become the eighth-largest economy in the world. Spain is a popular holiday destination for Europeans and has a rich culture.

Warm-up
Ask students where they went on holiday last month/summer/year. Elicit some answers and then ask them if it was a good holiday.

a Students read the questions and then skim the email to find the answers. Check answers as a class.

> **Answers**
> Harry was in Spain. Yes, it was.

b This exercise can be set for homework. Students read through the prompt questions.

Stronger classes: They can work out the questions and answer them and draft their emails. Remind them to refer to the model email in Exercise 11a if necessary. They can then write their final versions.

Weaker classes: Go through each question as a class. Give students time to answer each question and then refer them back to the model email in Exercise 11a. Students can then decide which answers will go in which paragraph and draft their messages. They can then check their drafts with you or a partner before they write a final version.

12 Last but not least: more speaking

a This can be set as homework. Ask students to find out as much as possible about themselves as small children and to find answers to the questions.

b Divide the class into small groups and ask them to show each other their photos. Students ask and answer the questions. As feedback, ask individuals to tell the class any particularly interesting things they learnt about the students in their group.

Check your progress

1 Grammar

a 2 Can, try on 3 Can, open 4 Can, play
5 Can, borrow

b 2 on 3 at 4 in

c 1 were 2 was 3 was 4 Were 5 wasn't
6 were 7 were 8 were

2 Vocabulary

a Months: June, August, April
Seasons: summer, winter, autumn

b 2 trousers 3 dress 4 jumper 5 socks
6 trainers 7 jacket

c 2 e 3 b 4 a 5 c

How did you do?

Check that students are marking their scores. Collect these in, check them as necessary and discuss any further work needed with specific students.

Memo from Mario

He was only 22

1 Sequencing *The Day the Music Died*

▶ In the lesson after dealing with the text on page 88, tell the students to close their books and put these utterances up all over the board:

> The plane wasn't in the air for very long
>
> there was snow
>
> Buddy Holly was very successful
>
> were in a small plane
>
> were stars too
>
> wrote a song about that
>
> it was called American Pie
>
> were all dead
>
> when there was a problem
>
> were singers
>
> They were Buddy Holly, Richie Valens and
>
> It was a very cold night
>
> Buddy Holly was only 22
>
> On 3 February 1959

▶ Ask the students to sequence the snippets by coming to the board and numbering them.

▶ At this stage do not offer help with the task. There may well be disagreements that the students will work out for themselves. This is good opportunity to really observe your students.

▶ Tell the students to open their books and compare their sequencing to the original text on page 88.

> **RATIONALE**
> This is a classical and useful technique for getting students to review a narrative structure.

2 Choral practice of *was and wasn't*

▶ Practise these lines with the group:

> John Lennon – hmm. He died, I think.
> Yes, in 1980, December 1980.
> He wasn't very old.
> He was only 40.
> Really sad, I was.

▶ Keep repeating the lines until most people have memorized them.

▶ Make sure the *wasn't/was* sound contrast is adequately pronounced and that the phrasing and pausing in the first two lines is clear.

▶ Ask a student to write up the lines on the board, helped by the others, not by you.

▶ Explain that you are going to experiment with uses of the voice. Lead the group in reciting the piece in the following ways (three times each):
> in a very light whisper
> in a loud whisper
> in a quiet voice
> in a deep sad voice
> in a high sad voice
> very, very slowly
> jerkily

▶ Divide the students into two groups and ask them to recite in canon. Start Group 1 on the first line and Group 2 on the third line and get both groups to recite the text three times.

▶ Bring the students back into one group. Tell them to chorus the first word of each line aloud and to say the rest of the line silently.

▶ Then tell them to chorus the first, third and final line, and to read the second and fourth lines quietly.

> **RATIONALE**
> This kind of choral work may appeal to the more musically-intelligent students. You may even want someone in the group to take over the recitation master role.
>
> As the students focus on the voice tasks, the sound and language patterns will filter happily into their linguistic subconscious

Unit overview

TOPIC: Famous women from the past

TEXTS

Reading and listening: an article about Rosa Parks
Listening: a radio quiz about past events
Reading: an article about Queen Elizabeth 1
Writing: a paragraph about a famous person for a school magazine

SPEAKING AND FUNCTIONS

Completing a questionnaire about past activities

LANGUAGE

Grammar: past simple: regular and irregular verbs (statements, questions and negatives)
Vocabulary: verb and noun pairs
Pronunciation: -ed endings

1 Read and listen

If you set the background information as a homework research task, ask students to tell the rest of the class what they found out.

BACKGROUND INFORMATION

Rosa Parks (4 February 1913 – 24 October 2005) was an African-American civil rights activist whom the US Congress later called the 'Mother of the Modern-Day Civil Rights Movement'. Parks became an international icon of resistance to racial segregation. She organised and collaborated with civil rights leaders, including Martin Luther King, Jr.

Warm-up

Ask students to name as many forms of transport as possible. Write their ideas on the board. In L1 if necessary, ask them when they travel by bus. Do they ever have to sit in a special seat?

a Students read the question.

Stronger classes: They can skim the text and find the answers.

Weaker classes: Read the text aloud as a class and then students find the answers.

Check answers.

Answer
It is about Rosa Parks, who refused to give up her seat on a bus. This started the movement to stop segregation of blacks and whites in the USA.

b ▶ **CD2 T51** Students read questions 1 to 5. Check any problems. Go through the first item as a class, if necessary. Play the recording for students to complete the exercise. Students can compare answers in pairs before a whole-class check. Play the recording again if necessary, pausing to clarify any problems.

TAPESCRIPT
See reading text on page 96 of the Student's Book.

Answers
1 Because a white man wanted her seat.
2 Because she was tired.
3 It was divided into a black world and a white world.
4 Because she broke the law by not giving up her seat.
5 Because they were angry that Rosa had been arrested.

2 Grammar

✱ Past simple: regular verbs

a **Stronger classes:** Students read through the example sentences. Ask them what they notice about the past simple form in each sentence and elicit that *start* and *walk* add -ed, *study* changes the y to i and adds -ed. Students can then complete the rule. Ask a few students to give you some examples of their own for these or different verbs in the past simple.

Weaker classes: Books closed. Write the following examples (or some of your own) on the board: *My brother watched TV last night. I studied Russian at school.* Ask students to identify the past simple form in each and elicit the rules for each verb (see Stronger classes procedure above). Students then open their books at page 99, read the examples and complete the rule. Then ask students to give you some examples of their own.

Answer
-ed, i

b Students read the gapped text quickly. Check any problems. Go through the example with the class.

Stronger classes: They can complete the exercise on their own.

Weaker classes: Elicit the past simple form of the verbs in the box and put them on the board. Students then use those forms to complete the text.

Do not check answers at this stage.

Answers
1 died 2 liked 3 liked 4 wanted 5 started
6 listened 7 studied 8 asked

Grammar notebook

Encourage students to note down the rules for the past simple and some examples of their own for each ending.

✱ OPTIONAL ACTIVITY

Call out some regular base forms of your own and ask students to give you the regular past simple form and then spell it out.

3 Pronunciation

See notes on page 109.

4 Grammar

✱ Past simple: irregular verbs

a **Stronger classes:** Students read the examples. Explain that these are irregular past simple forms, and elicit a few regular past simple forms so that students can see the difference. Students then go back through the article on page 96 and underline other past simple irregular forms. Check answers.

Students read through the verbs in the table. Go through the example as a class. Students then use the Irregular verb list on page 127 to help them complete it. Alternatively, ask them to predict the past simple forms for each verb and use the Irregular verb list to check their predictions. They can compare answers in pairs before a whole-class check.

Weaker classes: Books closed. Elicit a few regular past simple forms and write them on the board. Then write the following base forms (or ones of your own choice) on the board: *have, know, go*. Ask students if they can guess what the past simple forms of these verbs are. Explain that they are irregular so will not follow the pattern for regular verbs. Elicit or give the past simple forms of the base forms. Students then open their books at page 97 and read the examples.

Follow the procedure for Stronger classes from this point.

Answers
broke
got
went
had
knew
said
saw
spoke
took
thought
wrote

✱ OPTIONAL ACTIVITY

Stronger classes: Students can make sentences of their own using the past simple forms of the verbs in Exercise 3a.

Weaker classes: You can call out a base form from Exercise 3a and ask students to supply the past simple form.

b Students read through sentences 1 to 5. Go through the example as a class, drawing students' attention to the past simple positive form. Students complete the exercise. Check answers.

Answers
2 saw 3 went 4 got 5 thought

c Students read through the gapped text. Check any problems.

Stronger classes: They can complete the text with the past simple form of the verbs in the box.

Weaker classes: Elicit or give the past simple form of the verbs in the box and write them on the board. Go through the example as a class. Students complete the exercise.

Check answers as a class.

Answers
1 wrote 2 became 3 had 4 knew 5 went
6 spoke

Grammar notebook

Encourage students to start a section called *Past simple: irregular verbs*. Remind them to make a note of the past simple from this exercise and to write down translations if necessary.

OPTIONAL ACTIVITY

Past simple bingo. Students write down six verbs of their own choice in the base form. You then call out irregular past simple forms. The student who crosses off all their base forms first and shouts *Bingo!* is the winner. Check the verbs they wrote down and the verbs you called out to make sure they have marked off the correct ones.

5 Listen

If you set the background information as a homework research task, ask students to tell the rest of the class what they found out.

BACKGROUND INFORMATION

Beijing (population 11.940,000) is the capital and the second-largest city of the People's Republic of China, with nearly 12 million residents. It is renowned for its opulent palaces, temples, and huge stone walls and gates. Its art treasures and universities have long made the city a centre of culture and art in China. The city hosted the 2008 Olympic Games.

Neil Armstrong (born 5 August 1930) is an American aviator and a former astronaut, test pilot, university professor, and United States Naval Aviator. He was the first person to set foot on the Moon and spent 2½ hours exploring the lunar surface.

Michael Jackson (29 August 1958 – 25 June 2009) was an American singer and dancer. He was known as the King of Pop and was one of the most influential entertainers of all time. His songs include *Billie Jean* and *Thriller*.

a Divide the class into pairs. Students read through questions 1 to 5 and answers a to e. Go through the first question and answer as an example, if necessary. Students work in their pairs to ask and answer the questions. Monitor and check students are taking turns to ask and answer and that they are using the dates correctly. Make a note of any repeated errors to go through as a class after the exercise. Do not give answers at this stage.

b **▶ CD2 T54** Play the recording for students to listen and check their answers to Exercise 5a.

TAPESCRIPT

Host: Hello, and welcome back, and in the next round of our quiz we are looking at important dates, OK?

Woman: Yes, OK.

Host: And here is the first question. Singer Michael Jackson died on the 25th of June. In which year?

Woman: Er, I think it was in 2009.

Host: And 2009 is … absolutely correct. Jackson died on June the 25th 2009. Well done, Sarah. That's 20 points for you. And here's our next question. When did the first man walk on the moon? Was it a. on July the 20th 1949? b. on July the 20th 1969? or c. on July the 20th 1979?

Woman: Oh, er, the man's name was Neil Armstrong. And I think it was 1979, so 'c'.

Host: Well, Sarah, you're right about Neil Armstrong – but he didn't walk on the moon in 1979, it was on July the 20th 1969. So no points for that, I'm afraid. Don't worry. Let's look at the next question. You can get 40 points this time. This question is about the Olympic Games in Beijing, China. They started on August the 8th and ended on August the 24th. In which year? a. 2004? b. 2006? c. 2008?

Woman: That's easy. It was in 2008.

Host: That's absolutely correct. 40 points for you. The Beijing Olympic Games started on August the 8th and they ended on August the 24th 2008.

And now Sarah – 100 points on the all or nothing question. In Alabama, USA, in a famous incident, Rosa Parks did not give her seat to a white man. What year was that?

Woman: Er, oh, I'm not sure! Um … was it … 1958?

Host: Oh, I'm sorry, Sarah. It was in 1955, not 1958. Sorry about that, but you get a wonderful prize …

Answers
2 a 3 e 4 b 5 d

OPTIONAL ACTIVITY

Stronger classes: Students can write their own past simple quiz questions and work with a partner who must answer them correctly.

Weaker classes: Elicit some key dates and events in the students' own countries or in the world and students then use these to write their own quiz questions to ask a partner.

6 Grammar

★ Past simple: questions and negatives

a Students read through the words in the box and questions 1 to 3. Go through the first question as an example, if necessary. Give students a few minutes to complete the gaps.

Answers
1 did, die 2 did, walk 3 didn't walk

b Students read the examples. Elicit the negative (*didn't die*) and question forms (*Did ... walk / did ... begin*) and ask students how each is formed (negative uses *did* + *not*, questions use *did* + base form). Students then read and complete the rule before completing the table. Check answers as a class.

> **Answers**
> Rule: didn't; did
>
> Table:
> Question: Did
> Short answer: didn't

> **Language note**
> Students may produce question forms like *Did she liked the film?* Remind them that in questions we use *did* + base form. Remind students that we do not repeat the main verb in short answers in English.

c This exercise can be set for homework. Students read through sentences 1 to 5. Go through the example as a class, if necessary. Students complete the exercise. Check answers, making sure students are using the negative form correctly.

> **Answers**
> 2 didn't use
> 3 didn't watch the film.
> 4 didn't see a lot of interesting things.
> 5 didn't get a new computer.

d This exercise can be set for homework. Students read through sentences 1 to 5. Go through the example as a class, if necessary. Students complete the exercise. Check answers, making sure students are using the question form correctly.

> **Answers**
> 2 did it happen
> 3 did they study
> 4 did you have a pizza
> 5 did you go

Grammar notebook

Remind students to make a note of these rules and to write some examples of their own for past simple questions and negatives.

✱ OPTIONAL ACTIVITY

Whole class or groups. One student thinks of something they did last weekend. Other students must use the past simple to guess what the person did. The person replying must use short answers. Set a time limit to keep the activity fun. For example:

S2: Did you watch TV?
S1: No, I didn't.
S3: Did you go out?
S1: Yes, I did.

7 Speak

a Students read the questionnaire. Check any problems. Go through the first item as an example, if necessary. Give students a few minutes to complete the *Me* column.

b Divide the class into pairs. Ask a stronger pair to demonstrate the example question and answer. Draw students' attention to the use of the past simple question and the short answer. Students ask and answer questions to complete the *My partner* column in the questionnaire. Monitor and check students are taking turns to ask and answer and that they are using the question and short answer forms correctly. Ask pairs to feedback to the class on what they found out about their partner.

c Students work with a new partner. Ask a stronger pair to demonstrate the example question and answer. Draw students' attention to the use of the *Wh-* questions with the past simple and the past simple positive form in the answers. Give students a few minutes to exchange information. Monitor and check students are taking turns to ask and answer and that they are using the question and short answer forms correctly. Ask pairs to feedback to the class on what they found out about their partner.

8 Vocabulary

✱ Verb and noun pairs

a **Stronger classes:** Students read through the nouns in the box and look at the table headings. Go through the example as a class. Students complete the exercise. Check answers.

Weaker classes: Write the verbs from the table on the board and elicit any nouns that go with them which students already know. If they don't know any already, then give them an example of your own for each heading. Students then open their books at page 99 and read through the nouns in the box. Ask for volunteers to come up and write each noun under the appropriate heading. The rest of the class can decide if each noun is placed under the correct heading.

> **Answers**
> have: a coffee, (an) ice cream
> practise: English
> play: sports
> go to: bed, school, the cinema

b Students read through the list of nouns and classify them under the correct heading in the table in Exercise 7a. Check answers as a class.

Vocabulary bank Refer students to the vocabulary bank. Read through the words and phrases in open class and check understanding.

Get it right! Refer students to the Get it right! section. These exercises can be used as homework or for fast-finishers.

Vocabulary notebook

Encourage students to start a section called *Verb and noun pairs*. They can copy the completed table from Exercise 7b, or they can start a section for each verb and add nouns to it as they come across them.

✱ OPTIONAL ACTIVITY

Ask students to add some more nouns to the verbs in Exercise 7. Listen to their answers in open class and write some of the best ideas on the board.

Culture in mind

9 Read and listen

If you set the background information as a homework research task, ask students to tell the rest of the class what they found out.

BACKGROUND INFORMATION
Queen Elizabeth I (7 September 1533 – 24 March 1603) was Queen of England and Ireland from 17 November 1558 until her death. She was the fifth and last monarch of the Tudor dynasty. One of her mottoes was 'video et taceo' ('I see, and say nothing'). After her death, she was celebrated as the ruler of a golden age, an image that continues to this day.

Henry VIII (28 June 1491 – 28 January 1547) was King of England from 21 April 1509 until his death. He is well-known for his role in the separation of the Church of England from the Roman Catholic Church. He is also noted for his six wives, two of whom were beheaded.

Sir Francis Drake (1540 – 27 January 1596), was an English sea captain, privateer, navigator, slaver, pirate, and politician of the Elizabethan era. Queen

Elizabeth I awarded Drake a knighthood in 1581. He was second-in-command of the English fleet against the Spanish Armada in 1588.

James VI (19 June 1566 – 27 March 1625) was King of Scots as James VI from 1567 to 1625, and King of England and Ireland as James I from 1603 to 1625. He became King of Scots as James VI on 24 July 1567, when he was just thirteen months old. From 1603, he ruled the Kingdom of England, Scotland, and Ireland for 22 years until his death at the age of 58.

Warm-up

Books closed. Ask students if they know anything about the history of England. Can they name any kings or queens? Listen to some of their ideas in open class.

a Open books. Students look at the pictures and read the questions. Elicit their responses.

Stronger classes: They can skim the text and check their answers.

Weaker classes: Read the text aloud as a class and then ask students to check their answers.

b ▶ **CD2 T55** Students read through statements 1 to 8. You may want to pre-teach the irregular verbs *died* and *became*. Go through the first item as an example, if necessary. Students read the text again and complete the exercise. Check answers. Encourage them to correct the false answers.

10 Write

If you set the background information as a homework research task, ask students to tell the rest of the class what they found out.

BACKGROUND INFORMATION
Christopher Reeve (25 September 1952 – 10 October 2004) was an American actor. His most famous role was as Superman, in four films between 1978 and 1987. After becoming almost completely paralysed after a fall from a horse in 1995, he became famous for his fight against his disability.

a Look at the pictures with students and ask them if they have seen the Superman films. Tell them they are going to read an article about the actor Christopher Reeve. Pre-teach *back* and *wheelchair*. Students read the article.

b This exercise can be done in pairs and can be set for homework. Students decide on a famous person from their own country or elsewhere that they would like to write about.

Stronger classes: They decide on the key facts they want to include in their article.

Weaker classes: Refer students back to the Elizabeth 1 text on page 102 and the Christopher Reeve text. Encourage them to look at the text structure and decide on the sort of information they want to include in each paragraph.

Students can draft their articles and then check them with another pair/student. They can then write a final version.

Encourage students to add pictures or illustrations to their texts.

✳ OPTIONAL ACTIVITY

Display the texts on the classroom wall and encourage students to vote for the best texts. If there is a school magazine, students could submit their texts for publication.

Memo from Mario

What happened?

Riddles to practise irregular past forms

▶ Preparation: photocopy the riddles below.

▶ Explain the idea of a riddle. Tell the students that each riddle is spoken by a famous historical character. Read the first riddle and ask students if they can guess who the person was (Socrates).

▶ Write these names on the board:
Newton, Napoleon, Shakespeare, Cervantes, Galileo.

▶ Put the students into groups of three and hand out the riddles. Ask the groups to work out who each person was.

A

I thought a lot.
I spoke to my students a lot.
I was Greek.
They killed me.

B

I wrote extremely well.
I didn't get rich.
I was English.

C

I saw the stars through a telescope.
I knew the earth goes round the sun.
I was Italian.

D

I fought all the countries in Europe.
I killed thousands.
I died on an island.

E

I knew a lot about mathematics.
An apple fell on my head.
I wrote about gravity.

F

I was in prison.
I wrote a book about a tall, thin man and a short, fat man.
I was Spanish.

▶ Answers: B Shakespeare C Galileo D Napoleon
E Newton F Cervantes

▶ Now ask the students to work on their own and write two riddles about two other historical figures using the past simple.

▶ Help with past tense forms and new vocabulary.

▶ Ask various students to read out their riddles for the class to guess.

> **RATIONALE**
>
> Riddles are a useful vehicle for showcasing whatever grammar you want the students to work on, in this case irregular past tenses.
>
> The students' focus is semantic which hopefully allows the targeted verbs to percolate down into the subconscious, until they are needed for future use.

14 Things change

Unit overview

TOPIC: Comparing life in the past with life now

TEXTS
Listening: a dialogue comparing life now and in the past; photostory: So sorry
Reading: a text about an hotel owner in Thailand
Writing: a competition entry

SPEAKING AND FUNCTIONS
Describing things
Comparing people, places and objects

LANGUAGE
Grammar: comparison of adjectives; *than*
Vocabulary: adjectives and opposites
Pronunciation: *than* /ðən/

1 Listen

Warm-up

Divide the class into pairs. Tell students to ask and answer questions to find three things about them that are the same and three things that are different. You may like to give them an example to get them started by comparing yourself with one of the students. Write the answers on the board e.g. *Same: black shoes, blue eyes, like football. Different: hair, trousers, age.* Listen to some of their findings in open class.

a Students work in pairs and discuss which things are the same and which things are different in the pictures. Discuss their ideas as a class.

b ▶ CD2 T56 Ask students if they know anything about life in the 1960s. Listen to some of their ideas. Tell students they are going to listen to a teenager and his grandmother talking about life in the 1960s and life now. Play the recording while students listen and complete the exercise. Let them compare their answers with a partner before checking answers in open class.

TAPESCRIPT

Grandmother: I think life was great when I was a teenager. Yes, we had a lot of fun. Is it better now? I'm not sure. But it's very different! I think perhaps life is more interesting now – you know, there are computers and DVDs, and things like that. When I was young, of course, a lot of TV was in black-and-white, and we only

got programmes in the afternoon and evening! But I think that life is more difficult for today's teenagers – for example, my grandson Dave. His school work – he gets a lot of homework to do, and he's always got tests and exams – it wasn't like that for me. I was freer than him, I think. School life is more difficult now, certainly. But you know, the really big difference? I think people were friendlier in the 60s than they are now.

Dave: I think perhaps that some things are easier now – for example, with mobile phones and the internet, I can talk to my friends any time I want to. But I also know that some things now are difficult for my grandma. I'm sure that now, life is faster than in the 1960s, and I think that's hard for her. I mean, now she's older, so of course things are more difficult – like, going shopping in town, it's hard for her, the streets are very crowded, they're more crowded than before – and there are a lot more cars these days, the roads are much busier than in the 1960s. And I'm sure that things in the shops are more expensive. So perhaps life is worse for her now – but she's a very happy person!

Answers
2 G 3 G 4 D 5 G 6 D

c ▶ CD2 T56 Read through the sentences with students and check understanding. Play the recording again for students to decide if the sentences are true or false. Encourage students to correct the false statements. Check answers.

Answers
1 F (She thinks life was better in the 1960s.)
2 F (She watched TV in the evenings.)
3 F (She thinks it's difficult.)
4 F (The streets are very crowded.)
5 T

2 Grammar

✱ Comparison of adjectives

a ▶ CD2 T56 **Stronger classes:** Students read through the sentences. Go through the first one as an example, if necessary. Students complete the exercise. Play the recording from Exercise 1b again for students to check answers.

Weaker classes: Play the recording again and then students complete the exercise. Play it a second time to check answers.

TAPESCRIPT

See tapescript for Exercise 1b.

b Students read through the table. Elicit what they notice about the comparative form of *older* and elicit that -*er* has been added to *old*. Explain to them that the adjectives used in the sentences in Exercise 2a were used to show comparisons. Students now go back through the sentences in Exercise 2a and underline the adjectives and the words which show comparison. Go through the first item as a class, if necessary. Students then use this information to help them fill in the table.

Check answers as a class.

Answers
younger happier more more better worse

Students use the information from the table to complete the rule. Check answers.

Weaker classes: Elicit the rules as a class, then students complete the rule.

Answers
i
more
worse

To check understanding at this point, give students a few adjectives of your own and ask them to give you the comparative forms.

c Students read through adjectives 1 to 8. Check any problems. Go through the first one as an example, if necessary. Students complete the exercise. Remind them to think carefully about whether the adjective is regular, has a spelling change or is irregular. They can compare answers in pairs before a whole-class check.

Answers
2 taller 3 cheaper 4 funnier
5 more important 6 faster 7 more expensive
8 hotter

d Students read through sentences 1 to 6. Go through the example as a class, drawing students' attention to the adjective and its comparative form. Students complete the exercise.

Weaker classes: Elicit the adjectives students will have to use for each sentence as a class and write them on the board. Students then complete the exercise. Check answers.

Answers
2 fast, faster
3 funny, funnier
4 near, nearer
5 expensive, more expensive
6 tall, taller

✲ *than*

e Students read the example sentences. Ask them which other words are used with the comparative adjectives to show comparison, and elicit *than*. Ask them to provide another example of their own using an adjective from Exercise 2c.

Language notes

1 Students may produce statements like *Delhi is hotter that ...* because of the way their own language works. Remind them that in English we use *than* with comparative adjectives when comparing two things.

2 Remind students that we do not say *I am more tall than you*.

f Students now look at the sentences in Exercise 2d again and rewrite them using *than*. Go through the example as a class. Students complete the exercise. Check answers.

Answers
2 Planes are faster than trains.
3 Annie's joke was funnier than Mike's joke.
4 Moreton's nearer than Haytown.
5 The Plaza Hotel's more expensive than the Grand Hotel.
6 Andy's taller than Matt.

Grammar notebook

Remind students to copy their completed table into their notebooks and to make a note of any translations that they will find helpful.

✲ OPTIONAL ACTIVITY

Stronger classes: Elicit a selection of people, places and objects from students and write them on the board. In pairs, students must now make up a comparative sentence about two of the people or places, etc.

Weaker classes: Call out an adjective and ask students to give you the comparative form.

Pronunciation

See notes on page 110.

Speak

Divide the class into pairs. Ask a stronger student to demonstrate the example sentences, drawing students' attention to the use of comparatives. Students then exchange information about things and people using comparatives. Monitor and check students are taking turns to exchange information, and that they are using the comparative forms correctly. Make a note of any repeated errors to go through as a class after the exercise. Ask pairs to feedback to the rest of the class.

Read

If you set the background information as a homework research task, ask students to tell the rest of the class what they found out.

> **BACKGROUND INFORMATION**
> **Thailand** (population c.63 million) is in Southeast Asia, with Laos and Cambodia to the east, the Gulf of Thailand and Malaysia to the south, and the Andaman Sea and Myanmar to the west. The word *Thai* means freedom in the Thai language and is also the name of the majority ethnic group.

Warm-up

Ask students what they like about the place they live. Ask them to use adjectives in their answers and write some of the adjectives on the board.

a Look at the photos with students and ask them to describe what they see. Students read the text and answer the questions. Tell them not to worry about understanding every word, but to focus on finding the answers to the questions. Check answers.

> **Answers**
> He's the owner of a small hotel. He's from London.

b Read through the questions with students and check understanding. Students read the text and answer the questions. Go through the first item as an example, if necessary. Check answers as a class.

> **Answers**
> 1 He worked in a bank.
> 2 Six bedrooms and a small restaurant.
> 3 It's hard work. He does everything seven days a week.
> 4 Three years ago.
> 5 His friends.
> 6 The only thing he can hear is the sea.

✳ OPTIONAL ACTIVITY

Ask students to compare the place they live with the capital city of their country. If they live in the capital city, ask them to compare it to a small town. Ask them which they think is better, and encourage open class discussion.

6 Vocabulary

✳ Adjectives and opposites

a Students read the questions and sentences 1 to 3. Elicit the answer (sentence 3). Ask students to work out what the adjective is for each comparative adjective in sentence 3 (safe, quiet, relaxing).

b ▶ **CD2 T58** Give students a few minutes to read the words in the box and look at the pictures. Check any problems. Go through the example as a class, if necessary. Students complete the exercise.

> **Answers**
> 2 safe 3 noisy 4 modern 5 old-fashioned
> 6 boring 7 exciting 8 quiet

> **Language note**
> Remind students that in English adjectives do not agree with the subject. We don't say ~~three moderns houses~~. Remind them too that adjectives usually go before the noun they are describing, e.g. we say *a modern house* NOT ~~a house modern~~.

c Students read through adjectives 1 to 4. Go through the first item as an example, if necessary. Students complete the exercise. They can compare answers in pairs before a whole-class check.

> **Answers**
> 2 safe 3 quiet 4 old-fashioned

Vocabulary bank Refer students to the vocabulary bank. Read through the words and phrases in open class and check understanding.

Get it right! Refer students to the Get it right! section. These exercises can be used as homework or for fast-finishers.

Vocabulary notebook

Encourage students to start a section called *Adjectives and opposites* and to note down adjectives and any translations they find helpful.

✳ OPTIONAL ACTIVITY

Students can make up sentences using one or more of the adjectives in Exercise 6.

7 Speak

a Divide the class into pairs. Ask a stronger pair to demonstrate the example dialogue, drawing students' attention to the use of adjectives. Students exchange information about things in their life. Remind them to use adjectives where possible. Monitor and check they are taking turns to exchange information, and that they are using the adjective in the correct position and in the correct way. Make a note of any repeated errors to go through as a class after the exercise. Ask pairs to feedback to the rest of the class.

Weaker classes: They may find it helpful if you elicit different areas of their life they can talk about and put them on the board to refer to while they are exchanging information.

b Divide the class into pairs. Students read through the topics in the box. Check any problems. Ask a stronger pair to demonstrate the example dialogue, drawing students' attention to the adjective in the first statement and the comparative in the second statement.

Stronger students: They can choose their own topics or add to the topics in the box.

Photostory: So sorry

8 Read and Listen

Warm-up

Ask students what they remember about the previous episode of the photostory in Unit 12 and what happened (Izzie had an accident when she was skateboarding in the park).

a ▶ **CD2 T59** Ask students to read the question and predict the answer but do not comment at this stage. Play the recording while students read and check their predictions. Check answers in open class. If students ask questions about vocabulary, write the words on the board, but do not comment at this stage.

TAPESCRIPT

See the text on page 106 of the Student's Book.

> **Answers**
> No, Izzie isn't angry.

b Read through the sentences. Students read the text again and decide if the sentences are true or false. Students should correct the false sentences. Let students check answers with a partner before feedback in open class

> **Answers**
> 2 F (He didn't stop.)
> 3 T
> 4 T
> 5 F (She's not angry.)
> 6 F (She wants Darren to buy her an ice cream.)

9 Everyday English

a Read through the expressions from the dialogue with students. Do the first item as an example. Ask students if they can remember (without looking back) who said this (Mark). Students complete the exercise, only looking back at the dialogue if they need to. Check answers.

> **Answers**
> 1 Mark 2 Darren 3 Darren 4 Izzie

b Ask students to look at the expressions in the dialogue and in L1, discuss what they think they mean. Is a direct translation possible in their language? If not, discuss how they might express a similar meaning.

c ▶ **CD2 T60** Read through the sentences with students and clarify any problems with understanding. In pairs, students decide on the correct order for the dialogue. Check answers and ask students to practise the correct dialogue.

TAPESCRIPT/ANSWERS

Phil: Hi Maggie. Did you see the exam results? They came out today.

Maggie: Yes, I saw them – unfortunately.

Phil: Oh dear. What's the matter? Not good news?

Maggie: No. I'm sort of unhappy. I only got 80% in French. I wanted 90%.

Phil: Oh, French? You know, Tom Black got 93% in French.

Maggie: What? I don't believe it! He was always terrible at French.

Phil: Well, you see, he studied really hard this year. How about you, Maggie?

d Students read through the dialogues. Check any problems. Go through the first item as an example if necessary, showing students how only one option is possible. Students complete the exercise. They can compare answers in pairs before a whole class check.

> **Answers**
> 1 You see 2 What's the matter 3 sort of
> 4 I don't believe it

10 Improvisation

Divide the class into pairs. Tell students they are going

to create a dialogue between Mark and Izzie. Read through the instructions with students. Give students two minutes to plan their dialogue. Circulate and help with vocabulary as necessary. Encourage students to use expressions from Exercise 9. Students practise their conversation in pairs. Listen to some of the best conversations in open class.

11 Free Time ⊙ DVD Episode 7

a Look at the photo with students and ask them to describe what is happening and answer the questions. Divide the class into pairs and ask students to create a short dialogue for the people in the photo. Circulate and help with vocabulary as necessary. Listen to some of the dialogues in open class as feedback.

> **Answers**
> Mark and Jo. Students' own answers.

b Read through the instructions with students. In small groups, students think of ways to raise money for poor or sick people. Circulate and help with vocabulary as necessary.

c Divide the students into new groups. Students tell each other their ideas. Listen to some of the best ideas in open class and encourage further discussion. Play Episode 7 of the DVD for students to find out what happens.

12 Write

a Students read through the questions. Check any problems. Students then read the advertisement quickly and answer the questions. Check answers.

> **Answers**
> You can win 1000 Euros. You must write no more than 120 words.

b Students read Claudia's entry and decide which question she is answering. Draw students' attention to the use of comparatives in the text.

> **Answer**
> A

c This exercise can be set for homework.

Stronger classes: Using Claudia's entry as an example, students write their own entry. Remind them to plan first before drafting and then producing a final version.

Weaker classes: Students can work on this in pairs. Encourage them to plan and draft their entry before producing a final version. Once drafts have been checked students can write a final version.

13 Last but not least: more speaking

a Look at the photos and discuss the differences between them. Divide the class into small groups. Ask students to imagine what their country was like fifty years ago and to make a list of 5–10 differences.

b Students decide which things are better now and which things were better in the past.

c Students plan a presentation on their ideas. Encourage them to take it in turns to speak, and to use examples to explain their ideas.

d Groups give their presentations to the class. Give students a chance to ask questions and encourage further discussion.

Check your progress

1 Grammar

a 1 told 2 lived 3 went 4 became 5 thought
6 left 7 died 8 found 9 learned/learnt

b 2 wrote, didn't write
3 came, didn't come
4 ate, didn't eat

c 2 Spanish is easier than Portuguese.
3 My uncle's car is more expensive than my father's.
4 Your homework is more important than that computer game.
5 Her History teacher is better than my teacher.

2 Vocabulary

a have
a look   an ice-cream   a cup of tea

play
the piano   football   cards

go to
work   bed   the cinema

b 2 safe
3 modern
4 quiet

How did you do?

Check that students are marking their scores. Collect these in, check them as necessary and discuss any further work needed with specific students.

Memo from Mario

Things change

Extra practice of comparatives

▶ Ask each student to work on their own and write down the name of a personal hero. This could be a musician, a celebrity, a member of their family, a sportsperson, a political leader, etc.

▶ Ask them to write three sentences about their hero and to list six adjectives describing them.

▶ Organise the class into seated circles of between 10 and 12. In their groups, ask the students to say who their hero is and to say a few things about them.

▶ Each student takes a loose sheet of paper and writes their hero's name at the top of it. They pass this sheet to their right. Each student now has a sheet of paper with the name of the hero of the person on their left.

▶ Students compare this hero to their own hero. For example, if the student has written George Clooney and the neighbour has passed them a sheet with Lionel Messi written at the top, they could write: *I am Lionel Messi and I am younger than George Clooney.*

▶ Once the writing is done each student passes their sheet to the right again. Our student might write, having received a sheet headed by Madonna: *I am George Clooney and I am less famous than Madonna.*

▶ The exercise continues until the sheet gets back to the original 'owners'.

▶ After the students have read the comparative sentences written about their hero, ask them to choose the most interesting one to put up on the board. Now you have a board filled with comparative sentences written by the students themselves about something they care about.

> **RATIONALE**
> When learners write and talk about things of their own, and of things that are close to them, they tend to be much more present in the language class.

Pronunciation

Unit 1   Exercise 5

✳ *from*

a ▶ **CD1 T25** Play the recording and see if students can hear the different ways *from* is pronounced.

TAPESCRIPT
I'm from Poland.
Where are you from?
He's from England.

b Play the recording again, pausing for students to repeat each sentence. If students are having problems with the pronunciation, give them a few more examples of your own to drill as a class.

Unit 2   Exercise 6

✳ /ɪ/ and /iː/

a ▶ **CD1 T31** Play the recording for students to listen to the pronunciation of each word.

TAPESCRIPT
big   three

b **Stronger classes:** Students read through the list of words. Do the first item as an example, showing them how to classify the word according to its pronunciation. Students complete the exercise. Do not check answers at this stage.

Weaker classes: Write the headings on the board. Check students can hear the difference between the two sounds, playing the recording again if necessary. Give students a few minutes to read through the words in the box. Go through the first word as an example, asking a student to come and write it under the correct heading. Continue like this until students have classified all the words under the headings on the board.

c ▶ **CD1 T32** Play the recording, pausing after each word for students to check their answers.

Weaker classes: If there are still problems, play the recording again, pausing for students to repeat each word.

TAPESCRIPT/ANSWERS
/ɪ/: six, it, city, video
/iː/: he, we, cheap, fourteen

d ▶ **CD1 T33** Play the recording and see how quickly students can repeat the sentence. Listen to a few individual attempts in open class. For further practice at differentiating sounds ask students to add new words to the /ɪ/ and /iː/ columns.

TAPESCRIPT
He's in a video clip with six fit kids.

✳ OPTIONAL ACTIVITY
In small groups, give students a few minutes to see if they can think of any more words to add to each group.

Example answers
/ɪ/: Britney, lip
/iː/: tree, see, me, thirteen

Unit 3   Exercise 3

✳ /s/, /z/ and /ɪz/

a ▶ **CD1 T39** Students read through the verbs in the box. Go through the examples as a class, making sure students can hear the difference between each ending. Drill each sound, if necessary.

Stronger classes: They can try to classify each verb and then listen and check only.

Weaker classes: Play the recording once and then play it a second time for students to complete the exercise.

Check answers, playing and pausing the recording after each verb.

TAPESCRIPT/ANSWERS
/s/: stops, works, likes
/z/: goes, reads, learns, gives
/ɪz/: watches, studies, finishes

b ▶ **CD1 T39** Play the recording again, pausing after each verb for students to repeat.

Unit 4   Exercise 3

✳ /ð/ and /θ/

▶ **CD1 T45** Play the recording while students listen. Ask them if they notice the difference between the two sounds. If students are having problems with the difference, then remind them to position their tongue behind their front teeth for the /ð/ sound and to put their tongue between their front teeth, slightly sticking out, for the /θ/ sound.

Play the recording again if necessary to give students more practice.

TAPESCRIPT
/ð/ there mother the father
/θ/ thousand thirty think three

Unit 5 Exercise 3

* /v/ they've

a ▶ **CD1 T51** Students read through words 1 to 9. Play the recording, pausing after each word for students to repeat. Play the recording a second time if necessary.

TAPESCRIPT

1 they've 2 we've 3 you've 4 I've 5 very
6 five 7 verb 8 video 9 volleyball

b Students read sentences 1 to 3. Drill the sentences as a class.

c ▶ **CD1 T52** Play the recording for students to listen and check their pronunciation.

TAPESCRIPT

1 We've got five very long videos.

2 You've got the wrong verb.

3 I've got volleyball practice today.

Play the recording again, pausing after each sentence for students to repeat.

Unit 6 Exercise 4

* /w/ would

▶ **CD1 T61** Students read through questions 1 to 4. Check any problems. Play the recording for students to listen. Play the recording a second time, pausing after each question for students to repeat.

TAPESCRIPT

1 Would you like a sandwich?

2 Are you the new waiter?

3 What do you want to eat?

4 Where in the world are you from?

Unit 7 Exercise 6

* Compound nouns

a ▶ **CD2 T4** Students read through the words. Play the recording, pausing after each word. Ask students to identify where the stress falls (the first word), making sure they can hear this.

TAPESCRIPT

chat shows

game shows

sports programmes

soap operas

b ▶ **CD2 T4** Play the recording again, pausing after each word for students to repeat.

Unit 8 Exercise 3

* Linking sounds

a ▶ **CD2 T11** Students read through the sentences. Play the recording for students to listen. Ask students if they heard the *t* sound (no). Play the sentences again if necessary, to make sure students are clear on this area.

TAPESCRIPT

Don't laugh.

Don't cry.

Don't shout.

I don't like hamburgers.

b ▶ **CD2 T12** Students read the sentences. Play the recording for students to listen. Ask students if they heard the *t* sound (yes). Play the sentences again if necessary to make sure students are clear on this area. Ask them why they could hear the *t* in these sentences but not in the sentences in Exercise 3a and elicit or explain that it is because the *t* is before a vowel in the sentences in Exercise 3b. Play the sentences in Exercises 3a and 3b again, pausing for students to repeat.

TAPESCRIPT

Don't open the door.

Don't eat that.

I don't understand.

Don't ask me.

Unit 9 Exercise 4

* can/can't

a ▶ **CD2 T20** Play the recording for students to listen. Ask a stronger student to explain the difference in the sounds in *can* and *can't*.

TAPESCRIPT

1 He can write on a computer, but he can't walk.

2 She can ride a bike, but she can't swim.

3 They can learn to count, but they can't learn to talk.

4 I can use a computer, but I can't draw pictures with it.

b ▶ **CD2 T20** Play the recording again, pausing for students to repeat each sentence. Make sure students are pronouncing each *can/can't* correctly. Drill any problem sentences or drill *can/can't* in isolation.

c ▶ **CD2 T21** Students read the dialogues. Play the recording for students to listen. Play it a second time, pausing for students to repeat.

Unit 10 Exercise 6

✱ /h/ have

▶ CD2 T28 Play the recording for students to listen only. Play the recording again, pausing after each sentence for students to repeat. Make sure students are pronouncing the /h/ sound correctly. If there are still problems, drill a few words in isolation.

TAPESCRIPT

1 Hi! Can I help you?
2 He can walk on his hands.
3 Are you hungry? Have a hamburger.
4 Henry's having a holiday in Holland.

Unit 11 Exercise 7

✱ /æ/ and /e/

a **▶ CD2 T37** Students read the words in each column. Play the recording, pausing after each word for students to repeat.

TAPESCRIPT

/æ/ black jacket hamburger thanks January
/e/ yes red dress yellow September

b Students read sentences 1 to 3 silently. Drill each sentence as a class, focusing particularly on the /æ/ and /e/ sounds. If you feel students are still having problems, drill a few words from Exercise 7a in isolation.

c **▶ CD2 T38** Play the recording, pausing after each sentence for students to repeat.

TAPESCRIPT

1 I like the black jacket in the window.
2 I wear red in January and yellow in September.
3 She's wearing a black and red dress.

Unit 12 Exercise 3

✱ was/wasn't and were/weren't

a **▶ CD2 T43** Students read sentences 1 to 4. Play the recording, pausing after each sentence for students to repeat.

TAPESCRIPT

1 He was only 22.
2 They were in Iowa.
3 It wasn't a warm night.
4 They weren't in New York.

b **▶ CD2 T44** Play the recording, pausing after each question and answer for students to repeat. Make sure students are using the correct intonation of the questions and answers, and drill these in isolation if necessary.

TAPESCRIPT

1 Was he only 22?
  Yes, he was.
2 Were they in New York?
  No, they weren't.

c Divide the class into pairs. Ask a stronger pair to demonstrate the example dialogue. Students now continue asking and answering the questions from Exercise 2d on page 89. Monitor and check students are taking turns to ask and answer and that they are using the correct intonation and verb forms. Make a note of any repeated errors to go through as a class at the end of the exercise. Ask a few pairs to feedback to the rest of the class.

Answers

1 No, they weren't. They were in Iowa.
2 No, they weren't. They were on a plane.
3 Yes, they were.
4 No, it wasn't. It was a very cold night.
5 Yes, there was.
6 Yes, they were.
7 No, he wasn't. He was 22 years old.

Unit 13 Exercise 3

✱ -ed endings

a **▶ CD2 T52** Students read through the sentences. Play the recording, pausing after each sentence for students to repeat. Make sure students are pronouncing each ending clearly and play the recording again if there are any problems.

Stronger classes: You can ask students to read out the sentences with the correct pronunciation before listening. They can then listen and check.

TAPESCRIPT

1 We watched a film.
2 I called a friend.
3 He wanted an ice cream.

b **▶ CD2 T53** Play the recording, pausing after each sentence for students to repeat.

TAPESCRIPT

1 I phoned a friend.
2 I phoned my friend.
3 He talked a lot.
4 He talked to the teacher.
5 We visited a friend.
6 We visited the museum.

c **▶ CD2 T53** **Weaker classes:** Play the recording again, pausing after the first item. Go through this as an example, showing students which column it should go in. Play the rest of the recording for students to listen. Students complete the exercise.

Stronger classes: Students can complete the table in Exercise 3c and can listen and check only.

> **Answers**
> /t/: talked, watched
> /d/: phoned, called
> /id/: visited, wanted

✱ OPTIONAL ACTIVITY

Write the following verbs on the board and ask students to decide which column they would go in.

walked asked lived worked started stopped

Unit 14 Exercise 3

✱ *than* /ðən/

a ▶ **CD2 T57** Students read through sentences 1 to 5. Play the recording for students to listen. Elicit the pronunciation of *than* after they have heard all five sentences.

TAPESCRIPT

1 She's taller than me.

2 I'm older than him.

3 It's hotter than yesterday.

4 Our dog's bigger than yours.

5 This is more expensive than that one.

b ▶ **CD2 T57** Play the recording again, pausing after each sentence for students to repeat. Make sure students are pronouncing *than* correctly. If they are still having problems, drill one or two of the sentences as a class.

Get it right! key

Unit 1: Countries and nationalities

2 Polish
3 Japanese
4 Brazil
5 Italian
6 Germany
7 French
8 American; Australia

Unit 2: *(don't) like + sth + a lot/very much*

2 a   3 a   4 b   5 a

Unit 3: Present simple

1 starts
2 finishes
3 comes
4 speaks
5 like
6 listen
7 play
8 teaches

Unit 3: Pronouns

2 ... but his mother is Japanese.
3 I really love it.
4 ... but I don't like its screen.
5 Maria and her family ...

Unit 4: *there, their or they're*

1 There   2 they're   3 their   4 There
5 they're   6 their   7 there   8 their

Unit 5: *has* and *have*

2 have   3 has; hasn't   4 have   5 hasn't

Unit 6: Countable and uncountable nouns

2 I listen to some music ...
3 There are some apples ...
4 I've got lots of shopping ...
5 We've got some homework ...
6 There's an exercise about ...

Unit 7: Spelling – time words

2 I go running at six o'clock every morning.
3 I usually run for about 45 minutes.
4 I play football on Tuesday and Thursday.
5 We sometimes have a match at the weekend.
6 And I often go swimming on Saturday too.

Unit 9: *fun or funny?*

2 fun   3 funny   4 funny   5 fun

Unit 9: Verb + verb

1 swim   2 playing   3 playing   4 hit
5 doing   6 take

Unit 11: Time prepositions: *in, on* and *at*

2 in; in   3 In; at   4 on   5 on

Unit 11: Plural nouns: clothes

2 The players wear blue shorts and a white top.
3 You need warm socks to ...
4 Most men wear black trousers ...
5 Bring walking shoes or trainers.

Unit 13: Noun and verb pairs

1 have
2 have
3 go
4 have
5 go
6 play
7 go/get
8 have

Unit 14: Adjectives

2 ... the beaches were beautiful
3 I was surprised because ...
4 My new bedroom is bigger ...
5 ... with lots of interesting places.
6 ... snowboarding is easier than skiing

Project 1
A tourist leaflet

Warm up

You may find it useful to bring in some examples of tourist leaflets for students' own town to help students find information. You could also talk about your own town, and encourage students to ask questions.

1 Research

a Divide the class into groups of three or four.

Stronger classes: This part of the project can be set for homework. Each student can research the questions and then bring in the information they have collected to discuss in their group.

Weaker classes: Read through the prompt questions as a class and elicit suggestions and write them on the board. Students then research the questions further.

Encourage students to use different sources to collect their information from, e.g. books, magazines, newspapers, the Internet, etc. and to gather pictures at this stage because they will need these in Exercise 1b. Students then write notes for each question based on the information they have gathered.

b Give students time to find their pictures.

2 Make the leaflet

a Give each group a large piece of paper. Show students some of the real tourist leaflets if you have brought them in. Ask students to fold their paper in half, and then in half again. They can then cut the two folds at the bottom to make four separate pages. Alternatively, for smaller leaflets students can simply fold their paper in half to make two pages, and draw the map on page 1 only.

b Students read through the instructions. You could read through the sample leaflet about Izmir. In groups, each student takes a turn to write up some of the information they have gathered. Monitor and check students are taking turns to do this and that they are putting the right information on the right pages. Students can then read out or demonstrate how their leaflet works to the rest of the class.

★ OPTIONAL ACTIVITY

Display the leaflets around the class. Students can vote for the most interesting leaflet.

c If there is time, ask groups to think of a quiz about their own town/city. Encourage them to write questions and to think about the kind of quiz they are going to write, e.g. are they going to give

choices for answers, etc. If there's space, groups can transfer their quizzes onto their leaflets.

Stronger classes: Encourage them to write other questions which are not based on information in their leaflets.

Weaker classes: Students can write their questions based on the information in their leaflets only.

Students can prepare their quizzes and then ask their questions to other groups.

Project 2
A class survey

Warm up

Ask students what they like to do in their free time and elicit some suggestions.

1 Prepare the survey

Divide the class into groups of three or four.

a Students read through the topics. Encourage groups to choose one topic they all agree on for their survey.

b Students read through the example survey. Draw their attention to the formation of the questions and the types of questions to ask. Encourage each student in the group to come up with a question for the topic they selected in Exercise 1a and to write it down.

c Students then exchange information with another group and ask other students their questions, noting down the answers.

2 Write the report

a Read through the example as a class, drawing students' attention to the questions in Exercise 1b. Students give the information they found out to the other members of their group and write it down.

b Students can appoint a secretary to note down the information they have gathered. Go through the example report as a class, reminding them that a report should only give the main pieces of information about the number of people and the activities they researched. Give students time to write their reports and then read them out to the class.

★ OPTIONAL ACTIVITY

Find out if there is one free time activity which is more popular with the class than others.

Project 3

A poster presentation about a band or singer

Warm up

Ask students who their favourite band is. Ask them what kind of music they sing, how many members are in the band and where they come from. Ask students to read the text about the group Cobra Starship and help with any difficult vocabulary.

Divide the class into groups of three or four.

1 Research

a Stronger classes: This part of the exercise can be set for homework. Each student can research the questions and then bring in the information they have collected to discuss in their group.

Weaker classes: Read through the prompts as a class. Students then spend time gathering their information. Encourage them to use different sources to collect their information from, e.g. books, magazines, newspapers, the internet, etc. Students gather pictures of their favourite singer/band to use in Exercise 1c.

b If you have access to a computer, students can type this up. Students can appoint a secretary who is responsible for writing down all the sentences. Alternatively, each student could write a sentence of their own. Students now write a short text, based on the presentation text, about their favourite singer/band. Encourage them to answer all the questions from Exercise 1a and to divide the text up as in the presentation text.

c Give each group a large piece of card or paper to make a poster. If students have not already collected their pictures, then give them time to do this now. Each group then arranges their pictures and text and sticks them onto the poster.

d Students bring in a song by their favourite singer/band.

2 Prepare the presentation

Students discuss how they are going to present their poster, e.g. they can choose a spokesperson or they can take turns to read out the information. Students practise their presentation in their group.

3 Presentation

Each group presents their poster to the class. If students want, they can finish their presentations by playing a song by their favourite singer/band.

⭐ OPTIONAL ACTIVITY

All the posters can be displayed on the classroom walls and students can vote for the best one.

Project 4

A presentation on changes in your country

Divide the class into groups of three or four.

Warm up

Ask students how they think their own town/city has changed over the last 50 years.

1 Research

a Read through the prompts as a class. Encourage groups to choose one or two topics to focus on for their own town/city.

Weaker classes: It may be better for students to choose only one topic idea.

b Students read through the instructions and example questions.

Stronger classes: Give them time to prepare their questions on their chosen topic areas.

Weaker classes: Elicit information about the topic they chose in Exercise 1a and write it on the board to help them with their questions.

c This part of the project can be set for homework. Encourage students to interview different people in their family and to note down or record their answers.

Encourage students to do further research using the different sources mentioned and collect photos of their town/city 50 years ago.

2 Presentation

a Students put together all the information they have collected and decide which pieces they will use and how they will organise it. Students then write up (or type) the information they have selected and add any pictures or photos they have collected.

b Students then choose a spokesperson or they can decide to take turns to present their project. Students introduce their project to the rest of the class and present the information.

⭐ OPTIONAL ACTIVITY

Students can vote for the best project and the projects can then all be displayed in the class.

Workbook key

Welcome section

A

1 2 night 3 morning 4 evening

B

1 **a** ▶ **CD3 T2** TAPESCRIPT

1 Taxi!
2 Here's your **pizza**.
3 This is a good **DVD**.
4 They're in the **museum**.
5 I love **football**.
6 Oh, that's the **phone**.
7 Here's the **bus**.
8 I'd like a **sandwich**, please.
9 New York is a beautiful **city**.
10 This is our **TV**.
11 This is a nice **hotel**.
12 We're at the **airport**.

b See **tapescript** for Exercise 1a.

2 2 board 3 door 4 chair 5 desk 6 pencil
7 pen 8 notebook

3 **b** 2 pages 3 notebooks 4 sandwiches
5 cities 6 taxis 7 nationalities

c 2 three sandwiches
3 four men
4 two women
5 six children
6 four people

C

1 3 ✓ 4 a boring book 5 a good football team
6 ✓ 7 a new taxi 8 a bad hotel

2 2 a 3 an 4 a 5 a 6 an 7 an 8 a

3 **a** ▶ **CD3 T3** TAPESCRIPT
Lucy is fourteen.

b ▶ **CD3 T4** TAPESCRIPT/ANSWERS

1

My name's Kevin Thompson – Thompson,
that's T-H-O-M-P-S-O-N. Er ... and I'm from
Blackburn. That's B-L-A-C-K-B-U-R-N.

2

Man: OK, now can I have your name please?
Julie: Yes, I'm Julie Claymore. Julie C-L-A-Y-M-
O-R-E.
Man: Julie Claymore, right. And your city?

Julie: I'm from Newcastle.
Man: Sorry, what was that?
Julie: Newcastle. That's N-E-W-C-A-S-T-L-E.
Man: Fine. Thanks very much.

4 2 red 3 black 4 blue 5 brown 6 white
7 yellow

D

1 ▶ **CD3 T5** TAPESCRIPT/ANSWERS

1
Kim: The homework is on page 12. **OK?**
James: Yes, great. **Thank you**, Kim.

2
Ben: I **don't understand** these words.
Mike: No **problem**, Ben. I **can help** you!
Ben: Thanks, Mike!

3
Teacher: What's the answer, Kate?
Kate: Sorry, Miss. **I don't know!**

4
Paul: **Excuse me**, Miss.
Teacher: Yes?
Paul: **What does this mean**? This word here, on
page 28.
Teacher: Let me see.

2 2 eleven 3 fourteen 4 nine 5 five 6 twenty
7 seventeen 8 twelve

3 **a** 1 ninety
2 thirty-two, sixty-four
3 seventy-four, eighty-five
4 seventy-five, seventy-two
5 forty-one, forty-four

b ▶ **CD3 T6** TAPESCRIPT/ANSWERS
1 13 hotels
2 15 CDs
3 70 pencils
4 14 chairs
5 60 women
6 80 pages

1 He's a footballer

1 **a** 2 C 3 A 4 E 5 G 6 D 7 B

b 2 She's 3 You're 4 It's 5 Richard's
6 Australia's 7 I'm; What's

c 2 He's 3 it's 4 you're 5 It's

[d] 2 You are not; You aren't 3 He is not; He isn't 4 She is not; She isn't 5 It is not; It isn't

[e] 3 It isn't Japanese. 4 She's the winner. 5 It's boring. 6 You're not a film star. 7 It's expensive. 8 You're a bad dog.

[f] 2 Is she British? 3 Are you from Istanbul? 4 Am I right? 5 Is it a big city? 6 Is Brad Pitt a good actor?

[9] ▶ CD3 T7 TAPESCRIPT/ANSWERS
1 Is she American?
2 Are you from Japan?
3 Is he a good footballer?
4 Is it a cheap restaurant?
5 Am I the winner?
6 Is Broadway in New York?
7 Is the hotel expensive?
8 Is Maria from Spain?
9 Are you a singer?
10 Is the answer on page 5?

2 [a] 2 Portugal 3 Belgium 4 Poland 5 Italy 6 Turkey 7 Brazil 8 Britain

[b] Italian, Australian, Turkish, Polish, American, British, Belgian

[c] 2 She's from Russia. She's Russian.
3 He's from Spain. He's Spanish.
4 He's from America. He's American.
5 He's from Japan. He's Japanese.
6 She's from Turkey. She's Turkish.

[d] 2 Egypt / Egyptian 3 Argentina / Argentinian 4 Chile / Chilean 5 Peru / Peruvian 6 Korea / Korean 7 Colombia / Colombian 8 Thailand / Thai

3 ▶ CD3 T8 TAPESCRIPT/ANSWERS
1 It's Polish.
2 It's Australian.
3 She's in Russia.
4 He's from Germany.
5 He's Turkish.
6 I'm not from Canada.

4 [a] 2 e 3 c 4 a 5 f 6 d

[b] 2 What 3 Where 4 What 5 Where 6 Who 7 How 8 What

5 2 British (English) 3 They're 4 French 5 Italian 6 is

6 [b] Classroom things: pencil, chair, notebook, table
Classroom verbs: write, look at, say, ask, match

[c] *Example answers*
Countries: Poland; Nationalities: Spanish, Chinese, Polish; Jobs: actor, teacher, footballer

7 2 T 3 F 4 T 5 T 6 F 7 T 8 F

8 3 I'm 4 Wells 5 Is 6 No 7 isn't 8 What's 9 address 10 best 11 he 12 he 13 is 14 How 15 is 16 He's 17 fifteen

Unit check

1 1 Belgium 2 is 3 from 4 isn't 5 Polish 6 Who's 7 Is 8 actor 9 teacher

2 2 b 3 c 4 c 5 a 6 c 7 b 8 c 9 a

3 2 Colombian 3 Canada 4 Chinese 5 Portuguese 6 Greek 7 German 8 Ireland 9 Thailand

2 We're a new band

1 2 a S 3 e K 4 f C 5 b AM 6 d AM

2 [a] 2 You're 3 she's 4 It's 5 We're 6 You're 7 They're 8 He's

[b] 3 Tokyo isn't a city in China.
4 My favourite restaurant is/isn't expensive.
5 I'm not British. I'm …
6 Ferrari cars aren't cheap. They're expensive.
7 Daniel Radcliffe isn't a sports star. He's a film star.
8 We're / We aren't in Rome.

[c] 2 e 3 b 4 g 5 f 6 h 7 c 8 a

[d] 2 Are Ken and Sandy American?
3 Am I a good singer?
4 Where are you from, Sarah?
5 Is the film interesting?
6 Are you and Robert football players?
7 Is James Blunt popular in Belgium?
8 Are Julia and I good actors?
9 Who are you?
10 What is your phone number?

[e] *Example answers*
2 Yes, I'm quite a good singer.
3 No, I'm not. I'm from Milan.
4 Yes, we are. We're in a really good band!
5 No, they aren't. They're cheap.
6 No, she isn't. She's a teacher.
7 No, he isn't. He's American.
8 Yes, it's a very big school.

[f] 1 do 2 like 3 tennis 4 don't like 5 Do 6 like 7 No; don't

3 [a] 1 awful 2 fantastic 3 great 4 terrible

[b] *Example answers*
2 I really like mobile phones. I think they're fantastic.
3 I like tennis. I think it's excellent.
4 I really like hamburgers. I think they're great.
5 I like music. I think it's wonderful.
6 I don't like horses. I think they're awful.

c 2 dreadful 3 brilliant 4 disgusting
   5 useless 6 excellent

4 2 him 3 them 4 you 5 it 6 me

5 **a** ▶ CD3 T9 TAPESCRIPT/ANSWERS
   think, singer, film, cinema, big, women;
   see, please, read, museum, CD, people

   b ▶ CD3 T10 TAPESCRIPT
   1 Three big museums.
   2 We think he's Swiss.
   3 Fifteen CDs, please.
   4 The Italian singer is the winner.

6 1 Of course! 2 I'm sorry 3 Cool! 4 I know!

7 **a** 2 A'merican 3 Japa'nese 4 'terrible
   5 com'puter 6 'concert 7 seven'teen

   b 'awful
   'boring
   'interesting
   ex'pensive
   'wonderful
   'terrible

8 **a** ▶ CD3 T11 TAPESCRIPT

   Judy: Hi! Welcome to my homepage. My name is
   Judy Dahrendorf. I live in Santa Cruz in California
   and I really like rock music. Can you guess who
   my favourite pop stars are? Yes, you're right:
   they're the 'Kings of Leon'.

   Here are four things I want to tell you about them:

   There are four people in the band: three brothers
   and a cousin! Caleb, Nathan, Jared and Matthew
   Followill.

   My favourite King of Leon is Caleb. I think he's
   fantastic! And he's a wonderful singer!

   My favourite Kings of Leon song is *Closer*. All my
   friends say their favourite is *Use Somebody*. (I
   think it's really good, but it isn't my favourite.)

   The Kings of Leon are all American. Matthew is
   from Mississippi, and the other three are from
   Tennessee.

   Do you like my homepage? I hope so. And I hope
   you like K O L too!

   ANSWERS
   2 favourite 3 band 4 is 5 fantastic
   6 wonderful 7 really 8 American 9 from
   10 like

   b 2 T 3 F 4 T 5 F 6 F

Unit check

1 1 from 2 she's 3 are 4 them 5 aren't
   6 wonderful 7 film 8 together 9 we're

2 2 b 3 b 4 c 5 b 6 b 7 b 8 a 9 c

3 2 delicious 3 brilliant 4 disgusting 5 useless
   6 dreadful 7 terrible 8 excellent 9 fantastic

3 She lives in Washington

1 2 f 3 a 4 c 5 b 6 e

2 **a** 1 speak 2 stop 3 understand 4 listen
   6 play 7 study 8 read 9 watch 10 live
   11 write 12 work

   b 2 watches 3 goes 4 speaks 5 listens
   6 finishes 7 works 8 studies

   c 2 writes 3 watch 4 play 5 speaks
   6 live 7 understand

   d 2 We play tennis but we don't play
      computer games.
   3 Sam doesn't like dogs but he likes cats.
   4 Julie doesn't listen to CDs but she listens
      to MP3s.
   5 Tony and Jill watch cartoons but they don't
      watch football.

   e 2 Does 3 Does 4 Do 5 Do
   6 Do 7 Does

   f 2 Do you always finish your homework?
      Yes, I do. / No, I don't.
   3 Does your best friend like football?
      Yes, he/she does. / No, he/she doesn't.
   4 Do you and your friends play volleyball?
      Yes, we do. / No, we don't.
   5 Does your teacher speak English?
      Yes, he/she does. / No, he/she doesn't.
   6 Do your friends understand Russian?
      Yes, they do. / No, they don't.

3 ▶ CD3 T12 TAPESCRIPT/ANSWERS
   1 She likes it here.
   2 Does Anna learn music? /z/
   3 Sam watches films. /ɪz/
   4 She writes a lot of letters. /s/
   5 He lives in London. /z/
   6 The class finishes soon. /ɪz/
   7 Paul speaks Italian. /s/

4 **a** 2 cousin 3 brothers 4 grandmother
   5 aunt 6 Barbara's 7 parents 8 Barbara's
   9 David's

   b and **c** Students' own answers.

   d 1 mother-in-law 2 grandson
   3 granddaughter 4 grandchildren
   5 grandparents 6 father-in-law

5 2 your 3 his 4 her 5 our 6 its 7 their

6 2 grocery shop 3 flat 4 house 5 vegetables
   6 secretary

7 *Example answers*
work: in a hospital; play: tennis, the piano; watch: television, a film; write: an email, a letter; read: a book, a message; listen to: a band, your teacher

8 ▶ CD3 T13   TAPESCRIPT

Uncle: So tell me about your friend Rebecca. Her family lives in London, is that right?

Alice: Yes, that's right. She lives in London with her mum and her two brothers. They're eight and ten. Her mother's a nurse – she works in a hospital.

Uncle: And what are Rebecca's hobbies?

Alice: Well, she reads a lot. She doesn't watch a lot of TV, but she really likes books.

Uncle: And what do you do together, you and Rebecca? Do you go to concerts?

Alice: No, we don't, but we go to the cinema, and we play music together a lot. Also, we go to the same school, so I often study with Rebecca at her house.

2 ✗ 3 ✗ 4 ✓ 5 ✗ 6 ✓ 7 ✓

9 *Example answer*
Mateo's sister is Sonia and his brother is Marco. They're twelve and nine. His father works in a shop. Mateo's best friend is Franco. Mateo and Franco don't play tennis, but they play football together. Mateo speaks Italian and English.

Unit check

1 1 live 2 their 3 doesn't 4 Tara's 5 learn
6 speaks 7 volleyball 8 have 9 don't

2 2 b 3 b 4 a 5 a 6 b 7 c 8 c 9 c

3 2 grandfather 3 husband; wife
4 father-in-law 5 grandchildren
6 brother-in-law; mother-in-law; sister-in-law

4 Where's the café?

1 2 musician 3 bus 4→ collection 4↓ café
5→ theatre 5↓ tours 6 art

2 **a** ▶ CD3 T14 TAPESCRIPT/ANSWERS
1 139 2 318 3 651 4 807 5 714
6 10,000 7 2,924

b ▶ CD3 T15 TAPESCRIPT/ANSWERS
2 Fifty and twenty-five = seventy-five
3 Eleven and eighty-nine = (one/a) hundred
4 A hundred and ten and a hundred and sixty = two hundred and seventy
5 Two hundred and sixty-six and seventeen = two hundred and eighty-three

6 Three hundred and nine and a hundred and ninety-eight = five hundred and seven

3 ▶ CD3 T16 TAPESCRIPT/ANSWERS
1 I think he's thirty. /θ/
2 That's their father. /ð/
3 They buy clothes together. /ð/
4 Thanks for the birthday party. /θ/

4 **a** 2 are 3 are 4 's 5 's 6 are

b 1 there isn't 2 There are 3 there's
4 there aren't 5 There isn't 6 there's
7 There are 8 there's 9 There aren't
10 there isn't

5 **a** 2 h 3 c 4 e 5 b 6 g 7 d 8 f

b 2 primary 3 shopping centre 4 car park
5 leisure centre 6 police station

c *Example answers*
2 Is there a big post office in your town?
Yes, there is.
3 Are there any bookshops near your school?
No, there aren't.
4 Is there a good library in your school?
Yes, there is.
5 Is there a railway station near your home?
No, there isn't.
6 Are there any newsagents in your street?
No, there aren't.

6 2 Turn right. 3 Sit down. 4 Turn left.
5 Go home. 6 Look!

7 **a** 2 The park is opposite the post office.
3 The supermarket is opposite the library. The chemist is near / next to the supermarket.
4 The restaurant is between the bank and the newsagent.

b He wants to go to the chemist and the bookshop.

c 1 there is 2 down East Street
3 right 4 on the corner

8 1 I have no idea 2 actually 3 Really?
4 Wait a minute.

10 **a** 2 supermarket 3 Dixon's 4 Cycletech
5 bookshop

b 2 No, there aren't. 3 Yes, they do.
4 No, there isn't. 5 No, they don't.
6 No, she isn't. 7 Yes, there are.
8 Yes, there is.

11 Students' own answers.

Unit check

1 1 are 2 between 3 newsagent 4 train
5 opposite 6 takes 7 aren't 8 there's
9 market

② 2 c 3 c 4 a 5 c 6 b 7 b 8 b 9 a

③ 2 shopping centre 3 car park 4 department store 5 primary school 6 leisure centre 7 police station 8 secondary school

5 They've got brown eyes

① 2 brown 3 She hasn't got 4 likes 5 forest 6 stupid

② **a** 2 d 3 b 4 a

b 2 have got 3 's got 4 've got 5 've got 6 's got 7 's got 8 have got

c 2 Tom hasn't got a mobile phone.
3 Jessie and Tom haven't got a big family.
4 Tom's got a CD player.
5 Jessie's got brown hair.
6 Jessie and Tom have got brown eyes.
7 Tom hasn't got a computer.
8 Jessie's got a computer.

d 2 Has, got; Yes, he has.
3 Have, got; No, I haven't.
4 Has, got; No, she hasn't.
5 Have, got; Yes, they have.
6 Has, got; No, he hasn't.

e *Example answers*
2 I've got long fingers.
3 My sister's got a nice smile.
4 My parents haven't got an old car.

③ **a** 1 ear 2 eye 3 face 4 hair 5 mouth 6 nose 8 hand 9 finger 10 thumb 11 leg 12 foot

b 2 cheek 3 eyelash 4 earlobe 5 lips

c 2 eyes 3 nose 4 smile 5 good-looking 6 green 7 wavy

d 2 a 3 f 4 c 5 g 6 e 7 b

e ▶ CD3 T17 TAPESCRIPT
Now, I just need to get some details from you. What's your first name?
Right, and your surname?
Ah ... how do you spell that, please?
Thanks. Now, how old are you?
And what's your address?
Sorry, can you repeat that, please?
OK, fine. And what's your phone number?
And your mobile number?
Right, that's it, then. We'll send you your membership card in the next day or two.

④ ▶ CD3 T18 TAPESCRIPT
1 They've got wavy hair.
2 We've got twelve TVs.
3 Steve lives near the river.
4 He gives five interviews every day.
5 Vivien drives to the university.

⑤ 2 cat 3 budgie 4 hamster 5 guinea pig 6 rabbit 7 snake 8 spider 9 lizard

⑥ **b** Adjectives for hair: curly, straight, dark, fair
Other adjectives: interesting, boring, cheap, expensive, intelligent, stupid

⑦ ▶ CD3 T19 TAPESCRIPT
Sarah: Who's this? In the photo?
Joe: What photo? Oh – that's my sister's new boyfriend.
Sarah: Oh yeah? What's his name?
Joe: Gilles.
Sarah: What was that?
Joe: Gilles – G-I-double L-E-S. He's Swiss, but his family lives over here now.
Sarah: Swiss, right. So he speaks German.
Joe: No, he doesn't – he speaks French. He comes from Geneva. They speak French in that part of Switzerland.
Sarah: How old is he?
Joe: He's 21.
Sarah: He's got nice eyes. Are they green? It's a small photo.
Joe: No, they're blue. Look – you can see.
Sarah: Oh yeah, they're blue. He's quite good-looking, isn't he?
Joe: Oh, he's all right, I guess. Nothing special.
Sarah: Yes, he is! He's got really nice fair hair.
Joe: Yeah, well my sister thinks he's fantastic. She never stops talking about ...

2 Swiss 4 French 5 21 6 blue 7 fair

⑧ **a** Picture 3

b 2 No, he hasn't. He's got short black hair.
3 No, they aren't. They're from Hong Kong.
4 Yes, she has. She works in a restaurant.
5 No, she doesn't. She works in a library.
6 No, he doesn't. He studies Computer Science.

Unit check

① 1 isn't 2 he's 3 wavy 4 clothes 5 good-looking 6 haven't 7 fair 8 eyes 9 wears

② 2 a 3 c 4 b 5 b 6 a 7 b 8 b 9 c

3 2 wrist 3 cheek 4 lips 5 earlobe 6 neck
7 elbow 8 eyebrow 9 back

6 This is delicious!

1 2 mice D 3 sushi E 4 chicken A 5 snake F
6 dragonfly C

2 **a** ▶ CD3 T20 TAPESCRIPT/ANSWERS
1 beef C 2 tomatoes J 3 eggs M
4 chicken H 5 onions B 6 bananas A
7 cheese N 8 apples K 9 rice G 10 salt I
11 strawberries F 12 bread E 13 oranges L
14 sugar D

b Fruit: apples, strawberries, tomatoes
Vegetables: potatoes
Meat: beef, chicken
Groceries: salt, eggs, cheese, bread, rice

c 2 cereal 3 steak 4 yoghurt 5 cheese

3 **a** Countable: onion, carrot, apple
Uncountable: cheese, salt, sugar

b 2 C, U 3 U, C 4 U, C 5 C, U 6 C, U

c 2 some 3 an 4 a; some 5 some; some
6 a; a 7 some; an

d 2 some chips 3 an egg 4 some tomatoes
5 some honey 6 some bread
7 an ice cream 8 some water

e 2 these 3 This 4 Those 5 This 6 that

f 2 I'd like 3 Would you like 4 I'd like
5 Would you like

g 2 Yes, I'd like roast chicken, please.
3 Would you like vegetables or salad?
4 I'd like vegetables, please.
5 What would you like to drink?
6 Orange juice, please.
7 Would you like anything else?
8 No thank you.

4 **a** ▶ CD3 T21 TAPESCRIPT
1 The Swiss waiter's got wavy hair.
2 We want some white wine.
3 William's got a wonderful dishwasher.
4 Would you like some water with your
sandwich?

b ▶ CD3 T22 TAPESCRIPT/ANSWERS
1 Which answer is correct?
2 What's wrong with you?
3 Who's the winner?
4 Where does Wendy write letters?

5 1 Oh right 2 Yes please 3 Don't worry
4 No thanks.

6 **b** a/an: potato, lettuce, mushroom
some: water, meat, mayonnaise

7 **a** ▶ CD3 T23 TAPESCRIPT
Martin: Mum. I'm hungry. Can I have a
sandwich?
Mum: OK. What do you want? Chicken?
There's some nice chicken here.
Martin: No, not chicken. Are there any other
things?
Mum: Well, let's see ...
Martin: What about some roast beef?
Mum: No, sorry. I used the beef for your
father's lunch.
Martin: Oh, OK.
Mum: We've got some cheese here. You can
have a cheese sandwich.
Martin: Yeah, right. A cheese and salad
sandwich – that sounds good.
Mum: Cheese and salad? No, sorry, that's a
problem. We haven't got a lettuce. How
about ... cheese and tomato?
Martin: Yeah, OK. And some mayonnaise?
Mum: Yes, that's not a problem. So – a cheese
and tomato sandwich with mayonnaise, right?
Martin: That's great. But don't worry, Mum –
I can make it myself.

2 ✗ 3 ✓ 4 ✗ 5 ✓ 6 ✓

b A cheese and tomato sandwich with
mayonnaise.

8 Students' own answers.

Unit check

1 1 meal 2 meat 3 vegetables 4 fruit
5 dessert 6 have 7 sandwiches
8 an 9 some

2 2 a 3 b 4 b 5 c 6 a 7 a 8 b 9 c

3 2 salt
3 cereal
4 Chocolate
5 yoghurt
6 beans
7 Garlic
8 olive oil
9 salt

7 I sometimes watch TV

1 2 on an island 3 at home 4 teaches Calvin
5 Java 6 100 other children 7 doesn't like
8 haven't got

2 a Weekdays: Tuesday, Wednesday, Thursday, Friday
Weekend: Saturday, Sunday

b 2 On Thursday.   3 On Monday.
4 On Sunday.   5 On Tuesday.
6 On Wednesday.   7 On Saturday.

c *Example answers*
1 I play tennis with my friend on Monday.
2 I have a guitar lesson on Wednesday.
3 I go shopping with my parents on Saturday.
4 I do my homework on Sunday.

3 a 1 always   2 often   3 usually   4 sometimes
5 hardly ever

b 2 Robert often plays football with his friends.
3 Tony and Philip never take the school bus.
4 Beth hardly ever listens to classical music.
5 We always have pizza on Friday.
6 The music is usually fantastic on this programme.
7 My parents sometimes help me with my homework.

c *Example answers*
2 I sometimes have a burger at lunchtime.
3 I never go to bed before ten o'clock.
4 I usually listen to the radio in bed.
5 I hardly ever watch TV before school.

d 2 He plays football twice a week / at the weekend.
3 He writes letters once a week / on Sunday.
4 He walks to school five times a week.

e 2 Julie buys a newspaper seven times a week / every day.
3 Danny goes to the supermarket twice a week.
4 Denise goes to the cinema twice a month.
5 Greg goes to Paris / France once a year.

4 a soap opera, chat show, comedy, cartoon, game show, documentary, sports programme

b 2 sports programme   3 news   4 cartoon
5 soap opera   6 comedy   7 game show
8 documentary

5 a & b ▶ CD3 T24   TAPESCRIPT/ANSWERS
1 'breakfast   2 'weekday   3 'lunchtime
4 'homework   5 'strawberry   6 'newspaper
7 'dragonfly   8 'girlfriend

6 a 2 It's six fifteen. f   3 It's six fifty. e
4 It's seven ten. c   5 It's seven forty-five. d
6 It's seven thirty-five. a

b ▶ CD3 T25   TAPESCRIPT
1 What's the time? Er ... it's five to twelve.
2 Oh, look at the time! It's half past eight!
3 What time does the bus arrive? At ten past five.

4 School finishes at quarter to four.
5 Come on! The concert begins at nine o'clock.
6 When does the train leave? At twenty-five to eleven.

2 8.30   3 5.10   4 3.45   5 9.00   6 10.35

7 2 every day   3 always   4 also   5 sometimes
6 never   7 hardly ever

8 b Nouns: sandwiches, coffee, clothes
Verbs: buys, has, makes
Adjectives: black, delicious, expensive
Adverbs: never, sometimes, always

c *Example answers*
Jill never watches boring programmes.
Jack usually enjoys delicious pizzas.
Rosa always drives new cars.

9 a 1 Television in a British family

b 2 No, he doesn't.
3 Jamie likes cartoons and comedies.
4 Yes, he does.
5 Kim's favourite programmes are soaps.
6 She watches films at the weekend.
7 They watch football matches together.

10 a ▶ CD3 T26   TAPESCRIPT

Boy: Excuse me. Can I ask you some questions about TV?

Woman: Er ... oh yes, OK.

Boy: How often do you watch TV?

Woman: Not very often.

Boy: For example – twice a week? Three times a week?

Woman: Erm ... I think four times a week, usually. Yes. I hardly ever watch TV at the weekend.

Boy: OK. Thanks. And, what do you watch – what kinds of programmes?

Woman: Well, I usually watch comedies. And documentaries. I sometimes look at documentaries about animals and science.

Boy: Fine. OK. And what about soaps?

Woman: No, never! They're terrible!

Boy: Uh huh. And the news?

Woman: No, I hardly ever watch the news. I read a newspaper.

Boy: OK – thank you very much.

Woman: You're welcome.

She usually watches television four times a week.

b documentaries: sometimes
soaps: never
the news: hardly ever

Unit check

1 1 at 2 usually 3 on 4 comes 5 soap
6 days 7 news 8 do 9 every

2 2 b 3 a 4 b 5 b 6 a 7 c 8 b 9 c

3 2 game show
3 news
4 documentaries
5 twenty-five to ten
6 Saturday
7 Monday
8 comedy
9 cartoons

8 Don't do that!

1 ▶ CD3 T27 TAPESCRIPT

Steve: This film's awful. I'm bored. Really bored.

Julie: Me too. And I'm confused – I mean, I don't understand the story. What's that?

Steve: What?

Julie: That noise. What is it?

Steve: Hmm. I don't know. Stay here.

Julie: Don't go outside! I'm scared.

Steve: Don't worry, Julie. Everything's OK.

Julie: Steve? Where are you? Come back!

Julie: Help!

Steve: It's me!

Julie: Oh Steve – you idiot! Don't do that!

Steve: Sorry, Julie. It's just a joke.

Julie: Oh Steve. Sometimes you're really, really stupid.

2 confused 3 here 4 scared 5 worry
6 back 7 idiot 8 stupid

2 **a** 1 cry 2 laugh 3 shout 4 be

b 1 Write 2 Don't eat 3 Don't sit 4 Go
5 Talk 6 Listen 7 Ask 8 Don't tell

c 2 Don't open the window.
3 Look at the kangaroos.
4 Don't switch on the TV.
5 Don't talk in the library.
6 Go to bed.

3 ▶ CD3 T28 TAPESCRIPT/ANSWERS
1 I don't know why she isn't here.
2 Don't leave now.
3 Stop the music. I don't like it.
4 Please don't ask a lot of questions.
5 I don't understand why he's so angry.
6 Don't eat all the chocolate!
7 Don't open the box.
8 I don't think it's a good idea.

4 **a** 1 scared 2 worried 3 angry 5 happy
6 confused 7 sad 8 bored

b 2 bored 3 happy 4 confused
5 excited 6 worried 7 sad 8 angry

c ▶ CD3 T29 TAPESCRIPT
1 **George:** Sunday! It's terrible. I've got nothing to do, and it's raining and I can't go out. I don't think there's anything on TV at the moment, is there? Let me have a look ...
2 **Hazel:** Oh, that's wonderful! Oh, I can't believe it – that's fantastic! A trip to New York! I'm going to New York! What a fantastic prize!
3 **Carl:** No, no, hang on a minute. That can't be right. Three hundred and sixty-two, multiplied by thirty-three, and then ... No, that's not right. Um ... three hundred, plus sixty-two, <u>divided</u> by thirty-three ... Oh, this work is really hard! I'm going to stop and try again tomorrow.
4 **Fiona:** John, it's half past eleven and Maria isn't home yet. It isn't like her. She's usually home by 10.30. And she hasn't got her mobile with her so I can't ring her ...
5 **Mark:** Grrrr, this is awful! This stupid computer! What's wrong with it? It's so slow! Oh, come on, you stupid thing – this is driving me crazy!

2 Hazel is excited because she's the winner of a trip to the USA.
3 Carl is confused because the homework is difficult.
4 Fiona is worried because it's late and her daughter isn't home.
5 Mark is angry because there's a problem with the computer.

d 1 boring 2 worried 3 confusing 4 excited

e 2 relaxed 3 sleepy 4 upset 5 amused
6 frightened

5 1 I think 2 What's wrong 3 anyway
4 the thing is

6 *Example answers*
I feel scared in the dark.
I feel worried about the test tomorrow.
I feel happy when I see you.

7 2 F 3 F 4 F 5 T 6 T 7 F

8 Students' own answers.

Unit check

1 1 happy 2 fine 3 matter 4 angry 5 boyfriend
6 listen 7 don't 8 help 9 worried

2 2 a 3 c 4 b 5 c 6 b 7 c 8 a 9 c

3 2 excited 3 happy 4 scared 5 bored
6 sleepy 7 excited 8 angry 9 bored

9 ▸ Yes, I can

1 2 uses 3 take part 4 pushes 5 swim
6 pulls 7 ride 8 sits

2 **a** 2 He can't swim.
   3 They can play tennis.
   4 He can't dance.
   5 She can read.
   6 He can't ride a bike.

b 2 Can you swim? Yes, I can. / No, I can't.
   3 Can you play tennis? Yes, I can. / No, I can't.
   4 Can you dance? Yes, I can. / No, I can't.
   5 Can you read? Yes, I can. / No, I can't.
   6 Can you ride a bike? Yes, I can. / No, I can't.

c 2 can; can't 3 can 4 can't 5 Can; No; can't
   6 Can; can; can't

d *Example answers*
   1 I can't juggle, but I can walk on my hands.
   2 I can ride a bike, but I can't drive a car.
   3 My parents can send an email, but they
     can't send a text message.
   4 My best friend can sing, but he/she can't
     dance.
   5 A chimpanzee can't speak, but it can climb
     trees.
   6 Young children can go to school, but they
     can't go to work.

3 **a** ▶ CD3 T30 TAPESCRIPT/ANSWERS
   1 Can you <u>read</u>? <u>Yes</u>, I <u>can</u>.
   2 Can they <u>write</u>? Yes, they <u>can</u>.
   3 Can she <u>play</u> the <u>guitar</u>? <u>Yes</u>, she <u>can</u>.

b No. 'Can' is stressed in the answers, but
   unstressed in the questions.

c ▶ CD3 T31 TAPESCRIPT/ANSWERS
   1 I can <u>dance</u>, but I <u>can't sing</u>.
   2 He can <u>read</u>, but <u>he can't write</u>.
   3 Can she <u>play</u> the <u>piano</u>?
   4 Can you <u>do Sudoku puzzles</u>?

4 **a** 2 snowboard 3 play tennis 4 ride a horse
   5 rollerblades 6 swim 7 play basketball
   8 ski

b go: swimming, snowboarding
   play: basketball, volleyball, football
   do: gymnastics

c 2 score 3 draw 4 lose 5 win
   6 champions

5 **a** 2 Kevin likes playing tennis. He loves playing
     volleyball, but he doesn't like horse-riding.

He hates doing gymnastics.
   3 Brian and Louise like reading. They love
     playing computer games, but they don't like
     playing the guitar. They hate dancing.

b *Example answers*
   1 I like cycling. I love going to the cinema, but
     I don't like watching TV. I hate singing.
   2 My best friend likes dancing. She loves
     sending emails, but she doesn't like writing
     letters. She hates doing homework.
   3 My mum likes listening to music. She loves
     playing tennis, but she doesn't like watching
     tennis on TV. She hates walking the dog.
   4 My brother likes playing the trumpet. He
     loves going to concerts, but he doesn't like
     visiting his grandparents. He hates getting
     up in the morning.

6 **a** 2A 3E 4B 5D 6C

b Julia: netball, orienteering
   Craig: rugby, cricket, rowing

7 **a** /æ/: camel, gymnastics, fantastic
   /ɑː/: part, grass, laugh
   /eɪ/: rollerblade, strange, late

b *Example answers*
   /ɪ/: miss, cr<u>i</u>cket, w<u>i</u>n, w<u>i</u>nter
   /iː/: f<u>ee</u>l, l<u>ea</u>ve, n<u>ee</u>d, sl<u>ee</u>p
   /ɒ/: hang <u>o</u>n, h<u>o</u>liday, h<u>o</u>ckey, <u>o</u>xygen
   /əʊ/: g<u>o</u>, r<u>o</u>llerblading, sn<u>o</u>wboarding, b<u>oa</u>t

8 ▶ CD3 T32 TAPESCRIPT
   1 Tom never plays football – he doesn't like
     playing team games. But he sometimes runs in
     the morning and he likes doing gymnastics.
   2 A: Can Cristina ride a bike?
     B: Yes, she's really good at cycling. But she can't
        ride a horse, and I don't think she can rollerblade.
   3 A: What do you do in the winter, Matt?
     B: Well, I don't like snowboarding, but I often go
        skiing.
     A: What about football?
     B: No, I think football's boring.
   4 A: Pete, can you sing?
     B: Me? Oh, I'm a terrible singer! I love music,
        though. I can play the guitar and I'd like to
        learn the violin.

   2 A 3 B 4 B

9 **a** ▶ CD3 T33 TAPESCRIPT
   Interviewer: Today in the studio we're talking
   to Mark Cavalcanti. Mark is only 17 but he's
   already a star in British tennis. Mark, good
   morning.

   Mark: Good morning.

   Interviewer: Now Mark, your family name's
   interesting – Cavalcanti.

Mark: That's right. My grandfather's Italian.

Interviewer: So can you speak Italian?

Mark: I can understand some things but no, I can't speak it really. My parents grew up here in Britain so I'm British and we only talk in English at home.

Interviewer: And is tennis the only sport in your life?

Mark: No, not at all. I love swimming, and it's great exercise.

Interviewer: Are you a good swimmer?

Mark: Well, I'm OK. I like basketball too. I sometimes play in a local team. But my first love is tennis.

Interviewer: Are there any other tennis players in your family?

Mark: No, not really. My mother Helen loves watching sport, but she doesn't do any sport herself. And then there's Anna, my sister – she's 13 and she's really good at running. She wins all her races at school.

Interviewer: Great! But now let's talk about your tennis. There's a big match coming up in Australia ...

1 17   2 English   3 British   4 tennis
5 swimming   6 basketball   7 sister
8 watching sport   9 running

b Students' own answers.

Unit check

1 1 hockey   2 team   3 swim   4 races   5 free
6 can   7 loves   8 guitar   9 doesn't

2 2 a   3 b   4 c   5 c   6 a   7 a   8 a   9 b

3 2 go   3 swimming   4 play   5 score   6 do
7 draw   8 come   9 cycling

10 A bad storm's coming

1 2 once   3 the world   4 South Africa
5 dolphins   6 a storm is coming

2 **a** playing, doing, eating
writing, using, having
swimming, shopping, running

b 2 She's shopping   3 They're watching
4 I'm writing   5 They're sitting
6 We're doing   7 She's having

c 2 Alice isn't eating fish. She's eating chicken.
3 Dorothy isn't talking to George. She's sleeping.
4 Maria and Bill aren't listening to music. They're watching TV.

5 Pat isn't dancing. She's playing cards with Anne.
6 Wendy and Lisa aren't playing the guitar. They're singing.

d 2 Are you watching the news? No, I'm not.
3 Is Helen doing her homework? Yes, she is.
4 Are Ken and Neil playing tennis? No, they aren't.
5 Is Joe using the computer? No, he isn't.

e *Example answers*
1 I'm sitting in the classroom.
2 I'm studying English.
3 I'm using this book.
4 No, I'm sitting with my friend.
5 Yes, I'm wearing glasses.
6 My friends are listening to the teacher. Our teacher is talking to us.

f 2 I read; I'm reading
3 they're playing; They play
4 She's visiting; She often stays
5 He catches; isn't working

3 ▶ **CD3 T34** TAPESCRIPT
1 Harry's hobby is horse-riding.
2 I'm hardly ever hungry at home.
3 He's unhappy about his hair.
4 How often does Helen help you?
5 Hanna's having a hamburger at the Hilton Hotel.

4 **a** Across: 3 armchair   6 window   7 bed
8 door   9 table

Down: 1 sofa   2 fridge   4 cooker
5 toilet   7 bath

b 2 bathroom   3 bedroom   4 kitchen   5 hall

c 2 a   3 e   4 f   5 d   6 b   7 h   8 c

d ▶ **CD3 T35** TAPESCRIPT

I've got a bed and a desk in my room. There's a small table next to the bed. The desk is under the window and I've got my computer on the desk. There's a small armchair in the corner of the room. On the wall between the desk and the armchair I've got three pictures of my favourite pop stars. The door is near the armchair.

1 next to   2 under   3 on   4 between
5 near

5 1 lots of   2 all right   3 Why don't you
4 a bit of

6 Students' own answers.

7 **a** Sue: 2 ✗   3 ✓   4 ✗   5 ✓

b ▶ **CD3 T36** TAPESCRIPT
Dad: Hello.
Emma: Hi Dad. It's Emma.

Dad: Emma! Hello, love. Where are you?

Emma: We're in Empoli right now. We're staying in a beautiful hotel here – it's a really nice place.

Dad: So you're having a good time?

Emma: Oh yeah. And I'm speaking a lot of Italian now. It's great when people understand me – I'm feeling good about saying things in Italian now.

Dad: That's excellent. And is the food nice?

Emma: Fantastic! We all love the food here, and it's not only pizza. We're having great meals.

Dad: And what about the weather? Is it still raining? It's sunny here in England.

Emma: Oh, well it's still raining here and it's cold. But that's OK. We're still having a good time. Listen, Dad, I must go now. Some other people want to use the phone.

Dad: OK, love. But ring again on Friday, all right?

Emma: Yes, I will. Is everyone OK at home?

Dad: Yes, we're fine.

Emma: Well, give them my love. Bye, Dad.

Dad: Bye.

2 ✓ 3 ✓ 4 ✗ 5 ✓

(8) Students' own answers.

Unit check

(1) 1 bedroom 2 finishing 3 is 4 are
5 living 6 reading 7 in 8 aren't 9 they're

(2) 2 c 3 a 4 b 5 c 6 c 7 c 8 a 9 b

(3) 2 garden 3 fridge 4 garage 5 window
6 hall 7 garage 8 shelf 9 hanger

11 Special days

(1) 2 dinner 3 holiday 4 celebrate 5 bread
6 skirt 7 blouses 8 dancing

(2) **[a]** 2 December 3 April 4 October 5 June
6 May 7 February 8 November
9 March 10 September

[b] January; July

[c] Students' own answers.

[d] In the northern hemisphere: 1 winter
2 spring 3 summer 4 autumn

[e] *Example answers*
In spring I clean my bedroom and I sometimes paint it.
In summer I love swimming in the sea.
In autumn I have new teachers at school.

(3) 2 at 3 at 4 in 5 on 6 on 7 in
8 in 9 in

(4) **[a]** 2 scarf 3 jeans 4 shirt 5 jumper
6 trousers 7 T-shirt 8 socks 9 trainers
10 jacket 11 dress 12 shoes

[b] *Example answers*
1 I usually wear trousers and a jumper.
2 My favourite clothes are jeans and T-shirts.
3 I hate wearing a winter coat.
4 My best friend usually wears jeans.
5 I buy my clothes in a shop in town.

[c] 2 vest 3 wool 4 shorts 5 suit

(5) **[a]** ▶ CD3 T37 TAPESCRIPT
1 sad   said
2 bad   bed
3 man   men
4 dad   dead
5 sat   set

[b] ▶ CD3 T38 TAPESCRIPT/ANSWERS
1 I'm **sad**.
2 You aren't in **bed**!
3 Look at the **man**.
4 Is it **dead**?
5 They **sat** together.

[c] ▶ CD3 T39 TAPESCRIPT
1 Annie is Alan's best friend.
2 I'm helping Joanna in December and January.
3 Emma's jacket is black and yellow.
4 How many magazines is Danny sending?

(6) **[a]** 2 Can I borrow your dictionary?; I'm using it.
3 Can I come round to your place?; We've got visitors.
4 Can I see your homework?; Here you are.
5 Can I wear your sunglasses?; They're really expensive.
6 Can I talk to you?; What's the problem?

[b] 2 one 3 one 4 one 5 ones; ones
6 ones; ones

(7) 2 d 3 a 4 e 5 f 6 c

(8) **[a]** 1, 2, 3, 4 and 7

[b] Friday, Dave, Japanese, August, Tuesday, April

(9) ▶ CD3 T40 TAPESCRIPT

Assistant: Can I help you?

Nadia: Yes, I'm interested in a dress in the window.

Assistant: Yes – which one are you looking at?

Nadia: It's over there behind the shirts – next to that black jumper.

Assistant: Oh, yes, the green one. That's a lovely dress.

Nadia: How much is it?

Assistant: It's ... £49.

Nadia: Oh, OK. Can I try it on, please?

Assistant: I'm afraid we haven't got many sizes in that dress. Only ten or sixteen. What size are you?

Nadia: Twelve.

Assistant: No, sorry, we haven't got a twelve. Is there anything else I can show you?

Nadia: Well actually, those tops are nice. The pink one would look nice with my new trousers.

Assistant: Yes, or you can wear it with jeans or a skirt.

Nadia: OK, can I try it on, please?

Assistant: Yes, of course. The changing room's over there ...

2 c 3 c 4 b 5 a

10 2 black 3 white 4 red 5 black 6 black
7 grey / dark blue

Unit check

1 1 clothes 2 costume 3 trousers 4 huge
5 in 6 festival 7 parade 8 at 9 enjoy

2 2 c 3 a 4 b 5 b 6 c 7 a 8 b 9 c

3 2 boots 3 jacket 4 scarf 5 belt 6 sandals
7 shirt 8 top 9 socks

12 He was only 22

1 2 e 3 a 4 f 5 d 6 b

2 **a** 2 was 3 was 4 were 5 were 6 were
7 was 8 was 9 were 10 was 11 were
12 were

b 2 No, she wasn't. She was a film star.
3 No, they weren't. They were very sad when she died.
4 No, they weren't. They were comedies.
5 No, it wasn't. It was Stan.
6 No, they weren't. They were in black and white.

c 2 Were Jane and Diana in the park at 2.30? Yes, they were.
3 Was Julia in her bedroom at 9 o'clock? Yes, she was.
4 Were Paul and Carol in the supermarket at 10.15? No, they weren't.
5 Was Anna in the bookshop at 5.30? No, she wasn't.
6 Was Matt in the kitchen at 1 o'clock? Yes, he was.

3 **a** 2 last 3 last 4 yesterday 5 last
6 yesterday

b *Example answers*
1 I was in the bathroom at 8.15 yesterday morning.
2 I was at my friend's house at 5 pm last Friday.
3 Yes, I was.
4 No, we weren't at school because yesterday was Sunday.
5 No, I was at my friend's place last weekend.
6 My birthday was on (Monday) last year.

4 ▶ **CD3 T41** TAPESCRIPT

Alan: What kind of music do you like, Gran?

Gran: Well, my favourite group were the Beatles.

Alan: Oh right. Were they from London?

Gran: No they weren't! They were from Liverpool. Oh, they were fantastic, just wonderful.

Alan: How many of them were there – in the Beatles, I mean?

Gran: There were four of them – John Lennon, Paul McCartney, George Harrison and Ringo Starr. They were very young – and I was very young too! John was my favourite, but they were all great. All the girls in my school were crazy about them!

Alan: Right! Are their songs still on the radio?

Gran: Yes, they are. That song *Yesterday*, for example – that's a really famous Beatles song, they play that on the radio a lot.

2 Were 3 weren't 4 were 5 were
6 were 7 were 8 were 9 was 10 was
11 were 12 were

5 **a** ▶ **CD3 T42** TAPESCRIPT/ANSWERS
1 Were they in <u>London</u>? <u>Yes</u>, they <u>were</u>.
2 Were they <u>happy</u>? <u>No</u>, they <u>weren't</u>.
3 Were the <u>girls</u> at <u>home</u>? <u>Yes</u>, they <u>were</u>.
4 Was he an <u>actor</u>? <u>Yes</u>, he <u>was</u>.
5 Was she <u>worried</u>? <u>No</u>, she <u>wasn't</u>.
6 Was <u>Dave</u> at <u>school</u>? <u>No</u>, he <u>wasn't</u>.

b ▶ **CD3 T43** TAPESCRIPT/ANSWERS
1 <u>Helen</u> was in <u>hospital</u> on <u>Wednesday</u>.
2 Our <u>parents</u> were at the <u>library</u> <u>yesterday</u>.
3 <u>When</u> were you in <u>Paris</u>?
4 <u>What</u> was your <u>address</u>?

6 **a** 12th, twelfth
2, two, 2nd
15, fifteen, 15th
three, 3rd, third
one, 1st, first
fifty, fiftieth
22nd, twenty-second
thirty-one, 31st, thirty-first

b *Possible answers*
2 September 3 Friday 4 Sunday 5 Maths

c 2 Our national holiday is on the third of July.
3 Christmas Day is on the twenty-fifth of December.
4 New Year's Day is on the first of January.
5 The festival is on the ninth of October.
6 My party was on the thirtieth of August last year.

7 1 suddenly 2 you know 3 my fault
4 Poor you!

9 ▶ CD3 T44 TAPESCRIPT
1 the eleventh of December, two thousand and four
2 the twenty-fifth of November, nineteen eighty
3 the thirtieth of July, nineteen ninety-five
4 the thirteenth of September, nineteen fifty-nine
5 the thirty-first of August, nineteen ninety-nine
6 the third of March, two thousand and one

2 b 3 d 4 f 5 c 6 a

10 2 London. 3 In 1910. 4 In his first Hollywood film. 5 Because there were no words or music.
6 In 1920. 7 *Modern Times*. 8 In Switzerland.

Unit check

1 1 first 2 were 3 was 4 wasn't 5 way
6 afternoon 7 recording 8 weren't 9 fifth

2 2 b 3 a 4 c 5 b 6 a 7 b 8 c 9 b

3 2 third 3 morning 4 seventh 5 August
6 afternoon 7 **January** 8 night 9 twentieth

13 What happened?

1 1 tired 2 little 3 white 4 black
5 white 6 angry

2 **a** 2 changed 3 hated 4 studied 5 died
6 stopped 7 walked 8 started

b 2 stopped 3 worked 4 studied 5 walked
6 died

3 **a** ▶ CD3 T45 TAPESCRIPT
liked, travelled, called, watched
hated, started, landed, wanted

/t/ or /d/ travelled, called, watched
/ɪd/ started, landed, wanted

b ▶ CD3 T46 TAPESCRIPT
1 They visited a museum.
2 They landed on the moon.
3 The concert ended at 11 o'clock.
4 We waited at the station.

c ▶ CD3 T47 TAPESCRIPT/ANSWERS
1 We watched a film.

2 He lived in Barcelona. /d/
3 We helped Annie with her homework. /t/
4 They laughed at me. /t/
5 Sally stayed in a hotel. /d/
6 We opened our books. /d/

4 **a** Across: 3 became 4 ate 5 knew 7 saw
9 ran 11 thought 13 gave 14 took

Down: 2 found 3 began 6 wrote
8 went 10 had 12 got

b 2 took 3 went 4 got 5 chatted
6 had / ate

5 **a** 2 didn't play tennis. They played cards.
3 worked as a doctor. He didn't work as a waiter.
4 didn't phone my mum. I phoned my dad.
5 didn't dance. We watched TV.
6 parked near the library. She didn't park near the cinema.

b 2 went 3 saw 3 did; begin 4 did; go
5 Did; have 6 Did; sit 7 sat 8 did; have
9 had 10 did; get

6 **a** 2 go to 3 plays 4 have 5 having
6 going to

b make: a noise
do: a puzzle, housework
have: an accident, fun
take: a break, a photograph

7 2 e 3 a 4 f 5 d 6 b

8 **a** + -ed: answered, played
+ -d: danced, practised
y + -ied: married, cried
double letter: stopped, travelled

b /t/: asked, watched, looked
/d/: travelled, enjoyed, died
/ɪd/: hated, wanted, ended

9 ▶ CD3 T48 TAPESCRIPT

Sandro: Hello

Tony: Sandro, hi. It's Tony. I'm ringing from Cambridge.

Sandro: Tony, hi! How are you?

Tony: Fine! We arrived in London on Monday. The plane landed at 5.15 in the morning.

Sandro: Oh dear!

Tony: Yeah, really early. So we were in the city by 7.30. And we stayed in London for two nights.

Sandro: Where? In a hotel?

Tony: Yes, we were in a hotel for the first night. And then on Tuesday we stayed at my uncle's place.

Sandro: So what was London like? What did you do?

Tony: Well, we spent a lot of time at my uncle's

house – talking, you know. But we went all round the city in a tourist bus – that was really good. And we went for a boat trip on the river. Dad wanted to visit the British Museum too, but we didn't have time for that.

Sandro: So when did you leave for Cambridge?

Tony: On Wednesday. We got the early evening train and now we're staying with my cousins. They've got a great house here. Anyway, Sandro – how are things? How's Carla? I tried to ring her yesterday but …

2 B   3 C   4 C   5 B

10 Students' own answers.

Unit check

1 1 on   2 in   3 studied   4 nurse   5 hospital
6 stopped   7 didn't   8 were   9 died

2 2 a   3 c   4 a   5 c   6 b   7 c   8 a   9 b

3 2 c   3 b   4 a   5 c   6 c   7 a   8 a   9 b

14 Things change

1 [a] 2 c   3 f   4 a   5 d   6 b

[b] young, old; crowded, empty; different, the same; fast, slow; difficult, easy; happy, sad

2 [a] 2 hotter   3 happier   4 more difficult
5 unhappier   6 more expensive   7 better
8 hungrier   9 more mysterious   10 worse

[b] 2 A   3 A   4 B   5 B   6 Students' own answer.

[c] 2 taller   3 bigger   4 better   5 worse
6 more interesting

[d] 2 The dress is more expensive than the shirt.
3 The book is more interesting than the newspaper.
4 The city is busier than the village.
5 Marian's car is faster than Jack's.
6 The MP3 player is better than the CDs.

[e] *Example answers*
1 My best friend is taller than me.
2 My street is quieter than my friend's street.
3 My town is better than my grandmother's town.
4 School days are more boring than weekends.
5 Comedy programmes are funnier than news programmes.
6 History is more interesting than English.

3 ▶ CD3 T50   TAPESCRIPT/ANSWERS
1 She's underlined{younger} than him.

2 You're underlined{happier} than me.
3 The underlined{bank} is underlined{older} than the underlined{bookshop}.
4 underlined{Maths} is more underlined{difficult} than underlined{Science}.
5 The underlined{book} was more underlined{interesting} than the underlined{film}.
6 The underlined{shoes} were more underlined{expensive} than the underlined{trainers}.

4 [a] 2 g   3 d   4 h   5 e   6 c   7 a   8 b

[b] 2 safe   3 old-fashioned   4 modern
5 dangerous   6 noisy

[c] 2 unfriendly   3 clean   4 untidy
5 uncomfortable   6 heavy   7 light   8 dark

5 1 sort of   2 You see   3 What's the matter
4 I don't believe it

7 ▶ CD3 T51   TAPESCRIPT

I took this photo of my family last summer. My two brothers are on the left – Frank and Tim. Frank's the one with the curlier hair and he's a bit shorter than Tim.

That's my sister Anne on the other side – she's standing next to her friend Lisa. You can see they're both tall and they've got the same hair style. Lisa always wears more expensive clothes than Anne, but I think Anne always looks happier.

Then there's Dad here – he's playing cards with Uncle Bill. Dad's younger than Uncle Bill but he looks older and he's a bit fatter. And you can see he's winning the game because he's a better card player.

So that's everyone. Oh, there are the cats too. The big one's called Sandy. She's a bit boring – she just sleeps most of the time. The little one with Uncle Bill is friendlier and more interesting – he's called Pablo.

2 Tim   3 Lisa   4 Anne   5 Sandy   6 Uncle Bill
7 Dad   8 Pablo

8 *Example answer*
Alan's TV is more modern than Peggy's. His window is smaller and the street outside his room is busier and noisier. Peggy's chairs are older but more comfortable than Alan's. Outside her room, she's got a lovely garden and it is quieter. Her window is bigger.

Unit check

1 1 town   2 was   3 busier   4 more   5 crowded
6 old-fashioned   7 difficult   8 modern
9 easier

2 2 c   3 b   4 a   5 a   6 c   7 b   8 b   9 c

3 2 exciting   3 difficult   4 old-fashioned
5 quiet   6 light   7 dirty   8 heavy   9 dark

1 Saying *hello* and *goodbye*

Name ....

Class .... Date ....

Complete the dialogue with the words in the box.

~~My~~ this Hi I'm fine How

Simon: Hi. ⁰ .... *My* .... name's Simon.

John: Hello, Simon. ¹ .... John.

Simon: ² .... are you?

John: I'm ³ .... thanks. Simon, ⁴ .... is Mary.

Mary: ⁵ .... Simon.

Simon: Hello, Mary.

5

2 Countries and nationalities

Write the nationalities for the following countries.

0	Britain	*British*
1	China	....
2	Brazil	....
3	Spain	....
4	Russia	....
5	Canada	....
6	Poland	....

6

3 Numbers

a Write the numbers.

0	5	*five*		5	33	....
1	12	....		6	9	....
2	60	....		7	16	....
3	25	....		8	48	....
4	74	....				

8

b Write the numbers.

0	twenty-six	*26*
1	fourteen	....
2	sixty-eight	....
3	twenty-one	....
4	eleven	....
5	eighty-seven	....
6	fifty	....
7	thirty-two	....
8	ninety-nine	....

8

4 Time

Look at the clocks and write the times.

0   *nine o'clock*   1   _____   2   _____

3   _____   4   _____   5   _____

5

5 Question words

Complete the questions. Use *Who, What, Where* or *How*.

0   ___*How*___ old are you?   I'm 14.

1   _____'s your name?   My name's Ed.

2   _____ are you?   I'm fine, thank you.

3   _____ are you?   I'm Susan, John's sister.

4   _____ is Maria from?   She's from England.

5   _____'s the time?   It's 10.30.

5

6 Personal information

Match an item from column A with the correct information from column B.

	A		B	
0	Family name		a	0208 348 1276
1	First name		b	14
2	Address		c	Brown
3	Telephone number		d	carolinebrown@aol.com
4	Email address		e	47 The Vale, London NW11
5	Age		f	Caroline

5

7 Nouns

Label the pictures. Use the words in the box.

> man   door   hamburger   book   pen   CD
> computer   sandwich   window   phone   ~~chair~~

0 _____chair_____   1 _____   2 _____   3 _____   4 _____

5 _____   6 _____   7 _____   8 _____   9 _____

10 _____

☐ 10

8 Plurals

Write the plurals of these nouns.

0 chair   _____chairs_____

1 book   _____

2 hamburger   _____

3 sandwich   _____

4 pen   _____

5 computer   _____

6 door   _____

7 window   _____

8 phone   _____

9 CD   _____

10 man   _____   ☐ 10

9 Colours

Write the colours.

0 uble   _____blue_____

1 worbn   _____

2 agenor   _____

3 wolyel   _____

4 plerpu   _____

5 energ   _____   ☐ 5

10 Pronouns

Complete the sentences with the pronouns in the box.

| I̶ | He | We | They | you | She |

0   My name is Steven. __I__ am 14 years old.

1   Are _____ OK? Yes, I'm fine.

2   Peter is German. _____ is from Stuttgart.

3   Mary is American. _____ is from Seattle.

4   I have a sister. _____ are teenagers.

5   My parents are teachers. _____ are English teachers.

☐ 5

11 Object pronouns

(Circle) the correct pronouns.

0   Please give this book to (me) / I.

1   I can give you / your the answer.

2   That's Peter. Can you see he / him?

3   Victoria is here. Please talk to her / she.

4   We are brothers. Do you know us / we?

5   My parents aren't here. Please phone they / them.

☐ 5

12 Family

Complete the sentences with the words in the box.

| brother̶ | mother | wife | sister | father | husband |

0   David is Laura's ____brother____ .

1   Laura is David's _____ .

2   Charles is Mary's _____ .

3   Mary is Charles' _____ .

4   Charles is Laura's _____ .

5   Mary is David's _____ .

Charles   Mary

David   Laura

☐ 5

1 Saying *hello* and *goodbye*

1 I'm   2 How   3 fine   4 this   5 Hi

2 Countries and nationalities

1 Chinese   2 Brazilian   3 Spanish   4 Russian
5 Canadian   6 Polish

3 Numbers

a   1 twelve   2 sixty   3 twenty-five   4 seventy-four
5 thirty-three   6 nine   7 sixteen   8 forty-eight

3 Numbers

b   1 14   2 68   3 21   4 11   5 87   6 50   7 32   8 99

4 Time

1 one o'clock   2 four o'clock   3 twelve o'clock
4 ten o'clock   5 three o'clock

5 Question words

1 What   2 How   3 Who   4 Where   5 What

6 Personal information

1 f   2 e   3 a   4 d   5 b

7 Nouns

1 book   2 man   3 hamburger   4 sandwich
5 pen   6 computer   7 door   8 window
9 phone   10 CD

8 Plurals

1 books   2 hamburgers   3 sandwiches   4 pens
5 computers   6 doors   7 windows   8 phones
9 CDs   10 men

9 Colours

1 brown   2 orange   3 yellow   4 purple   5 green

10 Pronouns

1 you   2 He   3 She   4 We   5 They

11 Object pronouns

1 you   2 him   3 her   4 us   5 them

12 Family

1 sister   2 husband   3 wife   4 father   5 mother

Teaching notes for communication activities and grammar practice

Unit 1
Communication activity
Areas practised
The verb *be*: questions and short answers;
Question words *what, where, how old*;
Nationalities

- Divide the class into groups of five or six.
  Copy and cut up one sheet for each group.

- Give each student in the group a card. Tell
  them that they are the person on the card,
  and that they must not show their card to
  the other students.

- Explain that students must ask and answer
  questions using the correct form of the
  verb *be* to find out information about the
  other members in their group. Tell them that
  within their group there is a teacher, a singer,
  a model, an actor, a footballer, and a tennis
  player. Go through example questions with
  a stronger student. For example, *What is
  your name? Where are you from? How old
  are you? Are you a model/footballer?*

- Explain that they must write sentences about
  the other members of their group. Write
  an example on the board: *Paolo Pinto is a
  teacher. He is 34 years old. He is Brazilian.*

- Students complete the activity.

- Monitor and check students are forming the
  questions and answers correctly. Note down
  any repeated errors to go through as a class
  after the activity.

Grammar practice key

1
2 am/'m
3 Is
4 is/'s
5 are/'re
6 is /'s
7 is /'s
8 Are

2
2 You aren't my hero.
3 My brother isn't a footballer.
4 I'm not old.
5 She isn't Spanish.
6 It isn't a cheap computer.

7 I'm not a model.
8 You aren't a good singer.
9 Homework isn't great.

3
2 Is; it isn't.
3 Am; you are.
4 Is; she isn't.
5 Are; I am.
6 Am; you aren't.
7 Is; he is.
8 Are; I'm not.
9 Is; it is.

4
2 g   3 f   4 a   5 e   6 c   7 b

Unit 2
Communication activity
Areas practised
Do you like … ? / We (don't) like … ; Short
answers

- Divide the class into student A and B pairs.
  Copy the questionnaire for each student.

- Give students five minutes to fill in their
  own answers to the questions.

- Explain that students must take turns at
  asking their partner the questions on the
  questionnaire, putting a tick or a cross in the
  column. Tell them to answer questions with
  short answers and encourage them to use
  the positive and negative adjectives they
  learned in this unit. Ask a stronger pair to
  demonstrate.

  A: *Do you like computer games?*
  B: *Yes, I do. They're fantastic. / No, I don't.
     They're terrible.*

- Monitor and check students are using the
  question and answer forms correctly, noting
  down any repeated errors to go through at
  the end of the activity.

- Ask for class feedback about what students
  had in common with their partner. For
  example, *We like American films. We don't
  like homework.*

- Finally, conduct a class survey to find out
  what are the most and least popular things
  on the questionnaire. Is there something that
  everybody likes or dislikes?

Grammar practice key

1
2 Are
3 is
4 are
5 is
6 are
7 is
8 are
9 am

2
2 Is; he is.
3 Are; they are.
4 Are; we aren't.
5 Are; aren't.
6 Is; it is.

3
2 her; She
3 They; them
4 I; me
5 he; He

4
2 ✓
3 ✗ Are we right?
4 ✗ No, we aren't Chinese.
5 ✗ Yes, I like Tom Cruise.
6 ✗ He's a great actor.
7 ✓
8 ✗ I like them a lot.

Unit 3

Communication activity

Areas practised

Present simple: questions and short answers

- Divide the class into student A and B pairs. Copy and cut up one sheet for each pair.

- Give each pair a pack of 16 cards. Tell them to place the pack face down in the middle of the table.

- Explain that student A must pick up the top card and ask student B a question based on it, using the verb on the card. Student B answers the question and asks student A the same question. Ask a stronger pair to demonstrate.

   A: *Do you listen to classical music?*
   B: *No, I don't. Do you listen to classical music?*

- Students work through all the cards, then get together with another pair (Students C and D).

- Students A and C, and students B and D, then ask each other the same questions about their partners. For example, *Does he/she listen to classical music?* Tell them to make a note of the answers.

- When all the questions have been answered, check the answers to see how many were remembered correctly.

- Monitor and check students are forming the questions and answers correctly. Note down any repeated errors and go through as a class after the activity.

Grammar practice key

1
2 live
3 watches
4 goes
5 studies
6 play
7 reads

2
2 ✗ I like Green Day a lot.
3 ✗ Do you study Portuguese at school?
4 ✓
5 ✗ Karen plays tennis at the weekend.
6 ✓
7 ✗ We don't really like our house.
8 ✗ Do they live in a big city?

3
2 Kevin's
3 Sue's
4 Emily's
5 Mike's
6 Sue's
7 Mike's

4
2 his
3 her
4 their
5 our
6 my
7 your

Unit 4
Communication activity
Areas practised
There's / there are (statements, negatives, questions and answers); Prepositions of place; Places in towns

- Divide the class into student A and B pairs. Copy two sheets for each pair. Give each student the first picture.

- Explain that student A must study the picture for two minutes and try to remember everything about it. Meanwhile student B must write five questions about the picture to test student A's memory of it. For example, *Is there a ... ? Are there any ... ? Where is the ... ?*

- When the two minutes are up, students turn the pictures face down. Student B then asks student A the questions and notes how many questions are answered correctly.

- When all the questions have been answered, give students the second picture and reverse roles.

- Monitor and check students are forming the questions and answers correctly. Note down any repeated errors and go through as a class after the activity.

Grammar practice key

1
2 are
3 aren't
4 Are
5 isn't
6 Is
7 are
8 's

2
2 are
3 isn't
4 Is
5 Are
6 is
7 aren't

3
2 ✗ Are there any interesting museums?
3 ✗ There are lots of cheap computers in this shop.
4 ✗ There isn't a hospital near here.
5 ✓
6 ✗ There isn't a post office in this street.
7 ✓

4
2 c 3 a 4 b 5 c 6 a

Unit 5
Communication activity
Areas practised
has got (statements, negatives, questions and answers); Parts of the body

- Divide the class into student A and B pairs. Copy two sheets and cut up one sheet for each pair. Tell students to place the cut up pack face down on the desk and the complete sheet face up on the desk, so both students can see it clearly.

- Explain that student A must select two 'friends' from the cut up pack. Student A must not show these cards to student B.

- Student B looks at the complete sheet, and asks questions to try to find out who student A has selected. For example, *Has he got a big nose? Is she small?*, etc.

- When student B finds out who one of the friends is, student A puts that card down.

- When both friends have been found, students swap roles.

- Monitor and check the students are forming the questions and answers correctly. Note down any repeated errors and go through as a class after the activity.

Grammar practice key

1
2 Why do you like Brad Pitt?
3 Whis is the baby called Hilary?
4 Why have you got seven pets?
5 Why is Dan's hair a different colour?

2
2 a 3 e 4 b 5 c

3
2 Has ... got; hasn't
3 Has ... got; has
4 Have ... got; you have
5 Have ... got; we haven't
6 Have ... got; they have
7 Has ... got; he has
8 Have ... got; I haven't

4
2 ✗ Have you got a newspaper?
3 ✗ Why has your sister got blue hair?
4 ✗ They haven't got their books.
5 ✗ Why are chimpanzees and people similar?
6 ✓
7 ✗ I've got long curly hair.
8 ✓

Unit 6
Communication activity
Areas practised
I'd like … ; Sorry, I haven't got … ; Countable and uncountable nouns; Food vocabulary

- Divide the class into groups of three or four. Copy and cut up one sheet per group.
- Tell students to place the cards face up on the desk and sort them into countable and uncountable nouns.
- Tell each student to make a note of four things they want to buy from the other students.
- Mix up the cards and distribute them between the students of each group.
- Explain that students must take turns at asking each other for the items on their list. If a student has the item, the card is given to the student who asked for it and they swap roles. Ask a stronger pair to demonstrate.
  A: *I'd like some chips, please.*
  B: *Here you are. / Sorry, I haven't got any chips.*
- The object of the game is to collect all the items on the list.
- Monitor and check students are forming the questions and answers correctly. Note down any repeated errors and go through as a class after the activity.

Grammar practice key
1
2 sandwich (C)
3 homework (U)
4 chips (C)
5 coffee (U)
6 money (U)
7 Biology (U)
8 orange (C)

2 2 b 3 a 4 c 5 a 6 b 7 c

3 2 d 3 e 4 c 5 g 6 a 7 f

4
2 ✗ I would love some apples and bananas.
3 ✗ This newspaper is old.
4 ✓
5 ✗ She has got some work to do.
6 ✓
7 ✗ Give me that salt, please.
8 ✗ Try this tea. It's delicious!

Unit 7
Communication activity
Areas practised
Present simple; adverbs of frequency; time expressions

- Divide the class into student A and B pairs. Copy and cut up one sheet for each pair.
- Give each pair one pack each of the Activity cards and Frequency cards. Tell them to place them face down on the desk in separate piles.
- Students take turns at picking a card from the top of each pile. Each time they make a sentence about themselves, their friends or their family, according to the card they have picked. The sentences can be true or false. For example, *My uncle plays football every day.* Students should make a note of their sentences.
- When all the cards have been used, they join with another pair and read each other's sentences out. Students from the other pair try to guess if the sentences are true or false. The pair with the most correct guesses wins.
- Monitor and check students are forming the questions and answers correctly. Note down any repeated errors and go through as a class after the activity.

Grammar practice key
1
2 go
3 help
4 buys
5 like
6 play
7 watches
8 works

2
2 Sandra never goes to school.
3 Sandra helps her mother with the shopping twice a week.
4 Sandra's mother sometimes buys clothes for Sandra and her brothers.
5 Her brothers never like their clothes.
6 She plays volleyball with her friends once a week.
7 Sandra's father usually watches them.
8 He sometimes has to work at weekends.

2 We often go dancing on Friday evenings.

3 My aunt hardly ever uses her mobile phone.

4 I always watch the news in the evening.

5 Your answers are sometimes wrong.

6 My little brother is usually in bed at eight o'clock.

7 James never orders a starter.

2 ✗ She drinks tea three times a day.

3 ✗ Chat shows are always boring.

4 ✓

5 ✗ My mother sometimes watches football.

6 ✗ I buy a newspaper once a week.

7 ✗ Susan hardly ever wears black.

8 ✓

Unit 8

Communication activity

Areas practised

Imperatives: positive and negative

Useful expressions

It's your turn / my turn. That's right. / That's wrong.

You will need a dice and some counters for each group.

- Divide the class into groups of four or five. Copy and cut up one board game and one set of Chance cards for each group. Put the cards face down on the table.

- Students place their counters on the start square. The first student in the group rolls the dice and moves the number of squares shown on the dice.

- They must then look at the prompt on the square they land on and follow the instructions: if they land at the bottom of a ladder, they move to the top of it; if they land on the head of a snake, they move back to its tail; if they take a Chance, they follow the instructions on the card.

- Explain that students must follow the Chance card instructions correctly, or they have to pay the penalty written on the card.

- The game continues until everyone has reached the finish.

- Monitor and check students are performing the actions correctly. Note down any repeated errors and go through as a class after the game.

Grammar practice key

1 Forget

2 Open ... Don't talk.

3 Look ... Don't laugh.

4 Go away! ... Don't shout.

5 Hang on ... Don't forget.

2 d   3 f   4 a   5 g   6 b   7 c

Possible answers:

2 Read a book.

3 Give it some food.

4 Don't go near them.

5 Don't buy them.

6 Don't worry.

7 Don't watch it.

2 ✗ Don't walk on the grass.

3 ✗ Please try to be good.

4 ✓

5 ✗ Listen to your teacher.

6 ✗ Turn right, opposite the supermarket.

7 ✓

8 ✗ Please don't use my computer.

Unit 9

Communication activity

Areas practised

can/can't (ability); *like / don't like + -ing*; Sports vocabulary

- Divide the class into student A and B pairs. Copy and cut up one sheet for each pair.

- Give each pair a pack of 16 cards. Tell them to place the pack face down in the middle of the table.

- Explain that student A must pick up the top card of the pack and ask student B a question based on it, using the verb on the card. For example, *Can you juggle?*

- If student B answers the question positively, Student A asks a follow-up question: *Do you like juggling?* Then student B asks student A the same question(s).

- Students work through all the cards, then get together with another pair (students C and D).

- Students A and C, and students B and D then ask each other the same questions about their partners. For example, *Can he/she juggle? Does he/she like juggling?* Tell them to make a note of the answers.

- When all the questions have been answered, check the answers to see how many were remembered correctly.
- Monitor and check students are forming the questions and answers correctly. Note down any repeated errors and go through as a class after the activity.

Grammar practice key

1
2 Jenny can't juggle
3 Jenny can sing, but she can't play the guitar.
4 Mark can't sing, but he can play the guitar.
5 Mark and Jenny can drive a car.
6 Jenny can drive a car, but she can't ride a bike.
7 Mark can't count in Chinese.
8 Jenny can count in Chinese, but she can't read Chinese.

2
Students' own answers.

3
2 I love playing rugby.
3 She really likes watching soap operas.
4 My friend and I hate doing homework.
5 You love singing pop songs.
6 Simon likes listening to classical music.
7 We hate going shopping.
8 He loves walking in the park.

4
2 ✗ I can't understand cricket.
3 ✓
4 ✗ She doesn't really like driving.
5 ✗ I love playing football, but I don't like watching it.
6 ✗ Do you hate taking part in games?
7 ✓
8 ✗ Can you walk on your hands?

Unit 10
Communication activity

Areas practised
Present continuous: statements, questions and short answers; *Is there / Are there … ?*; House and furniture vocabulary

- Divide the class into student A and B pairs. Copy and cut up one sheet for each pair. Give each student a different picture. Tell the students that they must not show their pictures to their partners. Give them a few minutes to look at their pictures.

- Explain that they must ask and answer questions to find eight differences between the pictures. To do this, they will need to use the present continuous tense. Ask a stronger pair to demonstrate.
  A: *Is there a man cleaning the cooker?*
  B: *No. There's a woman cleaning the cooker.*

- Students complete the exercise.

- Monitor and check students are taking turns to ask and answer questions, and that they are using the forms correctly. Note down any repeated errors to go through as a class after the activity.

- Ask for class feedback. Did they find all eight differences?

Grammar practice key

1
2 's not raining
3 'm babysitting
4 aren't having
5 's cleaning
6 's taking
7 's singing

2
2 Is your friend reading a book?
3 Are you wearing new clothes?
4 What are you doing?
5 Are you sitting on a chair?
6 Are you having a good time?
7 Is your teacher sleeping?

3
Students' own answers.

4
2 ✗ My brother's not going to school today.
3 ✓
4 ✗ Harry and Phil are having a fight.
5 ✗ Why are you crying?
6 ✓
7 ✗ I'm hoping you can help me.
8 ✓

Unit 11
Communication activity

Areas practised
Can (permission); Prepositions *at, in, on*

- Divide the class into student A and B pairs. Copy and cut up the cards on the sheet and give a set of picture cards and a set of sentence cards to each pair.

- Students spread out all the cards face down on the table (not in a pile). Explain to students that they must turn over one picture card and one sentence card and see if they match. If the cards match, the student keeps them and has another turn. If they don't match, the student must turn the cards back over in exactly the same place. The winner is the student who has the most pairs when the game has finished and there are no more cards on the table.

- Ask a stronger pair to demonstrate. Ask them to read out the sentence they turn over. Ask the whole class if they think it matches the picture card which was turned over.

- The game continues like this until students have matched all the picture cards and sentences using their memory and the picture content to help them.

- Monitor and check students are taking turns to turn the cards over and helping each other find the pairs. Check that they are reading the sentences and not merely turning the cards over.

- Ask for class feedback. Students can come and stick their matching pairs on the board.

Grammar practice key

1 2 b   3 a   4 c   5 a   6 c

2
2 can; you can't
3 Can; he can
4 Can I; you can't

3
1 ones
2 one ... one; one
3 ones
4 one; one
5 ones; ones
6 one

4
2 ✗ Can I have that blue shirt?
3 ✗ Is Thanksgiving in November?
4 ✓
5 ✗ I like those white trainers, but I don't like the black ones.
6 ✓
   ✗ We love walking in the park in autumn.
8 ✗ Can I use your car, please?

Unit 12
Communication activity
Areas practised
Was: questions and short answers; Ordinal numbers; Dates

- Divide the class into groups of three or four. Make two copies of the sheet and cut up two sets of cards for each group. Cut the dates off one set of cards.

- Give a set of dated and undated cards to each group. Put the dated cards in a pile face down in the middle of the table. Tell students to distribute the undated cards equally among themselves. Explain that students have photographs of two travellers.

- Tell the first student to pick a dated card from the pile in the middle. If it is the same picture as one they have in their hand, they must put it at the bottom of the pile and pick another.

- The student looks at the picture and the date and asks the other students to guess where the traveller was on that date. For example, *Where was Mr Jones on the 5th of April? Where were Mr and Mrs Jones on the 10th of May?* Students take turns to ask questions based on the cards they have in their hands. For example, *Was she/Mrs Jones in Paris?*

- When a student guesses correctly they keep the two matching cards, and the next student takes a card from the pile in the middle. The game continues until all the cards are matched up, and the winner is the student with the most matching cards.

- Monitor and check students are forming the questions and answers correctly.

- Ask for class feedback. Students say where the traveller was on any given date.

Grammar practice key

1 2 a   3 c   4 a   5 c   6 a   7 b

2
2 We weren't in Rome last April.
3 Marcia wasn't with her friends last night.
4 There wasn't a swimming pool in the hotel.
5 You weren't very funny yesterday.
6 I wasn't at home all day yesterday.
7 They weren't in the park with their children.
8 Those weren't my sandwiches!

3

2 Were; Yes, they were.

3 Was; No, it wasn't.

4 Were; No, I wasn't.

5 Were; Yes, I was.

6 Was; Yes, she was.

7 Were; No, we weren't.

8 Were; Yes, they were.

4

2 ✗ Where was she last Sunday morning?

3 ✗ The weather was lovely last July.

4 ✓

5 ✗ The food wasn't very good.

6 ✗ Were your parents at the cinema last night?

7 ✗ There were lots of good restaurants near our hotel.

8 ✓

Unit 13

Communication activity

Areas practised

Past simple: questions and short answers; Verb and noun collocations

- Divide the class into groups of four or five. Copy and cut up one sheet for each group.

- Give each group a pack of twelve cards. Tell them to place the pack face down in the middle of the table.

- Explain that on each card is a picture of an activity, and that this is what they did last night.

- Explain that the first student in each group must pick up the top card and look at the activity on it. The other students in the group must ask *yes/no* questions and try to find out what the student did. Go through example questions with a stronger student: *Did you have a bath? Did you go to the cinema?* etc.

- The student who guesses correctly picks up the next card from the pile, and the game begins again.

- Monitor and check students are forming the questions and answers correctly. Note down any repeated errors and go through as a class after the activity.

Grammar practice key

1

2 married

3 organised ... didn't remember

4 opened ... arrived

5 cried ... died

6 didn't like ... changed

7 tried ... didn't listen

8 stayed ... played

2

2 The dog didn't destroy my homework.

3 We didn't finish the test before nine o'clock.

4 I didn't hate vegetables when I was small.

5 She didn't cry at the end of the film.

6 They didn't seem like nice people.

3

2 did you stay?

3 did you travel?

4 did you travel with?

5 did you return?

4

2 ✗ I didn't go to the cinema last night.

3 ✓

4 ✗ They didn't play football last week.

5 ✗ Where did you live when you were young?

6 ✓

7 ✗ When did Florence Nightingale die?

8 ✗ She studied Mathematics when she was at university.

9 ✗ What did you do last summer?

Unit 14

Communication activity

Areas practised

Comparison of adjectives

- Divide the class into groups of four. Copy and cut up one sheet for every group. Give a pack of cards to each group and tell them to distribute them evenly among themselves.

- The first student lays a card face up on the table. The second student lays one of their cards next to it.

- The second student must make a sentence comparing the two cards on the table. For example, *A castle is bigger than a house.*

- The next student lays a card next to the last card and also makes a comparative sentence, comparing their card to the last card laid down.

- If a student cannot make a correct or sensible sentence, they must keep their card and the next student has a turn.

- The first student to get rid of all their cards is the winner.

- Monitor and check students are forming the comparative sentences correctly.

Grammar practice key

1
2 more comfortable
3 longer
4 hotter
5 healthier
6 more fashionable
7 better
8 warmer

2
2 more interesting than
3 more popular than
4 curlier than
5 shorter than
6 sunnier than
7 more famous than
8 worse than

3
Students' own answers

4
2 ✗ Life is better today than it was when I was young.
3 ✓
4 ✗ I am busier today than I was yesterday.
5 ✗ Mike Myers is funnier than Jim Carrey.
6 ✓
7 ✗ Please try to be more careful next time.
8 ✗ The starter was bad, but the main course was worse.

TEACHING NOTES

RESOURCES

✳ Communication activity 1

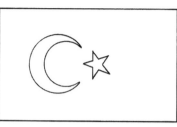

Paulo Pinto (34). Teacher

Suna Biret (26). Singer

Sally Thompson (19). Model

Gong Hu (27). Tennis player

Alessandro Ricci (22). Footballer

Jan Kolbe (37). Actor

Grammar practice 1

1 Complete the sentences with the correct form of the verb *be*.

1 Where .... *is* .... she from?

2 I .... fourteen years old.

3 .... he your best friend?

4 It .... a new computer.

5 You .... a great teacher.

6 The film .... boring.

7 Daniel .... my friend.

8 .... you from Los Angeles?

2 Make the positive sentences negative.

1 He's from Poland.
He isn't from Poland.

2 You're my hero.
....

3 My brother is a footballer.
....

4 I'm old.
....

5 She's Spanish.
....

6 It's a cheap computer.
....

7 I'm a model.
....

8 You're a good singer.
....

9 Homework is great.
....

3 Complete the questions and answers.

1 A: *Are you* .... from London?
   B: Yes, *I am* ....

2 A: .... it a good restaurant?
   B: No, ...

3 A: .... I the winner?
   B: Yes, ...

4 A: .... she your friend?
   B: No, ...

5 A: .... you a good golfer?
   B: Yes, ...

6 A: .... I boring?
   B: No, ...

7 A: .... he a film star?
   B: Yes, ...

8 A: .... you Turkish?
   B: No, ...

9 A: .... your phone number 670987?
   B: Yes, ...

4 Match the questions with the answers.

1 What's this in English?   a He's my dad.
2 Where are you from?   b It's in Canada.
3 How old is your   c 23 Peter Street,
  mother?   Warwick.
4 Who's this man?   d It's a pen.
5 How old are you?   e I'm 14.
6 What's your address?   f She's 42.
7 Where is Toronto?   g I'm from
                                Portugal.

RESOURCES

UNIT 1

 © Cambridge University Press 2010 Resources Unit 1

Communication activity 2

Do you like ... ? Questionnaire

	You	Your partner
computer games		
pizza		
Beyoncé		
big cities		
hamburgers		
homework		
Robert Pattinson		
Italian cars		
shopping		
mobile phones		
tennis		
Miley Cyrus		
expensive restaurants		
American films		
Eminem		
cats		
football		
British music		
school		
Rihanna		

UNIT 2

RESOURCES

Grammar practice 2

1 Complete the sentences with the correct form of the verb *be*.

1 They ___are___ from New York.

2 _____ John and Mark OK?

3 Volleyball _____ a great sport.

4 We _____ very lucky.

5 This _____ great coffee!

6 They _____ an awful band.

7 What _____ the right answer?

8 Where _____ they from?

9 I _____ correct.

2 Complete the questions and answers.

1 A: Are you French?
  B: No, *I'm not.* _____

2 A: _____ Robert Pattinson British?
  B: Yes, _____ .

3 A: _____ they your friends?
  B: Yes, _____ .

4 A: _____ you and your friend from Cambridge?
  B: No, _____ .

5 A: _____ we right?
  B: No, you _____ .

6 A: _____ this your car?
  B: Yes, _____ .

3 (Circle) the correct pronouns.

1 A: Do you like Jude Law?
  B: Yes. (He) / His is a great actor. I really like he / (him.)

2 Taylor Swift is awful. I don't like she / her at all. She / Her is a terrible singer.

3 The new Jonas Brothers CD is great. They / Them are my favourite band. Do you like they / them?

4 I / Me really like horses. But horses don't like I / me at all!

5 A: Do you like Mr Thompson?
  B: No, I think he / him is awful. He / Him isn't a good teacher.

4 Right (✓) or wrong (✗)? Correct the wrong sentences.

1 Greg and Kate is from Canada.
  Greg and Kate are from Canada.

2 Are they your mother and father?
  _____

3 Is we right?
  _____

4 No, we not Chinese.
  _____

5 Yes, I'm like Tom Cruise.
  _____

6 Him's a great actor.
  _____

7 Do you like her?
  _____

8 I like they a lot.
  _____

Communication activity 3

listen to	go	go	read
come from	play	play	have
have	watch	speak	speak
live	want	love	like

Grammar practice 3

1 Complete the sentences. Use the correct form of the verbs in the box.

> watch   ~~work~~   study   go   live   play   read

1 My father _____*works*_____ in a bank.
2 We _____ in a big house in Rome.
3 My brother _____ TV a lot.
4 She _____ to the cinema at weekends.
5 He _____ German at school.
6 I _____ tennis.
7 My uncle _____ the newspaper at work.

2 Right (✓) or wrong (✗)? Correct the wrong sentences.

1 Tony don't read Harry Potter books. [✗]
   Tony doesn't read Harry Potter books.

2 I likes Green Day a lot. [ ]
   ----

3 Is you study Portuguese at school? [ ]
   ----

4 Do you go shopping in town? [ ]
   ----

5 Karen play tennis at the weekend. [ ]
   ----

6 My family has a car and a computer. [ ]
   ----

7 We doesn't really like our house. [ ]
   ----

8 Do they lives in a big city? [ ]
   ----

3 Complete the sentences with the correct name and possessive *'s*.

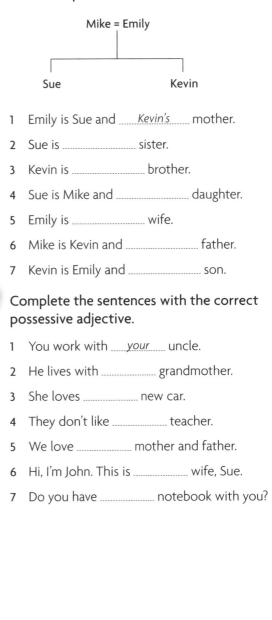

Mike = Emily

Sue   Kevin

1 Emily is Sue and _____*Kevin's*_____ mother.
2 Sue is _____ sister.
3 Kevin is _____ brother.
4 Sue is Mike and _____ daughter.
5 Emily is _____ wife.
6 Mike is Kevin and _____ father.
7 Kevin is Emily and _____ son.

4 Complete the sentences with the correct possessive adjective.

1 You work with _____*your*_____ uncle.
2 He lives with _____ grandmother.
3 She loves _____ new car.
4 They don't like _____ teacher.
5 We love _____ mother and father.
6 Hi, I'm John. This is _____ wife, Sue.
7 Do you have _____ notebook with you?

 © Cambridge University Press 2010   Resources Unit 3

RESOURCES

UNIT 3

Communication activity 4

Grammar practice 4

1 ⟨Circle⟩ the correct form of the verb.

1   There ⟨is⟩/ *are* a lot to do in my town.
2   There *is* / *are* three cinemas near my house.
3   There *isn't* / *aren't* any dinosaurs in this museum.
4   *Is* / *Are* there any good bookshops near here?
5   There *isn't* / *aren't* a newsagent next to Tony's Café.
6   *Is* / *Are* there a street market in this town?
7   There *'s* / *are* a lot of young people at this concert.
8   There *'s* / *are* a dog in your garden!

2 Complete the sentences with *is, are, isn't,* or *aren't.*

1   There ___aren't___ any old buildings in the city centre. (✗)
2   There _____ some good cafés near my school. (✓)
3   There _____ a pencil on my desk. (✗)
4   _____ there a dishwasher in your house?
5   _____ there any cartoons on TV?
6   There _____ a big library at the university. (✓)
7   There _____ any cars in this town. (✗)

3 Right (✓) or wrong (✗)? Correct the wrong sentences.

1   There are any girls in my family.   ⟨✗⟩
    There aren't any girls in my family.
2   Is there any interesting museums?   ☐
    ‑‑‑‑‑‑‑‑‑‑‑‑‑‑‑‑‑‑‑‑‑‑‑‑‑‑‑‑‑‑‑‑‑‑‑‑
3   There is lots of cheap computers in this shop.   ☐
    ‑‑‑‑‑‑‑‑‑‑‑‑‑‑‑‑‑‑‑‑‑‑‑‑‑‑‑‑‑‑‑‑‑‑‑‑
4   There isn't no hospital near here.   ☐
    ‑‑‑‑‑‑‑‑‑‑‑‑‑‑‑‑‑‑‑‑‑‑‑‑‑‑‑‑‑‑‑‑‑‑‑‑
5   Is there any milk in the house?   ☐
    ‑‑‑‑‑‑‑‑‑‑‑‑‑‑‑‑‑‑‑‑‑‑‑‑‑‑‑‑‑‑‑‑‑‑‑‑
6   There aren't a post office in this street.   ☐
    ‑‑‑‑‑‑‑‑‑‑‑‑‑‑‑‑‑‑‑‑‑‑‑‑‑‑‑‑‑‑‑‑‑‑‑‑
7   Are there any actors in this classroom?   ☐
    ‑‑‑‑‑‑‑‑‑‑‑‑‑‑‑‑‑‑‑‑‑‑‑‑‑‑‑‑‑‑‑‑‑‑‑‑

4 ⟨Circle⟩ the correct answers, *a, b* or *c.*

1   The bookshop is _____ to the café.
    a ⟨next⟩   b behind   c in front
2   There's a post office _____ of the supermarket.
    a behind   b opposite   c in front
3   Wait for me _____ of Mill Street and Croft Road.
    a on the corner   b between   c near
4   The bank is _____ the chemist and the bookshop.
    a in front   b between   c next
5   Excuse me, is there a restaurant _____ here?
    a next   b between   c near
6   There's a newsagent _____ the library.
    a opposite   b in front   c next

✳ Communication activity 5

Sarah

Laura

Kate

Anna

Dave

Mark

Tom

Nick

Grammar practice 5

1 Put the words in the correct order to make questions.

1 she / why / has / eyes / got / blue
Why has she got blue eyes? .... ?

2 Brad Pitt / you / why / like / do
.... ?

3 called / baby / is / why / Hilary / the
.... ?

4 seven / got / you / have / pets / why
.... ?

5 hair / Dan's / a / colour / is / why / different
.... ?

2 Match the answers with the questions in Exercise 1.

1   a   Because he is good looking.

2   b   Because I love dogs and cats.

3   c   Because he thinks it's fashionable.

4   d   Because her mother and father have got blue eyes.

5   e   Because that is her grandmother's name.

3 Complete the questions and answers.

1 A: _Have_ you _got_ a pen?
   B: Yes, I _have_ .

2 A: .... Sally .... any brothers?
   B: No, she ....

3 A: .... your horse .... long legs?
   B: Yes, it ....

4 A: .... I .... a nice smile?
   B: Yes, ...

5 A: .... we .... any money?
   B: No, ...

6 A: .... your friends .... bicycles?
   B: Yes, ...
   A: .... Alan .... green hair?
   B: Yes, ...

8 A: .... you .... a pet spider?
   B: No, ...

4 Right (✓) or wrong (✗)? Correct the wrong sentences.

1 Paula has gots a big family.   ✗
Paula has got a big family.

2 Has you got a newspaper?   ☐
....

3 Why is your sister got blue hair?   ☐
....

4 They hasn't got their books.   ☐
....

5 Why chimpanzees and people are similar?   ☐
....

6 My friend's father has got green eyes.   ☐
....

7 I's got long curly hair.   ☐
....

8 Have Tom and Alice got a little house?   ☐
....

RESOURCES

UNIT 5

✳ Communication activity 6

Grammar practice 6

1 Underline the noun in each sentence. Then write *C* (countable) or *U* (uncountable).

1 Do you like tennis? ___U___

2 I'd like a sandwich, please. ___

3 We don't want any homework, thank you.
   ___

4 These chips are delicious. ___

5 Would you like some coffee? ___

6 Have you got any money? ___

7 Biology is really interesting. ___

8 Here, take this orange. ___

2 Complete the sentences. (Circle) the correct answers, *a, b* or *c*.

1 What is ___ book on my desk?
   a these   b those   c (this)

2 I'd like one of ___ onions, please.
   a this   b those   c that

3 ___ lamb is wonderful.
   a This   b These   c Those

4 Do you know ___ man over there?
   a this   b these   c that

5 Look at ___ little spider on my hand.
   a this   b those   c that

6 Mmm. ___ chips are fantastic!
   a This   b These   c That

7 He lives in one of ___ small towns in America.
   a this   b that   c those

3 Put the sentences in the correct order to make a conversation.

a Yes, I'd like some cheese too, please.

b Good morning.

c Yes, I'd like a kilo of onions, please.

d Good morning.

e Can I help you?

f That's €6, please.

g OK. Would you like anything else?

1 ___b___   ___Good morning.___

2 ___   ___

3 ___   ___

4 ___   ___

5 ___   ___

6 ___   ___

7 ___   ___

4 Right (✓) or wrong (✗)? Correct the wrong sentences.

1 Would you like a bread?   ✗
   Would you like some bread?

2 I love some apples and bananas.   ☐

3 These newpaper is old.   ☐

4 I'd like an onion, please.   ☐

5 She has got a work to do.   ☐

6 Would you like an orange?   ☐

7 Give me those salt, please.   ☐

8 Try these tea. It's delicious!   ☐

RESOURCES   UNIT 6

✳ Communication activity 7

Activity cards

watch TV	go to school	go shopping	listen to music	eat fish
play football	read a book	wear a hat	check your email	go swimming

Frequency cards

once a	twice a	x times a	every
always	usually	often	sometimes
hardly ever	never	day	week
month	year	morning	evening

UNIT 7

RESOURCES

Grammar practice 7

1 Complete the text. Use the present simple form of the verbs in the box.

> buy   ~~live~~   watch   go
> play   like   work   help

My name is Sandra, and I (1) ....*live*.......... with my family in London. I have two brothers. They (2) .... to school five days a week. I don't go to school. I am nineteen years old. On Wednesday and Saturday I (3) .... my mother with the shopping. Sometimes my mother (4) .... clothes for me and my brothers. My brothers never (5) .... their clothes because they are not fashionable. On Sunday I (6) .... volleyball with my friends. My father usually (7) .... us, but sometimes he (8) .... at weekends.

2 Correct these false sentences about the text in 1.

1   Sandra's brothers go to school every day.
    Sandra's brothers go to school five days a week.

2   Sandra goes to school once a week.
    ....

3   Sandra helps her mother with the shopping three times a week.
    ....
    ....

4   Sandra's mother always buys clothes for Sandra and her brothers.
    ....
    ....

5   Her brothers usually like their clothes.
    ....

6   She plays volleyball with her friends twice a week.
    ....

7   Sandra's father hardly ever watches them.
    ....

8   He never has to work at weekends.
    ....

3 Write the sentences. Put the adverbs in the correct place.

1   Simon checks his email. (never)
    Simon never checks his email.

2   We go dancing on Friday evenings. (often)
    ....

3   My aunt uses her mobile phone. (hardly ever)
    ....

4   I watch the news in the evening. (always)
    ....

5   Your answers are wrong. (sometimes)
    ....

6   My little brother is in bed at eight o'clock. (usually)
    ....
    ....

7   James orders a starter. (never)
    ....

4 Right (✓) or wrong (✗)? Correct the wrong sentences.

1   I go often shopping with my sister.   ✗
    I often go shopping with my sister.

2   She drinks tea three time a day.   ☐

3   Chat shows always are boring.   ☐

4   He usually gets up at seven o'clock.   ☐

5   My mother watches sometimes football.   ☐

6   I buy a newspaper one time a week.   ☐

7   Susan ever hardly wears black.   ☐

8   French homework is never interesting.   ☐

RESOURCES   UNIT 7

Communication activity 8

20 go back two squares	**21** take a CHANCE	**22** go back five squares	**23**	**FINISH**
19 take a CHANCE	**18**	**17**	**16** take a CHANCE	**15** go forward two squares
10	**11** take a CHANCE	**12** go forward three squares	**13**	**14** take a CHANCE
9 take a CHANCE	**8** go back one square	**7**	**6** take a CHANCE	**5**
START	**1**	**2**	**3** go forward one square	**4**

Chance cards

Don't close your eyes for one minute. (Penalty: miss next turn.)	Sit on the desk. (Penalty: go back three spaces.)
Look at the teacher for one minute. (Penalty: go back two spaces.)	Open and close the classroom door. (Penalty: miss next turn.)
Say the alphabet from A–Z. (Penalty: go back four spaces.)	Don't speak for one minute. (Penalty: go back two spaces.)
Get up. Don't sit down for one minute. (Penalty: miss next turn.)	Tell the person next to you to do something. (Penalty for person next to you: miss next turn.)

Grammar practice 8

1 Circle the imperatives.

1 Tom: It's lunchtime, Harry.

   Harry: (Wait) a minute. I've got work to do.

   Tom: (Forget) about work. I'm really hungry!

2 Open your books at page 34. Don't talk.

3 Sue: Look at that man's hair!

   Kate: Don't laugh. That's my dad.

4 Mary: I don't want to talk to you. Go away!

   John: OK, OK. Don't shout.

5 Mark: Bye, Mum!

   Mum: Hang on, Mark. Don't forget your
            sandwiches.

   Mark: Oh, thanks.

2 Match the two parts of the sentences.

1 Don't open   a   me, because I don't
                           know.

2 Don't listen   b   my chocolate!

3 Don't park   c   at her clothes.

4 Don't ask   d   to that awful music.

5 Don't write   e   the window.

6 Don't eat   f   in front of the hospital.

7 Don't laugh   g   your name on the
                           library books.

3 Write the imperatives.

1 This food is disgusting.
   Don't eat it.

2 I'm bored.
   ....

3 The dog's hungry.
   ....

4 I'm scared of horses.
   ....

5 These shoes are really expensive.
   ....

6 I'm worried about the English test.
   ....

7 This is a really boring film.
   ....

4 Right (✓) or wrong (✗)? Correct the
wrong sentences.

1 Sit down and you open your books,
   please.   ☒
   Sit down and open your books, please.

2 Don't walks on the grass.   ☐
   ....

3 Please to try to be good.   ☐
   ....

4 Don't forget to check your email.   ☐
   ....

5 Listen you to the teacher.   ☐
   ....

6 Turning right opposite the supermarket.   ☐
   ....

7 Don't call me again.   ☐
   ....

8 Please don't to use my computer.   ☐
   ....

© Cambridge University Press 2010   Resources Unit 8

RESOURCES

UNIT 8

Grammar practice 9

1 Look at the table and write sentences with *can/can't*.

	Mark	Jenny	Me	My friend
juggle	✓	✗		
sing	✗	✓		
play the guitar	✓	✗		
drive a car	✓	✓		
ride a bike	✓	✗		
count in Chinese	✗	✓		
read Chinese	✗	✗		

1 Mark / juggle

   Mark can juggle. ....

2 Jenny / juggle

   ....

3 Jenny / sing / play the guitar

   .... , but ....

4 Mark / sing / play the guitar

   ....

5 Mark and Jenny / drive a car

   ....

6 Jenny / drive a car / ride a bike

   ....

7 Mark / count in Chinese

   ....

8 Jenny / count in Chinese / read Chinese

   ....

2 Complete the table with information about yourself and your friend. Write six true sentences using *can/can't*.

Example: I can't drive a car, but I can ride a bike.

1 ....

2 ....

3 ....

4 ....

5 ....

6 ....

3 Write the sentences. Use the *-ing* form of the verb.

1 John / hate / swim / in the sea

   John hates swimming in the sea. ....

2 I / love / play / rugby

   ....

3 She / really / like / watch / soap operas

   ....

4 My friend and I / hate / do / homework

   ....

5 You / love / sing / pop songs

   ....

6 Simon / like / listen / to classical music

   ....

7 We / hate / go / shopping

   ....

8 He / love / walk / in the park

   ....

4 Right (✓) or wrong (✗)? Correct the wrong sentences.

1 My sister is really like watching gymnastics.   ☒

   My sister really likes watching gymnastics.

2 I can't understanding cricket.   ☐

   ....

3 Greg can read Japanese.   ☐

   ....

4 She doesn't really likes driving.   ☐

   ....

5 I love playing football, but I don't liking watch it.   ☐

   ....

6 Do you hate take part in games?   ☐

   ....

7 I can't send email from this computer.   ☐

   ....

8 Can you to walk on your hands?   ☐

   ....

RESOURCES   UNIT 9

Communication activity 10

PHOTOCOPIABLE © Cambridge University Press 2010 **Resources Unit 10**

UNIT 10

RESOURCES

Grammar practice 10

1 Complete the sentences. Use the present continuous form of the verbs in the box.

sing	clean	not have	take
not rain	~~come~~	babysit	

1 A: How is your holiday?

   B: Terrible. We __'re coming__ home.

2 A: What's the weather like.

   B: Well, it _____, but it's cloudy.

3 A: What are you doing at the moment?

   B: I _____ for my cousin's children.

4 A: Why are you leaving?

   B: Because we _____ a good time.

5 A: Where is Dave?

   B: He _____ his room.

6 A: What's Max doing?

   B: He _____ a picture of his house.

7 A: What's that terrible noise?

   B: That's my dad. He _____ in the bath.

2 Put the words in the correct order to make questions.

1 you / your / doing / are / homework

   Are you doing your homework ?

2 a book / friend / your / reading / is

   _____ ?

3 clothes / wearing / you / are / new

   _____ ?

4 doing / you / are / what

   _____ ?

5 you / sitting / chair / a / on / are

   _____ ?

6 having / a / are / time / good / you

   _____ ?

7 teacher / is / sleeping / your

   _____ ?

3 Write true answers to the questions in 5.

1 _Yes, I am_ .

2 _____ .

3 _____ .

4 _____ .

5 _____ .

6 _____ .

7 _____ .

4 Right (✓) or wrong (✗)? Correct the wrong sentences.

1 Dan is read a book in his bedroom.   ✗

   Dan is reading a book in his bedroom.

2 My brother not going to school today.   ☐

3 Are you using this computer?   ☐

4 Harry and Phil have a fight.   ☐

5 Why do you crying?   ☐

6 Who is looking after Judy?   ☐

7 I am hope you can help me.   ☐

8 Theresa is making a milkshake.   ☐

RESOURCES

UNIT 10

✳ Communication activity 11

The film starts at 8.30.	We usually go skiing in winter.	We go to the beach every day in summer.	I like staying in bed on Sunday.	Can I try on these trainers?
Can I use your computer?	Can I read your newspaper?	He often goes swimming on Saturday.	Nice trousers!	It's my birthday in February.

Grammar practice 11

1 Complete the sentences. (Circle) the correct answers, *a, b* or *c*.

1 It's John's party on ....

    a August   b two o'clock   c (Friday)

2 The concert finishes at ....

    a Saturday   b 10.30   c winter

3 We usually go skiing in ....

    a winter   b Tuesday and Thursday
    c nine o'clock

4 Does he always get up at .... ?

    a spring   b Sunday   c five o'clock

5 There's a good programme on TV at

    ....

    a eleven o'clock   b autumn   c Monday

6 On .... we have fish for dinner.

    a six o'clock   b spring   c Friday

2 Complete the dialogues with *can* or *can't*.

1 A: ..... *Can* ..... I try on these trainers, please?

   B: Yes, of course .. *you can* .. .

2 A: Sally, ... I use your computer?

   B: No, sorry, ... I'm doing my
   homework on it.

3 A: .... my little boy play with your
   dog?

   B: Yes, ... She's a good dog.

4 A: Is that ice cream nice?

   B: Yes, it's delicious.

   A: .... try some?

   B: No, ... Go and buy one!

3 Complete the sentences with *one* or *ones*.

1 A: Look at those shoes. They're fantastic!

   B: The red .. *ones* .. ?

   A: No, the black ....

2 A: Can I try on the red dress, please?

   B: Which .... ? The .... in
   the window?

   A: Yes. That .... , please.

3 A: My trainers are old.

   B: Do you want some new .... ?

4 A: Do you like the new record shop?

   B: Which .... ?

   A: The .... on the corner, opposite
   the café.

5 A: Do you see those boys over there?

   B: Which .... ?

   A: The .... in the jeans and black
   jackets.

6 A: Does he want a scarf for Christmas?

   B: No, he's got ....

4 Right (✓) or wrong (✗)? Correct the wrong sentences.

1 Kevin starts work in eight o'clock.   [✗]

   Kevin starts work at eight o'clock.

2 Can I have got that blue shirt?   [ ]

3 Is Thanksgiving on November?   [ ]

4 The party starts at seven o'clock on
   Saturday.   [ ]

5 I like those white trainers, but I don't
   like the black one.   [ ]

6 Can I try on this red dress?   [ ]

7 We love walking in the park on autumn.   [ ]

8 I can use your car, please?   [ ]

RESOURCES

UNIT 11

 © Cambridge University Press 2010 Resources Unit 11 163

Communication activity 12

Mrs Jones	Mr Jones
3 March	5 April
Mr and Mrs Jones	Mr and Mrs Jones
10 May	15 June
Mrs Jones	Mr Jones
2 July	20 August
Mr and Mrs Jones	Mrs Jones
25 September	7 October
Mr Jones	Mr and Mrs Jones
8 November	13 December
Mr and Mrs Jones	Mr Jones
20 January	19 February

UNIT 12
RESOURCES

Grammar practice 12

1 Complete the sentences. (Circle) the correct answers, *a*, *b* or *c*.

1   My grandfather .... a very good footballer.

   a weren't   **b** (wasn't)   **c** were

2   .... you ill last week?

   a Were   **b** Was   **c** Wasn't

3   .... that your mother on the phone?

   a Weren't   **b** Were   **c** Was

4   Where .... your friend's apartment building?

   a was   **b** were   **c** wasn't

5   That .... a very nice thing to do.

   a were   **b** weren't   **c** wasn't

6   How many people .... there last night?

   a were   **b** wasn't   **c** was

7   Dan and Sue .... here on the fourth of July.

   a was   **b** were   **c** wasn't

2 Make the positive sentences negative.

1   That was a good film.

   That wasn't a good film.

2   We were in Rome last April.

   ....

3   Marcia was with her friends last night.

   ....

4   There was a swimming pool in the hotel.

   ....

5   You were very funny yesterday.

   ....

6   I was at home all day yesterday.

   ....

7   They were in the park with their children.

   ....

8   Those were my sandwiches!

   ....

3 Complete the questions. Then answer the questions using the clues to help you.

1   _Was_ there a restaurant in the hotel? ✓

   Yes, there was.

2   .... the children happy? ✓

   ....

3   .... the weather good? ✗

   ....

4   .... you out late every night? ✗

   ....

5   .... you up early every morning? ✓

   ....

6   .... Susan on the beach every day? ✓

   ....

7   .... you all happy to come home? ✗

   ....

8   .... your parents at home when you returned? ✓

   ....

4 Right (✓) or wrong (✗)? Correct the wrong sentences.

1   I am at the museum at one o'clock yesterday. ✗

   I was at the museum at one o'clock yesterday.

2   Where she was last Sunday morning? ☐

   ....

3   The weather were lovely last July. ☐

   ....

4   Suddenly, there was a knock on the door. ☐

5   The food weren't very good. ☐

   ....

6   Was your parents at the cinema last night? ☐

   ....

7   There was lots of good restaurants near our hotel. ☐

   ....

8   What was that man's name? ☐

RESOURCES   UNIT 12

✳ Communication activity 13

Grammar practice 13

1 Complete the sentences. Use the past simple form of the verbs.

1 Steve _____cooked_____ (cook) a great meal last night.

2 She _____ (marry) a soldier in 2002.

3 Simon _____ (organise) this party, but he _____ (not remember) to invite Sonia.

4 They _____ (open) the hotel restaurant when we _____ (arrive).

5 I _____ (cry) when my cat _____ (die).

6 Her boyfriend _____ (not like) it when she _____ (change) the colour of her hair.

7 We _____ (try) to tell her, but she _____ (not listen).

8 He _____ (stay) at home and _____ (play) computer games all day yesterday.

2 Make the positive sentences negative.

1 I cycled 20 kilometres on Saturday.

I didn't cycle 20 kilometres on Saturday.

2 The dog destroyed my homework.

_____

3 We finished the test before nine o'clock.

_____

4 I hated vegetables when I was small.

_____

5 She cried at the end of the film.

_____

6 They seemed like nice people.

_____

3 Write the questions.

1 When _did you arrive_ _____ ?

We arrived at 8.30 in the morning.

2 Where _____ ?

We stayed at the Marina Hotel.

3 How _____ ?

We travelled by car.

4 Who _____ ?

I travelled with my best friend.

5 When _____ ?

We returned at 10 o'clock last night.

4 Right (✓) or wrong (✗)? Correct the wrong sentences.

1 Did you enjoyed the film? [✗]

Did you enjoy the film?

2 I wasn't go to the cinema last night. [ ]

_____

3 What did she want? [ ]

_____

4 They didn't played football last week. [ ]

_____

5 Where was you live when you were young? [ ]

_____

6 Did you go to work yesterday? [ ]

_____

7 When died Florence Nightingale? [ ]

_____

8 She study Maths when she was at university. [ ]

_____

9 What did you last summer? [ ]

_____

RESOURCES

UNIT 13

Communication activity 14

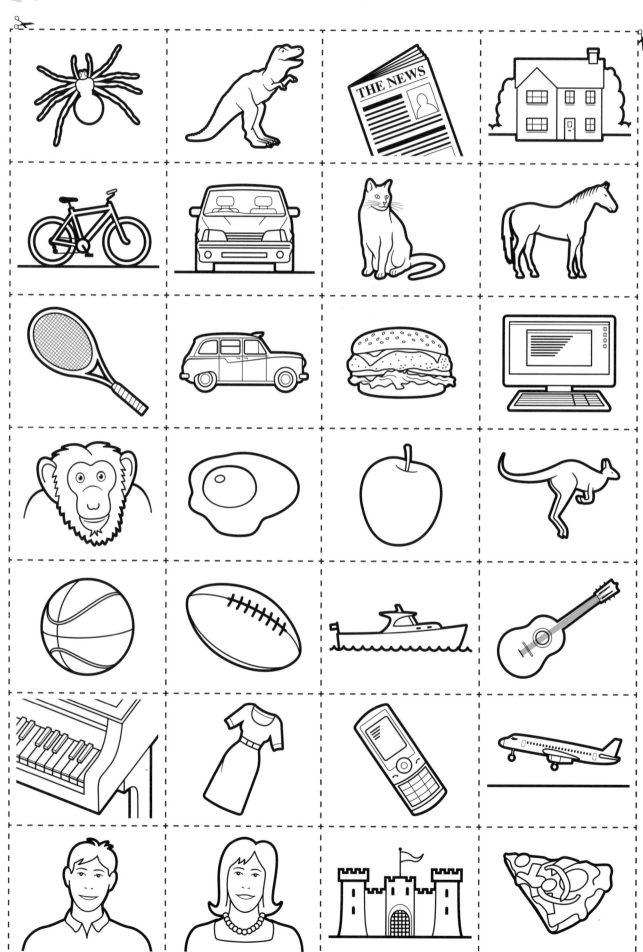

UNIT 14

RESOURCES

Grammar practice 14

1 Complete the sentences. Use the comparative form of the adjectives.

1 Stephanie is pretty, but Pamela is
....*prettier*.... .

2 Your bed is comfortable, but my bed is
....

3 I have got long hair, but my sister's hair is
....

4 Yesterday was hot, but today is ....

5 White bread is healthy, but brown bread is
....

6 Tom wears fashionable clothes, but Mark's
clothes are ....

7 I am a good singer, but you are ....

8 This jacket is warm, but that jacket is
....

2 Complete the sentences. Use the comparative form of the adjectives.

1 These shoes are .....*cheaper than*..... those
shoes. (cheap)

2 I think books are usually ....
films. (interesting)

3 Football is .... cricket.
(popular)

4 Tanya's hair is .... yours.
(curly)

5 My little finger is .... my
thumb. (short)

6 August is .... May. (sunny)

7 Madonna is .... Shakira.
(famous)

8 I feel .... I felt yesterday.
(bad)

3 Complete the sentences. Use comparative adjectives.

1 my father / my mother
My father is older than my mother.

2 my best friend / me
....

3 English / French
....

4 today / yesterday
....

5 America / Italy
....

6 dogs / cats
....

7 women / men
....

4 Right (✓) or wrong (✗)? Correct the wrong sentences.

1 Our house is more big than your house. [✗]
Our house is bigger than your house.

2 Life is gooder today than it was when I
was young. [ ]

3 Love is more important than money. [ ]

4 I am more busier today than I was
yesterday. [ ]

5 Mike Myers is funnier Jim Carrey. [ ]

6 I thought my room was dirty, but yours
is dirtier! [ ]

7 Please, try to be carefuller next time. [ ]

8 The starter was bad, but the main course
was more bad. [ ]

RESOURCES

UNIT 14

Acknowledgements

The publishers are grateful to the following contributors:
Vanessa Manhire and Hazel Meek: editorial work
Pentacor: text design and layouts

The publishers are grateful to the following illustrators:

David Benham 130, 146, 152, 166

Rosa Dodd (NB Illustration) 164

Andrew Hennessey 131, 150, 162

Humberto (Sylvie Poggio) 148, 156, 160

Graham Kennedy 142

Red Jelly 120

Mark Watkinson (Illustration) 154, 158, 168